# Language Loyalty, Language Planning and Language Revitalization

**BILINGUAL EDUCATION AND BILINGUALISM**
**Series Editors:** Professor Colin Baker, *University of Wales, Bangor, Wales, Great Britain* and Professor Nancy H. Hornberger, *University of Pennsylvania, Philadelphia, USA*

**Recent Books in the Series**
Continua of Biliteracy: An Ecological Framework for Educational Policy, Research, and Practice in Multilingual Settings
*Nancy H. Hornberger (ed.)*
Languages in America: A Pluralist View (2nd edn)
*Susan J. Dicker*
Trilingualism in Family, School and Community
*Charlotte Hoffmann and Jehannes Ytsma (eds)*
Multilingual Classroom Ecologies
*Angela Creese and Peter Martin (eds)*
Negotiation of Identities in Multilingual Contexts
*Aneta Pavlenko and Adrian Blackledge (eds)*
Beyond the Beginnings: Literacy Interventions for Upper Elementary English Language Learners
*Angela Carrasquillo, Stephen B. Kucer and Ruth Abrams*
Bilingualism and Language Pedagogy
*Janina Brutt-Griffler and Manka Varghese (eds)*
Language Learning and Teacher Education: A Sociocultural Approach
*Margaret R. Hawkins (ed.)*
The English Vernacular Divide: Postcolonial Language Politics and Practice
*Vaidehi Ramanathan*
Bilingual Education in South America
*Anne-Marie de Mejía (ed.)*
Teacher Collaboration and Talk in Multilingual Classrooms
*Angela Creese*
Words and Worlds: World Languages Review
*F. Martí, P. Ortega, I. Idiazabal, A. Barreña, P. Juaristi, C. Junyent, B. Uranga and E. Amorrortu*
Language and Aging in Multilingual Contexts
*Kees de Bot and Sinfree Makoni*
Foundations of Bilingual Education and Bilingualism (4th edn)
*Colin Baker*
Bilingual Minds: Emotional Experience, Expression, and Representation
*Aneta Pavlenko (ed.)*
Raising Bilingual-Biliterate Children in Monolingual Cultures
*Stephen J. Caldas*
Language, Space and Power: A Critical Look at Bilingual Education
*Samina Hadi-Tabassum*
Developing Minority Language Resources
*Guadalupe Valdés, Joshua A. Fishman, Rebecca Chávez and William Pérez*
Language Loyalty, Continuity and Change: Joshua A. Fishman's Contributions to International Sociolinguistics
*Ofelia García, Rakhmiel Peltz and Harold Schiffman*

**For more details of these or any other of our publications, please contact:**
**Multilingual Matters, Frankfurt Lodge, Clevedon Hall,**
**Victoria Road, Clevedon, BS21 7HH, England**
**http://www.multilingual-matters.com**

BILINGUAL EDUCATION AND BILINGUALISM 59
Series Editors: Colin Baker and Nancy H. Hornberger

# Language Loyalty, Language Planning and Language Revitalization

## Recent Writings and Reflections from Joshua A. Fishman

Edited by

Nancy H. Hornberger and Martin Pütz

MULTILINGUAL MATTERS LTD
Clevedon • Buffalo • Toronto

This volume has been compiled to mark the occasion of Joshua A. Fishman's 80th birthday and is being published in conjunction with a companion volume edited by Ofelia García, Rakhmiel Peltz and Harold Schiffman, entitled *Language Loyalty, Continuity and Change: Joshua Fishman's Contributions to International Sociolinguistics*. Both books are available from Multilingual Matters Ltd.

**Library of Congress Cataloging in Publication Data**
Fishman, Joshua A.
Language Loyalty, Language Planning and Language Revitalization: Recent Writings and Reflections from Joshua A. Fishman/Edited by Nancy H. Hornberger and Martin Pütz.
Bilingual Education and Bilingualism: 59
Includes bibliographical references and index.
1. Sociolinguistics. 2. Fishman, Joshua A. I. Hornberger, Nancy H. II. Pütz, Martin. III. Title. IV. Series.
P40.F57 2006
306.44–dc22                  2006010927

**British Library Cataloguing in Publication Data**
A catalogue entry for this book is available from the British Library.

ISBN 1-85359-901-8/EAN 978-1-85359-901-9 (hbk)
ISBN 1-85359-900-X/EAN 978-1-85359-900-2 (pbk)

**Multilingual Matters Ltd**
*UK*: Frankfurt Lodge, Clevedon Hall, Victoria Road, Clevedon BS21 7HH.
*USA*: UTP, 2250 Military Road, Tonawanda, NY 14150, USA.
*Canada*: UTP, 5201 Dufferin Street, North York, Ontario M3H 5T8, Canada.

Typeset by Techset Ltd.
Printed and bound in Great Britain by the Cromwell Press Ltd.

# Dedication

*From Nancy*: To my husband Stephan, who has nurtured and shared with me the love and practice of multilingualism and intercultural under-standing in our own family *and* to our children, Ch'uyasonqo and Kusisami, who have been a constant inspiration to me for three decades now, and who have in their own young adult lives taken on the love and championing of "little" peoples in the far reaches of the world, that Joshua A. Fishman exemplifies and exhorts us to in his life and work.

********************

*From Martin*: To my wife, Natascha, who brings such joy to my life and makes it all worth doing. I'm grateful for her patience and constant support especially during the initial stages of the editing of this book.

# Contents

# Acknowledgements

Above all, we thank our mentor Joshua Fishman and his wife Gella Schweid Fishman for the extraordinary opportunity to celebrate with them Joshua's 80th birthday and his lifetime sowing, tending, and reaping in sociolinguistic and minority language revitalization fields. We treasure the very warm welcome the Fishmans gave us at their home in New York City on the occasion of the interview with which we open this volume entitled *Language Loyalty, Language Planning, and Language Revitalization: Recent Writings and Reflections from Joshua A. Fishman.*

We are particularly grateful for the Fishmans' first visit to Landau, Germany (LAUD Symposium 2004) where Joshua was invited as a keynote speaker and where the idea to present a Festschrift to his 80th birthday originated.

Warm thanks are due our colleagues Ofelia García, Rakhmiel Peltz and Harold F. Schiffman, for their initiative and collaboration in planning the birthday celebration and in preparing the companion volume to this one, entitled *Language Loyalty, Continuity and Change: Joshua A. Fishman's Contributions to International Sociolinguistics.*

We gratefully acknowledge invaluable and timely assistance received from our graduate students in putting the volume together. In particular, we thank Koblenz-Landau University's Pamela Reis (Landau Campus) and University of Pennsylvania Educational Linguistics Forum (ELF) 'elves' – PhD students Julia Deák, Cynthia Groff, Francis Hult, Sean McGrew, Katherine Mortimer, Shannon Sauro, Laura Sicola and Tamara Warhol – for their help with editing at the proof stage; thanks also to Jinwei Dong, Visiting Scholar at Penn from Guangdong University of Foreign Studies in China, who kindly assisted with proofreading. We are especially grateful to Penn Educational Linguistics PhD candidates Shannon Sauro, for transcribing the entire four-hour interview with Fishman, and Francis Hult, for his strategic and ever cheerful assistance and initiative in every aspect of this Fishman 80th birthday celebration effort.

Abundant appreciation goes to our publisher Multilingual Matters for their unfailing commitment to intergenerational multilingualism and their support for this project strategically, financially, administratively, editorially and substantively. Not only Mike and Marjukka Grover, but also especially their son Tommi Grover, as well as Ken Hall, Kathryn King and Anna Roderick have helped speed this volume on its way. We are grateful to Colin Baker, co-editor of the Bilingual Education and Bilingualism series in which these two Fishman celebration volumes appear, for his endless encouragement, enthusiasm, and wise editorial counsel.

Mouton de Gruyter Publishers generously donated the copyright fees for all the contributions reprinted here from their publications. We are deeply appreciative of their sponsorship of the volume. Their solidarity with this publication seems especially fitting since their own publications, the *International Journal of the Sociology of Language* and the book series *Contributions to the Sociology of Language,* are virtually synonymous with the name Joshua Fishman – general editor of both the journal and the book series since their founding in the 1970s and up to the present.

The sources for all the extracts published in this volume are given in the listing of contents. We are extremely grateful to all the publishers concerned for kindly granting permission to reproduce their copyright material here.

# *Foreword*

A visit to the Fishman home is unforgettable.

At the end of the table sits a triglossic, heavyweight intellectual. Nearby is a vast library of books, all neatly ordered. Sharing much of the wisdom of his forefathers, he also kindly distributes food and beverage around the table. The conversation is quiet; the atmosphere is friendly; everything is welcoming. We sit, listen and learn. Joshua Fishman is speaking.

I remember the shift of topic well: Joshua's deep love of Gella, their children and grandchildren; the love of languages transmitted by his parents; gems of wisdom about religion, psychology and pedagogy; his concern for ethnic and religious life.

We eat alongside a 20th-century discipline 'great', but are really sitting as disciples at the feet of a Freud or Keynes. Behind the gentle smile is a person of universal understandings, a founding father, a truly remarkable thinker and original scholar.

Visiting this book is equally unforgettable.

This is because Joshua Fishman needs to be read and re-read by future generations. In his writing there is a condensation of wisdom, a vision composed in one century but even more relevant in the next. The book contains an excellent recent selection of his deep insights and vast understandings that need inter-generational transmission. While his writings continue, this collection is a priceless legacy that needs preservation and re-presentation to future generations.

Joshua Fishman's reverence for the small languages and peoples of this world, the holiness of his international humanity, and his fight for language freedoms, make him one of the world's most remarkable scholars. His mountain-top view of downtrodden ethnic groups and dying languages creates a universal vision of a new land.

Those who work at the sharp end of top-down and bottom-up language planning know that Fishman is a prophet in his own time. For example, his understanding that intergenerational language transmission is the crucial foundation of all language planning is now understood by grounded language planners. But not yet by many academics. He is light years ahead.

In leaving Joshua and Gella's home, there is a sense of having visited a mansion of ideas, insights, humanity and history. In entering this book, you will walk into the same mansion. Sit, listen and learn. The great rabbi of language is speaking.

Colin Baker

# Introduction

Nancy H. Hornberger and Martin Pütz

As a founding figure in sociolinguistics in the 1950s, widely influential in creating and developing the sociology of language as an academic field, and a prime mover in the scholarship and practice of language planning, Joshua Fishman is perhaps best known and loved internationally and at home for his pioneering and enduring work in language loyalty, language maintenance and shift, and language revitalization. This volume brings together a selection of Fishman's most recent writings on endangered languages and language revitalization, along with an interview reflecting on his recent and lifetime's work on these themes.

The volume includes selected writings from works published within the past 20 years and selected excerpts from an interview dialogue between Professor Fishman and the volume editors carried out in 2005, as Fishman approached his 80th year. The writings are organized into four sections – two core sections focusing on reversing language shift and on the status of threatened languages, respectively, anchored by an introductory section of Fishman's personal perspectives on the field of sociolinguistics and a concluding section sampling his work on Yiddish language revitalization, integral to his overall sociolinguistic work (and taken up in more detail in Volume 2 of this 80th birthday celebration set).

In the interview with Professor Fishman in May 2005, we invited him to reflect back on the writings collected here and on his work as a whole. Having been privileged to be present at the original spoken presentation of several of the papers collected here, and deeply inspired both by those experiences and by Fishman's written opus, we bring to the interview our own personal and professional perspectives and an appreciation of Fishman's profound influence on our own careers. At the same time, we join with Fishman in a critical appraisal of what has and has not been accomplished in both scholarly and practical work on language loyalty and language revitalization.

As for the writings collected here, Part 1, Personal Perspectives on Sociolinguistics, includes a couple of biographical pieces, one an autobiographical reflection on Fishman's life in relation to his work and the other his memories and reflections on the early days of American sociolinguistics. Two additional pieces eloquently put forth Fishman's personal perspectives on (1) the case for the fundamental importance to sociolinguistics of sociological concepts and methods on a par with linguistic ones (an essay structured around the five books of the Pentateuch, thus metaphorically underlining the foundational nature of Fishman's sociological 'creed' *vis-à-vis* sociolinguistics); and (2) the meaning and value of the concept of diglossia, clarifying his own usage of the term in relation to others' usage and to the concept of societal multilingualism.

Part 2, on Loyalty, Shift and Revitalization, brings together significant theoretical and empirical expositions of Fishman's highly influential Reversing Language Shift (RLS) Framework, beginning with his first published article on the topic in the *Journal of Multilingual and Multicultural Development* (1990) and ending with reflections on the specific case of Australian Aboriginal and immigrant languages, as originally published in the Australian journal *Vox*. Also included are two encyclopedic overview pieces on RLS and language revitalization, respectively, as well as an essay on worrisome problems in the study of language maintenance and language shift.

Part 3, Globalization, Power and the Status of Threatened Languages, moves from the focus on on-the-ground efforts to reverse language shift to macro and micro perspectives on the growing threat to 'small' languages posed by increasing globalization, specifically the power of English-only in the United States and global English on a world scale. Internationally revered as champion of the 'little languages', Fishman here writes eloquently of the principle of ethnolinguistic democracy and of the value of our involvement with 'minor, endangered languages' not only because 'they need our help most, [and] because by doing so we become more human', but also because it will make us 'more sensitive, more humble and more cautious language policy researchers and language policy implementers as well' (1987: 15).

Part 4, Yiddish Language and Culture, closes out the volume with two samples from Fishman's close and detailed work on Yiddish, elucidating larger sociolinguistic concerns. The first essay explores the terrain of language attitudes, specifically positive ethnolinguistic consciousness, in this case the sanctification of Yiddish through associating it with 'individuals whose sanctity cannot be doubted' and with 'texts of unimpeachable authorship' (2002: 138). The second offers a perspective on and persuasive argument for the holiness of bilingualism, not only implicitly as the sociocultural norm worldwide, but also explicitly in many cases where it involves one or more 'holy' languages, as in the case of Yiddish. Fishman reminds us here, as he has throughout his half century career, that the bulk of the human population is and always has been bi- (or multi-) lingual and, furthermore, that 'we owe to the sociolinguistic enterprise the realization that bilingualism... may very well be the sociocultural norm' (2002: 16). Fitting reminders with which to conclude our selection of Fishman's sociolinguistic writings on language loyalty, language planning and language revitalization.

# An Interview with Joshua A. Fishman

*On 17 May 2005, volume editors Nancy H. Hornberger (NHH) and Martin Pütz (MP) interviewed Joshua A. Fishman (JAF) in his home in the Bronx, New York. We asked him to reflect on some of the themes in articles and papers included in this volume, in the light of a lifetime of work in language loyalty, language planning and language revitalization. Following is an edited and abridged transcript of that interview.[1]*

**NHH:** Well, we definitely want to begin by first of all thanking you for letting us do this and come invade your private space and talk to you. So, we thought we'd follow the approach you did in that lovely essay you wrote in 1991 called 'My Life through My Work and My Work through My Life' (Chapter 1, this volume), a little bit of a topical approach rather than a strictly chronological one. And we're going to come back to your early days in Yiddish, especially at the end, but I thought we'd start right now placing you starting at Columbia, then Center for Advanced Studies in Stanford, and getting into your teaching at Penn and then Yeshiva. We'll start in that time period, which I guess is already many years.

**JAF:** That's almost 60 years ago.

**NHH:** Picking up a little bit on the themes that you mentioned in that essay, of early influences from your life that also continued throughout your life, such as the multidisciplinary perspective and the love for writing and publishing. Well, actually, we'll come back to that in a minute, but first we want to start by asking you about your years at Columbia a little bit, the influence of Weinreich in getting you started at Columbia, and the Yiddish Scientific Institute (Yivo).

**JAF:** Weinreich had nothing to do directly with getting me started at Columbia, although it's impossible for me to say that it wasn't in the back of my mind or maybe even closer to the front. But he had nothing directly to do with picking a department or a major. Obviously I had been to their home by then several times over a period of years.

**NHH:** How did that evolve? How did you start going to their home?

**JAF:** Like many things, it starts innocently from the side, from the corner, then moves toward center stage. There was a Yiddish children's camp, summer camp up here in upstate New York in a newer town called Newburg. The camp was called Nayvelt.[2] Nayvelt has a double meaning to

1

the Yiddish speaker because Theodor Herzl's (1896) famous book was about Nayland – his book, in German, was titled *Der Judenstaat* (in English, *A Jewish State*). And this camp was a socialist camp. It was socialist in ethos; it had no direct link to any party. It was socialist in terms of its emphases on social justice – the annual end of season holiday was called Nayland.

**NHH:** New land?

**JAF:** New land. We spent a whole summer planning a better society. These were war years already. And at that time enemies of the state were being arrested in the United States, communists mostly. Of course Nazis were being arrested if you could find any. Overnight, all the Nazis disappeared. I know because I grew up in a German/Jewish neighborhood in Philadelphia, and before Pearl Harbor there were lots of Nazis among the Germans because they would march through the local park. The Bund and the flags with the swastika and everything would march through the local park. Can you imagine doing this in a neighborhood that was half Jewish?

**NHH:** And this was when you were high school aged?

**JAF:** Yes.

**MP:** What year was that?

**JAF:** I went to high school from, let's say, 1940 to 1944.

**NHH:** I think that's right because you were at Penn 1944 to 1948.

**JAF:** And the German-American kids went to the same high school as we, the Jewish-American kids, did, and there were very frequent fights between the two sets of boys. You know, for anti-Semitism on the one part and on the other hand for being called pro-Hitler. And then in social studies class, the different points of view as to American neutrality were very prominent. There were kids who were very much in favor of doing everything we could to help Britain even if it meant risking war. We had a teacher who was a pacifist, and he said, 'That's going to bring a war, you know'. And we said, 'Well it's worth it. It's worth a war to free the world of Hitler'. And kids would sit, you know, and say, 'The U.S. is supposed to be neutral. It says it's neutral, and it's lying about it. It's not being fair'. Both those discussions went on very frequently, you know. The class would meet every day.

And the teacher's being a pacifist didn't help things either because he kept saying we were both wrong. He was opposed to war of any kind. You know, in the middle of this war in Europe for a teacher to say that, that was quite something. And he was a real intellectual. He'd tell us, 'Don't buy war bonds because they won't be worth in dollars what you spent to buy them by the time you cash them in, because the inflation after the war is going to be something you wouldn't believe'. But what did we know about inflation? We never had experienced any inflation. I knew about inflation because I collected stamps and I saw those German stamps that said 18 million Marks on them. 18 million Marks to mail a letter! I realized that's inflation.

**NHH:** So, through the camp you made a connection with Weinreich.

**JAF:** 1940. I was a counselor, and my assistant counselor was Gabriel Weinreich, Uriel's younger brother. He grew up to be a physicist and a person of distinction in his own right. And Uriel came to visit him during the summer. Uriel was working that summer in a different camp together with another friend of ours. And he hiked that day. He walked and hitch-hiked to get to visit us, and he slept in a tent at night that he had brought along so as not to have to incur any expense. The whole idea was to spend as little as you possibly could, and they made their own sandwiches. So I met Uriel that summer too, and Gabi and I became very fast friends.

There were very few kids around of any kind of American background that you could talk to about the war in Europe and find out about Vilna. I found out that those Jewish kids growing up in Vilna could speak some Polish because the government required them. You know, it was part of Poland, under protest from Lithuania, which always considered it their lost capital. They could go to the post office to buy stamps, but they would practice how to say what they wanted, so that when they got to the window they would say it right. Otherwise, the postal clerk would criticize them for their Jewish accent in Polish. But they knew no Lithuanian. Lithuanian, that was below contempt. No one would bother to learn Lithuanian. Who else could I find these things out from? I was always interested in languages and peoples and Jews and Gabi Weinreich was like a walking treasure on these topics.

**NHH:** He had lived there as a young boy?

**JAF:** Yes, he had just come from there. He had escaped from Vilna with his mother. You see, when the war broke out, Weinreich senior and Weinreich Uriel were off at a conference in Copenhagen, at a linguistics conference – and the war began. Now everybody knew that some war was coming. They all said later that they knew, but obviously they didn't know well enough to stay home. If they had known, they wouldn't have gone off to Copenhagen, and they couldn't return to Vilna. So they then booked passage to the United States, directly from Copenhagen – and they made it pretty quickly. You know the war didn't impact Scandinavia yet, and that's where the conference was. And Gabi and his mother Regina were left stranded in Vilna. And Vilna initially was under Soviet Russian control. Then when the Nazis declared war on Russia, they pushed the Russians out of Vilna, so it was under Nazi control. And only after, toward the end of the war, the Russians got back there. So while it was under Russian control, she got some kind of sponsorship from the American Jewish Labor Committee. The Committee got the U.S. government's permission to bring in some-thing like 100 Jews of great cultural importance. So Gabi's mother and he were among those, and they got a ticket with the Trans-Siberian Railroad all the way across Siberia, through to Japan, across the Pacific, and then to San Francisco. And then took the train to New York.

**NHH:** So he was telling you all about that?

**JAF:** Yes! Now where else could I hear stories like that? Where could I find out things like that? That's obviously thrilling history. So, that's how I got to meet him, and after the summer was over, he invited me to come visit them in New York. Well, I lost little time in doing that, and Max Weinreich wasn't at home at the time, so I met Uriel and I met his mother. And just as I was about to leave – you know, this again involved a 3–4 hour train trip, Max Weinreich arrived and invited me to come to the Yivo conference and gave me a five dollar check for the ticket. I mailed him a five dollar check after I got home, which of course he ripped up. He didn't cash my five dollars, and I didn't cash his five dollars – except I didn't rip his check up.[3] And that's how I came to my first Yivo Conference in 1946.

**NHH:** So you were saying that he only indirectly is related to your studying at Columbia.

**JAF:** Well, being in New York meant being near Max Weinreich and his family. First of all, they had weekly Yiddish-reading evenings, Yiddish literature evenings, literary evenings. They invited a few other people. Many of them were Yiddish newspaper-affiliated writers and so I met Yiddish literary figures. Some of them were just arriving in 1944, from France. There was a Yiddish conference in New York, a world conference, and Yiddish writers from all over the world came to New York – and when they did, they tried to stay here. Many succeeded, but many had to go back to France.

**NHH:** So it was a very lively intellectual atmosphere.

**JAF:** It was. It was much more than I'd had in Philadelphia. Any young Jewish intellectual in those days was in Philadelphia only as long as it took to come to New York. As soon as you could manage, you got a job in New York, either as a Yiddish teacher or as a member of one or the other of the newspaper staffs, and you stayed in New York. So there was practically nobody in Philadelphia except the autodidacts like my father, of which there were several. Totally self-educated in Yiddish, through Yiddish, in world literature. From Shakespeare to Karl Marx to whatever you want, science, natural science. We had all those books in Yiddish. But more than anything else, there were no young people like me in Philadelphia, who spoke the language well and with some kind of intellectual understanding of its origins, and with some kind of political understanding as to how it had figured in the immediate pre-Holocaust period in Poland.

Did you see that paper of mine about the language issue among Jewish political parties in Poland before the war? It's titled something like 'The Language Issue among Jewish Political Parties in Poland'. It covers about a dozen parties and shows you whether they were pro-Yiddish, neutral or anti-Yiddish; whether they were secular or religious; whether they were Zionist, socialist or non-partisan. And it shows you the implicationality of these dimensions, because as soon as you took a position on any one of them, you were taking positions on all three of them so that if you took the position pro-Yiddish, then you were certainly not strongly Zionist. You could have been maybe labor-Zionist. The implicationality was striking.

Anyway, I was a kid like that in an environment where there were other kids who went to the public and Yiddish schools that I went to, but they didn't live with it day by day in their minds.

**NHH:** Your parents were born in Poland?

**JAF:** No, my mother was born in the Ukraine, near the river which forms the boundary with what is now Moldavia, what was then Bessarabia. The Dnestr – it was called the Dnestr. And my father lived on the other side of that river, in Moldavia, right on the river in a town called Soroke. So they were from Moldavia and the Ukraine, respectively.

**NHH:** But you were born here.

**JAF:** Yes. My father came in 1910. And my mother was trapped there in Olt Konstantin with her mother and younger brothers during the war and couldn't get out of the Ukraine even though her father and older brothers had already left for the United States before. So she lived through all the revolution and the pogroms, the Ukrainian pogroms, the white pogroms. I'm sure there were red pogroms too. Every force had made its own pogroms against Jews. And issued its own money, you know, so the money of the previous regime was no good after a few weeks. Yes, so she came in 1920, ten years later than my father.

**NHH:** But they already knew each other? No, they met here.

**MP:** That was just a coincidence that they lived so close together in the Ukraine and Moldavia.

**JAF:** Yes. That's why they spoke the same dialect. That was important, so I wasn't exposed to any dialect variation at home.

**MP:** So they spoke a Russian dialect at the time, at home?

**JAF:** Yiddish, only Yiddish. They spoke Russian on the rare occasion that they wanted to say something to each other that I shouldn't understand. This used to be, in other homes, the occasion on which Yiddish was used among the adults. My speaking Yiddish, let's say in 1930 when I was four years old, was as much of a noteworthy occasion on the street that when I came into the grocery and said what it was that I wanted to buy, in Yiddish, there would be a hush in the store. It was as if a dog were talking, like a parrot. What I'm saying to you is that, you know, twenty, fifteen years later, there was still no young person speaking Yiddish – although they had all gone to school, we had a youth club, we spoke Yiddish at the youth meetings. The school was especially successful at doing that, you know. It's the old story. The school can produce more speakers than the society can reproduce, so as soon as the club was over we would go back to speaking English with each other. And I thought that was so sad.

**NHH:** At Columbia, you studied psychology and you've written about how that proved to be a basis from which you could then later go into linguistics, history, sociology.

**JAF:** You know I had co-majored in history at Penn before coming to Columbia. You really didn't think then, as nowadays, that history was only for historians. I took the history of the English language. I took a whole year of the history of England. What kind of American intellectual would not know the history of England? I took a course in Russian history. I'd studied a lot of history, but curiously enough, I had studied almost no sociology in college. You know the way it is in the United States – every kid from a home with books knows about psychology. Psychology – that reverberates with Americans because it's individually-focused and Americans like anything that's individually-focused; they can grab it and do something with it, 'gain friends and influence people'. So, I didn't know much about sociology. I knew about history. I knew about psychology.

So it was after coming to Columbia that I realized my mistake, but it was too late. They wouldn't admit me to sociology as a graduate student because I hadn't had any undergraduate sociology. I'd had one course in undergraduate sociology. Actually, it was a graduate course. It was my very final semester. You know, I had this four-year Mayor's scholarship to Penn. And it was in the last semester, when I had completed not only all the undergraduate requirements but I'd completed most of the graduate requirements too for the master's, that I undertook the luxury of sociology. And it was a course that used the old *Encyclopedia of the Social Sciences*, which was a twenty-five volume set; and everybody was assigned a volume. I was assigned volume A, so I gave my report on anthropology. That's how I learned about anthropology. That was something! Rex Crawford was the professor – he had been a governor of Puerto Rico, one of the New Deal governors of Puerto Rico.

So, at Columbia I took psychology and sociology courses that were open to me. I tried to tell my professors that I was interested in the sociology of language. I really tried to tell it to them once or twice, but they had no idea what it was, and to say that they were uninterested in it is beside the point. They couldn't be interested in it if they had no idea what it was all about. So they were kind enough to tell me, to pat my head, and say, 'Go ahead and finish your dissertation and do whatever you like after that!'

**MP:** So the sociology of language was not a concept at the time. Not yet, not at all. Are you the one who invented the term, sociology of language?

**JAF:** I don't think so. I think it had existed in Europe for a long time.

**MP:** *Soziologie der Sprache.*

**JAF:** Even outside of its German context, which was very specific and unfortunately contaminated, the French were into sociology of language too. And there was even an American book on the sociology of language by someone named Hertzler (1965).

**NHH:** How did you get to 'sociology of language' in the beginning?

**JAF:** Well, my first real book publication was *Language Loyalty in the United States* (Fishman, 1966). It rang a bell in Europe because it had a chapter on German by Heinz Kloss (1966). It had a chapter on Ukrainian. It had a chapter on French, and a chapter on Yiddish. I didn't publish the Yiddish chapter in the book, much to Gella's consternation, because I published it in Tom Sebeok's series on Anthropology and Folklore, I think it was called. Ferguson taught it in his class and he said, 'Everybody liked it except the Jewish students who felt very uncomfortable'. It was still very early to mention Yiddish in polite society, in intellectual society. We were the first generation of Jewish college-goers, in a sense we were immigrants there and not merely children of immigrants.

**MP:** Heinz Kloss was a well-known academic in Germany at the time. Did you also collaborate with him somehow?

**JAF:** I discovered Heinz Kloss after the war. How did I discover him? At Stanford, at the Center for Advanced Study in 1963. I used to take off an afternoon a week and go down to the library. The Stanford library was very deficient at the time. It had no usable catalog, and you just found whatever you found: these are the economics books, here are the history books. It was not a very advanced system. So I found the whole collection of the publications of the *Auslandsdeutsche Volksinstitut*, that somehow they got out – I never found out the story about how they obtained it all. And Heinz Kloss published in that series, primarily on Germans in the United States. Since I was just writing up my *Language Loyalty in the United States* then – I wrote that up while I was at the Center – I salivated.

**NHH:** It was like a goldmine.

**JAF:** Yeah, I salivated reading that. I found out where Kloss was, and I wrote to him, and we got to corresponding. I asked him, would he like to do the overview on German language maintenance efforts in the USA. I realized that he could do that out of the back of his mind, but American researchers couldn't do it if you gave them ten years to do it. So he did. His English was atrocious at the time, so I rewrote it. But I couldn't retype it. I didn't have a computer then, 1963. There were no computers at that time. I was already straining the center staff typing my chapters for *Language Loyalty*, and if I had given them a manuscript by a fellow named Heinz Kloss, they would have just thrown it out. So I would correct it by hand and send it back to him to have him find a typist. And we worked, and we struggled with it. He was the kind of fellow that perseverates about anything he wrote for weeks after he's written it, and would drop me some lines, like – 'on page six, on line twelve, change "never" to "hardly ever"'.

**NHH:** Well, we wanted to ask you a little bit about people like Kloss, Ferguson, others of your colleagues with whom you've worked closely. I was thinking of asking you about a memorable experience or insight from each one, but that's probably too many. I'll name a few names, maybe if you want to talk about any of them – Haugen, Ferguson, Gumperz, Hymes.

**JAF:** Haugen is, unfortunately I would say, quite forgotten by now. At that time, he took command of the room. He was tall, well-spoken, and we were at the Center the same year, which means we had a whole year together to eat lunch every day if we wanted to. One of the interesting things he told me was when I came up with some kind of content categories for classifying interview material that were five in number. And he told me, 'you can't do five.' How come we can't do five? He said, 'Things in nature never divide up into five things. It's one, then it's two, and each one of them splits, so it's four.' He was referring to binomial expansion.

**NHH:** Not even threes.

**JAF:** So, I said how come we have five fingers? He was very serious about that as a kind of intellectual realization that he was sharing with me. That for social phenomena, five is a spurious number. You can't come up with five, although you could have both 1's and 4's.

Once, he said to me, 'You know what you're studying – he meant the attrition of minority languages in the United States – it's a very sad topic, a very sad topic. I wonder if you have difficulty sleeping at night. I know that same sadness about the demise of Norwegian in the United States.' I said, 'No, it doesn't bother me excessively. You know, the same way that human life is sad. Do you believe that pessimism is the only valid conclusion to come to about life, that we're all headed downward, even as we speak to each other? Instead,' I said, 'I think about all the creative pleasure the leaders of these groups have.'

I tell you, he was so impressed by his own seniority in the field, rightfully so. He had been president of the Linguistic Society of America. He was highly thought of by his colleagues, not necessarily in sociolinguistics, and I must say, as an individual, he always came through for me. If I ever asked him to write an article, he always would. He would realize that for a young person to be able to bring an article by Haugen into a book or into a conference was an accomplishment.

But I once had a public argument with him at the Georgetown University Round Table meetings. He said something about interference. You know, I was a young whipper-snapper. I was maybe beginning to be somewhat known, but I was far from Haugen. And in the discussion, I said, 'In sociolinguistics, there is no such thing as interference. Interference constitutes just a variety of speaking, a kind of speaking, and you have to try to locate it functionally, but you can't in any way downgrade it. If you don't downgrade dialect because it's a variety of speaking, then interference is also; in certain social circles, and on certain topics, between certain informants, there's a lot of it.'

James Alatis, who was the chair of the meeting at that time, smelled the conflict in the air, and he said, 'I don't know, it can't be both what Haugen says and what Fishman says. Why don't we give them both a chance to restate their positions.' So both positions became more rigid on restatement. Haugen was not accustomed to being disagreed with. I must say, he treated me very gingerly. I think he was a gentleman. I wasn't trying to attack Haugen. I had nothing against Haugen, actually great respect, first for his *Norwegian Language* (Haugen, 1953), which I, as you know, annotated page by page, volume one. And which I used as an introductory text for 'Sociology of Language' which I first taught at Penn in 1959–60.

Later on, I got to know him at the Center for Advanced Study.

**MP:** Perhaps I can follow up on the issue of sociolinguistics and the sociology of language. At the '64 Summer Linguistic Institute at Bloomington, Indiana, as you say, American sociolinguistics was born. In your article 'Bloomington, Summer 1964: The Birth of American Sociolinguistics' (Chapter 2, this volume), you talked about the 'two cultures' problems in sociolinguistics, referring to the linguists and anthropologists on the one hand and societally-oriented linguists like yourself on the other.

**JAF:** No, societally oriented non-linguists.

**MP:** Non-linguists. Would you consider yourself to be a non-linguist?

**JAF:** Yes.

**MP:** Would you say that this division between micro versus macro sociolinguistics is still valid today, or has it even become more profound? And further would you still say, as you did ten years ago, that sociology has become and remains a junior or even a silent partner in the formation of sociolinguistics? In other words, has the sociological perspective again to be put back into the sociolinguistic enterprise?

**JAF:** I think it's more or less the case, as I look back today, that sociolinguists do not know sociology and that their work is sociologically uninformed, that it would be stronger, fuller, more provocative if that were not the case, that there is no respect for them in social science circles. I'm not saying you have to actually have two different programs at the university, one in sociolinguistics and one in sociology of language. I don't think that would be possible; I don't think it would be desirable. I don't believe in politicizing young people prematurely. They know what they hate even before they know anything about how to do what they like. So I wouldn't drive two sets of students apart on this ground, between sociolinguistics and sociology of language. Particularly since there's no sociology of language. There's no faculty for that. There are no courses for that, so what's the point?

But it's an emphasis. It's a particular emphasis which has not gone unrecognized. Lots of people are doing sociology of language and calling themselves sociolinguists, so it's one of these things where you have to watch what they're doing rather than what they call themselves. What they call themselves has all kinds of implications for their position, for their colleagues, for their department, for their funding, and these are all immaterial. Their funding is immaterial (laughs) – cognitively, conceptually, intellectually immaterial.

**MP:** Only a small proportion of the sociolinguistic literature is getting through to sociology in fact. Do you deplore this fact, and how do you account for this? I mean, why is it that sociology does not seem to be interested that much in sociolinguistic studies and findings, and are you somehow jealous of the psycholinguistic discipline, which seems to find recognition in both linguistic and psychological circles?

**JAF:** Sure, I'm jealous.

**MP:** But how does it come about that sociology is not so much interested in these sociolinguistic findings?

**JAF:** Because the history of sociology has been one of no attention to language from the very outset. Whereas the history of psychology has had very long attention to language, not only because of psychology and its interest in memory and learning and so forth, all of which involve language to a large extent, but because of psychology's proximity to education, which is again a language discipline, a language pursuit. Sociology, on the other hand, has none of that, and actually was so much taken with its own intellectual discovery of globalization, which started 150–200 years ago, that sociologists believed that it was beside the point to study about language and ethnicity. These are all things that were going to disappear. Not only that they *should* disappear, as Marx believed, but that they were going to *inevitably* disappear, as Weber and Durkheim suggested. They were convinced that all these were non-productive aspects of the past – languages, and religions, and ethnicities. There was no point to it – to focusing on that.

Now, it had not always been so, particularly not in Germany, and certainly also not in France. In Germany, there were lots of sociologists that were taken with language. I don't know if we should call them sociologists or social philosophers, or whatever, but you can't say that Herder was not interested in language. There were some less known ones that easily fell into racism, but racism, you know, was an intellectual topic. The human race naturally falls into certain types, and those who felt that it did were very interested in language. And of course anthropology was very interested in language. The difference between anthropology and sociology; we used to have a dean at Yeshiva University who said the difference between anthropology and sociology is: if it's in the city, it's sociology; if it's in the jungle, it's anthropology.

**MP:** It's a weird perspective.

**JAF:** No, it's just a methodology perspective.

**MP:** That was my second question in fact. The concepts language maintenance and language shift are studied by different methods, I mean, depending on the academic discipline of the scholar. As regards the methodological framework, would you say that the sociologist's perspective, that is examining survey data from as many communities as possible, is more revealing than the anthropologist's participant observation or the ethnographic account of language and culture? In other words, in how far would you say that the sociological paradigm is a more appropriate type of methodology if it is at all? Or would you say the two ideally complement each other and should be applied as such to an analysis of language maintenance and shift? So can you get the two together?

**JAF:** I believe in that very much–

**MP:** But it's not realistic.

**JAF:** –but I don't know anybody like that.

**MP:** Right. So we have to invent such a person.

**JAF:** So you have to invent such a person, and who has to do the inventing? A person who is not that kind of person has to invent it and to train students like that. And you have to have at least two people train them because it takes two people nowadays to do that, which you hope in the future will take one person.

For example, when I was starting the sociology journal, the *International Journal of the Sociology of Language* (Berlin/New York: Mouton de Gruyter) I wanted another editor to be a linguist, an anthropological linguist for the journal, that would really complement me by being sensitive to areas that I was untrained in. There's a difference between trained sensitivity and just intellectual, general theoretical awareness. So I asked Ferguson would he co-edit the journal with me, before I started it. And he agreed with me that it would be a good thing to have a linguist as co-editor, but he didn't want to do it. Ferguson was very laid back in terms of administrative responsibility. He didn't like to do it. He didn't do it well. He let things slide, and he realized that I was not that kind, and it would just ruin our friendship.

**NHH:** It's true. He doesn't have edited volumes really, Ferguson. Except with Heath (Ferguson and Heath 1981).[4]

**JAF:** Yeah, and he has his own. Toward the end of his life he published his *Sociolinguistic Perspectives* book (Ferguson, 1996).

**MP:** Another important concept, of course, is diglossia. And one of the persons who criticized the concept is the Welsh scholar Glyn Williams. You probably know him because you wrote the Foreword to his book. In his sociological critique of sociolinguistics (Williams, 1992), he was very critical of your concept of diglossia and also your conception of society, by which you seem to suggest that linguistic changes are to be seen as the result of changes in society. And that this, according to Williams, resulted in a highly mechanical process, as he puts it, involving a degree of inevitability, as a consequence of which, conflict is absent. So Williams concluded that there is, I quote, 'an implicit claim that the elimination of minority languages is a natural, evolutionary process which makes struggle irrelevant' (Williams 1992: 100). Now there is certainly some truth in that.

**JAF:** I think that must be a misreading. I mean, he cannot have read anything by me, if he says something to the effect that my work is based on the implicit assumption that minority languages will vanish.

**MP:** Also at the time, your book on *Reversing Language Shift* (Fishman, 1991) was out, wasn't it? I mean that's full of the struggle of trying to overcome.

**JAF:** I think that's a little later.

**MP:** Williams' book was in 1992. Your *Reversing Language Shift* book was 1991.

**JAF:** He couldn't have read it by then.

**MP:** I liked his book in general. Quite some good and critical remarks, not just about your work, but also about Hymes and Labov, and some other sociolinguists.

**JAF:** He is a very good critic of everybody. He is a good critic of anybody and everybody, but I would say, since it is thoroughly within the French philosophical school, it has this peculiar disregard for data and for data collection, and data analysis, and revision of theory based on data. So that there's no data there. There's a constant argument at a high level of abstraction, which I find it hard to follow. You know, I feel like stopping after each paragraph and saying, now show me the data for that. I once did that with an anthropologist. I probably wrote about this, I don't remember.

**NHH:** With a French anthropologist?

**JAF:** No, I did that with Gumperz. Gumperz came back from his Norwegian experience up there in that little town (e.g. Blom & Gumperz, 1972).

**NHH:** Hemnesberget.

**JAF:** Hemnesberget. And I said, 'Oh gee, I'd like to read the paper.' He said, 'I don't have a paper, but I'll let you listen to the tapes.' I remember when I was a student, one of my professors who was a great methodologist said, 'One thing you can be sure of: the theory for any paper is shorter than the data. If you have a theory where you can't differentiate between the theory and the data or the theory is the data, then there's something wrong.'

So I listened to his tapes, and I said to him, 'John, I see one half of the tape has to do with them when they're coming home for Christmas and the students are getting together. And the other half has to do with the same students, but not at a party, a serious discussion, and I'd like to see the data. Make a table out of that so I can tell that for student A, he is taking part in the following settings. In one he is speaking this. In the other he is speaking that. In the third he is speaking a little of both.' He said, 'It's all too in flux. You have to understand the flux of human conversation.' I said, 'I don't mind. Flux is flux, but a published paper has to organize the flux for the purposes of understanding and discussion. You can't have a discussion which is in flux. The data may be in flux, but your discussion can't be in flux.' You know, he never forgave me for that. He was really very hurt and I was really sorry. Seemingly, he had been attacked at Berkeley for all of this ethnomethodology as not being scientific, and he thought I was doing that too. I actually thought that what I was doing was encouraging him to meet that kind of criticism. As a methodology, I don't oppose that kind of data as data collection, but I don't like it for data analysis. I can't tell the difference between the data and the analysis.

So, I have that problem with Williams too. And now, as far as the absence of conflicts, you know, he is a Marxist. And the absence of data of conflict in Marx would be the absence of Marx *per se*, since he understands all of life, all of society, as conflict.

**MP:** Did you give him a response at the time? Did you respond to his criticism?

**JAF:** No. I didn't respond to Williams' criticism, and I don't see anybody else criticizing me for the lack of conflict in my work, which must mean that either they don't have that impression or they don't do that kind of analysis. For example, even Phillipson, who thinks that I don't realize how much damage is being done by English to other languages around the world, doesn't say I have no appreciation of language conflict or that I think that there is no damage or that I think all the languages will disappear. There's a certain extremism about Williams, a philosophical extremism.

**MP:** Another important topic is the notion of power. As you know, we had it as a central issue at our LAUD Symposium in Landau (April 2004). In your contribution to the Proceedings (Pütz, Fishman, & Neff-van Aertselaer, forthcoming), you state the following: 'Sociolinguistics has too seldom paid adequate attention to the centrality of "power" in human behaviour and to "social power" more explicitly in its study of language in society' (Fishman, forthcoming). Now, my question is, has not the concept of power always been a central issue of the sociology of language? I mean, right from the beginnings, even if sometimes it has only been a hidden statement, but somehow it has always been there.

**JAF:** I'm willing to assume it's hidden, but I'm not willing to assume that it's central. Otherwise, you wouldn't have had such a dickens of a time trying to define it and make it operational. If it were even consciously considered as important, it would have been operationalized. It would have been put to use, rather than as a metaphor. No reason in our society not to acknowledge it. But it's true in the social sciences generally. Anthropology doesn't talk about power.

**NHH:** Well, I tend to think we assumed it was there, but it was not possible to operationalize it.

**JAF:** Well, operationalization, measurement is a philosophical topic. We may disagree on that, but... Thorndike, the old Edward Lee Thorndike would say: 'if it exists, whatever you're talking about, if it exists, it exists to some degree. If it exists to some degree, then it can be measured.'

**NHH:** Okay.

**JAF:** You can't both say it exists, but it can't be measured. That's a very American positivistic, dry as dust empiricism approach. But, you know, there's a terrible price to be paid if you disregard that entirely. You have to struggle as a scientist to say things in ways that others don't say them, that lead to recognition of their more-or-less nature.

**NHH:** I think you can observe and describe, and I guess the next step is to measure, right? Well, as you say, it's a philosophical issue.

**JAF:** It has to do with what is reality, and there's nothing more philosophical than discussing reality. Because then you have to discuss what is the real reality.

**MP:** Back to the official English Only movement. It was a prominent issue in the United States in the 1980s when you wrote an article on that issue (Chapter 10, this volume). Today, generally, the question of English dominance is still, even now more so, a hotly debated issue in academic circles and is often conceptualized in terms of dichotomies such as the ecology of language paradigm and the domination of English paradigm in a way, in the sense that Skutnabb-Kangas and Phillipson (e.g. 1994) put it. They also refer to the terms 'linguistic human rights', 'linguicism', 'linguistic imperialism', 'linguistic genocide'. Would you say that these terms are somehow exaggerated, or would you say they are in place given the fact also that some psychologists of language, such as Edwards (e.g. 2004), criticize 'the new ecology of language' because the whole movement is seen as being too naïve, too romantic about these things and language should be seen as a medium of communication rather than a medium of identity? Would you support this claim or this criticism of Edwards?

**JAF:** Well, I don't see why it can't be both things. Why does it have to be driven in a different direction than they're driving it, just because they're one-sided? Edwards is very one-sided in a statement of that kind. Language is one of those things that is both referent and process.

**MP:** Skutnabb-Kangas too is very much one-sided. So they are to be seen as being at extreme poles of the continuum.

**JAF:** Yes, and therefore not as good points of departure for a full appreciation of language. It's no surprise that sociology, and anthropology, and psychology, and history, and religion, and philosophy, all of these consider language. Because there's some aspect of reality that they want to supplement, they want to add to the picture. And therefore I think Skutnabb-Kangas and Phillipson may be the romantics that really think that every language can be and should be and must be saved, but I don't see that Edwards has a leg to stand on, to say that they're over-emphasizing language and identity. You'd have to do a serious study to say that; you'd have to find some people in the general population who have different degrees of language and identity. Edwards hasn't done that. Edwards has, for the last quarter century, criticized language and identity movements. And it's not because he thinks that it's just communication. He's not really that one-sided, but whenever he gets into a furor about some of his opponents, or people he's opposed to, he'll come up with a statement which is more extreme than he really believes. Because he really does realize that language is related to identity to some people most of the time, to some people some of the time, and to some people even all of the time. And that there are different movements and there are different intensities of this relationship. It's not good for students either, to oppose an extreme view by another extreme view which is easily disproven.

**NHH:** You've also written that the idea that ethnocultural identity is so closely linked to language that it can't exist without it, is disprovable. You've said that. And you have also said that you yourself are not as primordialist as some would make you out to be.

**JAF:** Oh, I'm not a primordialist. I don't think you can be a social scientist and a primordialist. But it's true that to this very day, when I come into class, I'm going to find a class made up of a hundred percent primordialists. The naïve student is fully convinced by his parents, by his pastors, by his community organizations that language is part of the basic material of humanity, of God, of society, that you cannot disentangle language from those things. And there's a kind of deep mystery there in their minds: they believe in the mysticism of it all.

**NHH:** Well, I was thinking of my experience with Quechua activists and other indigenous language activists and advocates. So, I'm often asked, 'Isn't the objective reality that these languages are dying? So, what do you do in the face of that?' And I say, 'Well, on the other hand, here are these people, speakers of these languages that are – you mentioned it earlier, I think – committing tremendous amounts of energy and creativity to promoting these languages, developing them, keeping them alive. And who is to say that one reality is more real than the other?' How do we reconcile that?

**JAF:** Well, I think you do it the way Nancy Dorian does it. She says all these efforts on behalf of languages accomplish something that would not be accomplished without them. So, to some extent, they create the reality that they hope to save. Maybe not to the extent that they'd like to.

You see, this is what I did that was so shocking that I could be accused of being a primordialist. You don't have to read far into what I've written to read all the correlational or causational or theoretical construction. You know for primordialism, you don't need any correlation because there are deep, eternal identities involved. But it turns out that social class intensifies this or that. You keep on trying, through language planning, to foster the language. Language planning and primordialism don't go together. Right? You don't have to do language planning if it's already in there in the warp and woof of the deep identity. If it's there, you don't have to reverse language shift because you're never going to get free of that deep structure. I think it's just so shocking for the social science world to see someone trying to show the prevalence of the primordialist idea in European thought.

That's all I've said. I've said we've got to study this, to understand these people because they're talking about something very important to them, very central to the way they understand God and life and society. That was shocking because I think no one had done that since – I won't say since Herder, but you have to go back a good bit to find that. Of course, in a sense Wundt was still saying that, but he was writing in German, which no one understands anymore. And secondly, he was writing in psychology, and third of all, he was writing about primitive peoples, so that left us out scot-free. We could feel good about that.

**MP:** Perhaps one important thing, Joshua. Some people want to strengthen the English dominance paradigm, and they are talking about issues such as the costs are too high to promote minority education, and that refers to the cost-benefit argument. And multilingualism in general is not economically beneficial. I know you wrote a paper about that too, the cost-benefit argument. And language differences constitute a barrier to international exchange, especially now in the context of globalism. Or take the argument of nation building for which a national or mutual language, such as English as official language, is said to prevent tribalism, ethnic divisions, rivalry, and all that, and the latter implying the danger of fostering isolation from other nations and from global communication. Now, what would be a response to all these allegations, all these arguments put forward against the promotion of multilingualism?

**JAF:** I don't like science at that level. We're not running a political campaign, and we're not running for president. Study! Get the data on that!

**MP:** Would you never want to give advice to language planners? To put theory into practice?

**JAF:** The advice has to come from data.

**MP:** But you have the data.

**JAF:** I have the data. I have studied whether gross national product is in any way impacted negatively by more or less multilingualism. Are countries that are more or less multilingual more or less productive in gross national product? So, we have all the countries of the world, for each of them there is a measure of the extent to which they speak the major language in that country. If the percent is one, if one is the major language in the country, one percent of the people speak it, there must be an awful lot of other languages that are less than one. So, it's a measure of linguistic diversity, the proportion of speakers of the major language. I use that only because it's available.

**MP:** Have you ever been involved in discussions with governments, for example, who like to implement certain strategies or language policies, giving advice for Basque or for Frisian, or other languages?

**JAF:** They only ask me how to improve their research. They don't ask me about the economic circumstances because they all realize that the factory can work in Dutch. The factory can work in Spanish. Therefore, they're engaged in identity politics, not in manufacturing politics. If it's self-bankrupting because they cannot keep up a modern industry in Basque, well they would be the first to know it. Basque happens to be one of the high employment areas in Spain, and they're the most insistent on doing it in Basque even though everybody speaks Spanish in those factories. The factory ostensibly operates in Basque, all the signs, all the instructions, all the regulations, all the communications from management.

**MP:** So they know the answers by themselves. They don't have to ask a sociologist of language. Is that what you mean, more or less?

**JAF:** That's not what they ask me. Maybe they ask Glyn Williams that. He wants them to do it in Welsh. He does want to see them do it in Welsh. He is a very adamant Welsh patriot and activist. He's willing to engage in conflict. I remember this: he debated a colleague named Glyn Lewis. Glyn Lewis said at a meeting at which Glyn Williams was present – because Lewis had worked all his life for Welsh, he was His Majesty's and then Her Majesty's Inspector for Welsh in Wales – and he said his life had taught him that you can lead a horse to water, but you can't make him drink. And Glyn Williams said, 'You can make it drink!' (laughter). That was the big difference between them. So maybe they're asking Williams how to make them drink.

But I think that's all assuming that the language scholar must be a propagandist for use of small languages in all circumstances, and I have never said that. In fact, the reason I don't have conflict as an obvious part of my theories is because I'm always trying to point out how there are still a lot of functions for the small language. It doesn't mean it won't need help, but there are still a lot of functions. In fact, I'm trying not to have all the languages have the same functions because that would be ruinous for the small languages. So what that means is giving them fewer functions at certain levels and in certain areas of life. I'm not sure they would like it, and everybody has gotten to think of that as a kind of enfeeblement of the small language. It's not going to be used for the power functions much. But I don't think they are going to be used much for all functions. There'll be a small academic, activist, romantic, patriotic front that will use them for all functions, and most other people will just use it for some functions. And wherever you go around the world and you watch that, that's what the case is.

In Ireland, at the University of Cork, where I visited in the same day two graduate classes in astrophysics, one was held in Irish, and one was held in English. And the one in Irish had two students, and the one in English had twelve. It was the same professor. And I said, 'What's the sense of this? You could have one class with fourteen students. Why do you have one with two? And that one has no textbooks.' He said, 'I want them to know that's the reality that there are only two if you do it in Irish. That's not the fault of the language. The language is not at fault here.'

**MP:** So English is not a 'killer language'? You don't like that metaphor?

**JAF:** If it were sufficient to understand English with that metaphor then you wouldn't have English under the auspices of all these small languages in the school systems that they control. They all want to have English too, or Spanish or whatever the local big language is. Where is it – I think in some state in India, where this week it turned out that they wanted to be sure to have English in grade one for everybody.

**NHH:** When you were a child you collected stamps and vowed you would visit as many countries as you could one day, and you have visited I don't know how many countries.

**JAF:** I got an invitation to Japan today.

**NHH:** And I'm interested also in where you've lived internationally. I know that you've lived in Jerusalem, but are there other parts of the world where you've spent weeks or months?

**JAF:** We lived for half a year in Holland and also in Hawaii. We spent almost a year in Hawaii.

**NHH:** At the East-West Center. Was that part of the four nation project?

**JAF:** That's where we formulated it. That's where it was planned.

**NHH:** And then you directed it out of Israel.

**JAF:** Yes, we each of us went off to some country, and since I was the director, I directed it from the country I went to. In fact, Israel was not initially in the plan. But Jernudd and Rubin said, 'Listen, you've got to go to Israel. Hebrew is a major language planning story. You're the right person for that. It'll look silly if you don't do Israel.' So you know, I'm not going to be in the position of vetoing Israel.

**NHH:** Well, that kind of brings us also to Yiddish. We wanted to ask you a little bit about the role of Yiddish in both your life and your work. I mean it's a huge question, but a few specifics. For example, the role of Yiddish schools – you were a student, you were a teacher, you've done research on the ethnic mother tongue schools. Do you want to comment on the role of Yiddish schools in your life and in your work?

**JAF:** It's obvious to me that so much of my work derived at one level of abstraction or another, which means either very directly or less very directly, from my interest in Yiddish, or my experience, or my observations, or my perseverances, or my worries, or my hopes, or my frustrations in the world of Yiddish, in connection with Yiddish. I never go through a day that I don't think about the problem of Yiddish. It's my problem of Yiddish, you know. That's what I think of: what do I give my children and my grandchildren when the world which I could give them has been killed? Then what do I give them? Now if I could give them that world, they might reject it. They might say it's old-fashioned or not American, but I don't even have that option.

It's like being cut off from the mother ship when you're flying in the stratosphere, and just floating out there. We come from a certain world. That world doesn't exist anymore. Now of course, you can give them memories, but they're already second-hand memories. I can tell them about my youth growing up in Philadelphia, but it's less interesting than Vilna in representing something fully formed. You know what I mean? Vilna, in a sense, had everything. It had the modern sector, the orthodox sector, the Hebrew sector, the Yiddish sector, the Polish sector. There were Polonized Jews, not many.

So I would say you don't have to dig too deep to find the key, the link to Yiddish, and you can know when you've found it if you find a study connecting it or mentioning Yiddish in connection with a certain topic.

**NHH:** You had said that you worried sometimes that you might be accused of being too Yiddish-centric in your sociolinguistic work but that that actually hasn't happened.

**JAF:** It hasn't happened, maybe because of the kindness of folks like you that would never say anything like that – although you know it's been said about other people by other people.

**NHH:** About Yiddish in particular or?

**JAF:** No, about being Jewish. You know this French linguist, a great man in the previous century. André Martinet. Well, it turns out that whatever moved him, you know he had been chair of Linguistics at Columbia, he knew both Weinreich and Greenberg when they were very young. He wrote the introduction to Uriel Weinreich's *College Yiddish* text. But since they and some other Jewish linguists rejected what he considered to be his theoretical masterpiece, his great opus in linguistic theory, he wrote about them all, that like all Jews, they were monists and they cannot abide a tripartite theory because it reminds them of the Trinity. No one's ever said anything like that to me. I have nothing against monistic theories or Trinitarian theories in principle.

**NHH:** No, in fact you've proposed some trinities in your work.

**JAF:** I have?

**NHH:** Bilingual education typology.

**JAF:** I guess I have.

I think I have been lucky or maybe it's just a way of thinking, to find the general issue no matter what the specific data is. Actually, the specific data may be Yiddish, or the specific concern may be Yiddish. It's quite true you know, in terms of *Language Loyalty*, which was my first claim to fame, as a book. You know the paper on the Whorfian Hypothesis (Fishman; 1960, see also 1985) had already appeared before that, and it could be that more people have come across my name in that connection than any other.

I was tooling up to get to work in this area and Gella and I both had a mentor, who was the director of a Yiddish camp called Boiberik. Boiberik is a fictitious resort town in Sholem Aleichem's stories. It's a vacation town, a summer vacation town, and therefore for a children's camp operated in Yiddish, for children speaking Yiddish, to be called Boiberik, you know it had a double meaning – a nice name and it meant a vacation place, a literary and a restful place. I remember its director, Leybush Lehrer, recommended Haugen to me. He had read Haugen. This was '58 to '60 – Haugen's book had already come out (1953). He said to me, 'You know, we don't really understand what's happening here. Here we're living in the United States, we don't really know how other languages are coping with their problems. Do they have the same problems that we have? Or are we the only ones? We are the only ones that have no country anymore. We came from someplace which doesn't exist anymore. They all have some place to go back to. We have no place to go back to. We're all involuntary exiles.'

So, I won't say I wouldn't have done the study without his goading, but that stayed in my mind you know. It's true. What did he have in the back of his mind? He said, 'You know, maybe the Italians, maybe they know how to do it. They never experienced the social mobility that we experienced.' See, even he was talking about it in general terms. Well, of course, he was a psychologist. He was a trained psychologist. He had a master's degree from Clark University – imagine, an immigrant boy from Warsaw. He wrote a textbook in psychology in Yiddish – there must have been people who needed it, or maybe he needed it to be out there. 'Maybe the Italians. You never know, you may find out there are other groups like that, small groups, large groups, east groups, west groups, Christian groups, non-Christian groups, all kinds of comparisons here that you can make.'

**NHH:** He actually talked about that with you at that time?

**JAF:** Yeah, well, I had had many of these ideas already, but the fact that he felt that he didn't know. He was a man who read the literature; he read Haugen, he must have read other psycho-educational literature for sure. He has one book called *People are Like That, Azoy zenen Mentshn* in Yiddish (1934).

**NHH:** Great title.

**JAF:** Yeah. Then he has another book called *Jews are Like That, Azoy zenen Yidn* (1959).

**NHH:** So he wrote originally in Yiddish.

**JAF:** Oh yes. He wrote only in Yiddish. I mean, maybe he wrote a paper or two in English, so that his colleagues in Jewish education, who couldn't read Yiddish or wouldn't, would know what he was up to.

**NHH:** Beyond Yiddish providing the specific case from which you then could find general answers, I think – you've talked about this too, and I think about it a lot – it also provided you or provides you with a minority perspective, being on the periphery. Right? Because of its status as not only a little language, but also a discriminated language.

**JAF:** Doubly discriminated. Discriminated externally, discriminated internally.

**NHH:** Don't you think that infuses all your work, that view from the margins?

**JAF:** From the periphery, from the margin.

You know Sholem Aleichem has a story about a boy called Motl. It's a 1910 or 1912 story of coming to America from the little town. People were already coming to America.

**NHH:** That's when your father came.

**JAF:** Yeah. And pretty much the same area. My mother was almost directly from the same area that Sholem Aleichem wrote *Fiddler on the Roof* about. The first dramatic thing about the book is that the boy's father dies. He coughs, and coughs, and coughs, and spits up blood, and dies. Of course, the family has no money to buy any kind of medication and he dies. And then the boy hasn't been bar mitzvahed yet, but he has to learn to say Kaddish, the prayer for the dead, although it's not really absolutely obligatory for boys who are not yet of the age to say Kaddish, but still it's no more than you owe your dad to say that during the services. So, it's a real struggle for him. There's a long Kaddish. There's a short Kaddish. You have to know when to say which, and for the whole eleven months, you have to go to the services several times a day, and it's a real responsibility, which is an onerous one.

But on the other hand, he has all kinds of favors shown to him. People invite him to meals. People give him toys. People pat him on the head. The teacher in the elementary school doesn't whip him when he misbehaves. So he comes up with the phrase, 'It's really good for me because I'm an orphan.' So, that's what I think of in connection with this external view from the margin. I'm an orphan. I'm here on the margin, on the outside, and it gives me perspective, gives me an odd perspective.

**NHH:** And many blessings.

**JAF:** Yeah. Well, you know, I guess if you're going to be an intellectual seriously, you have to try to be an outsider too. To depart from the established thinking, to really think in an unestablished fashion – it's very hard to do that. So much of your thinking is following in the groove.

I wrote a paper about stereotyping, I don't know if you've ever seen it. Stereotyping *per se* is really groove thinking – fast answers to problems. You just go to the usual answer and there you've got it. You don't have to waste your time thinking. And there's a natural human propensity in that direction, and you have to struggle against it. Now taking it outside that framework, people doing research have to struggle against the groove too.

And I remember once Ferguson said to me that he had a very deep distrust of scholars who come up with the accepted answer to a question (laughter). If there's anything that you expect of a scholar, it's that he should come up with some crazy idea that ordinary people wouldn't understand. It wouldn't occur to them. In fact, you know, Jews praise various rabbinic commentators because of their abstruseness – 'who would have thought of that?' It's called distancing your thinking from common sense.

**NHH:** You mean there's a phrase for that?

**JAF:** There's a phrase for that. Distancing your thinking from common sense. If you want to come up with a – maybe an excessively convoluted – theory, but the result is something which wasn't expected. Distancing your thinking from common sense.

**MP:** Joshua, what are your plans for the future? Are you now working on papers or new books that we can await?

**JAF:** You know, there are ever so many books in press right now because of you folks and other folks. I think maybe all in all, five or six books are in press. The ones that I know of are my own book on language planning, corpus planning. I think I told you about it. Everybody's done status planning. And I finally thought the students were getting the short end of the stick because they had no real idea what moves the corpus planner in a particular direction. It's a fascinating story about the corpus planners. You know, some languages did have to be made up from the whole cloth. Unbelievable. So that's in press with Lawrence Erlbaum (Fishman, 2006).

Then, Guadalupe Valdés already has our joint book in press, on heritage language. We wrote that volume and there are papers that our student assistants wrote, too. That's with Multilingual Matters (Valdés, Fishman, Chavéz & Pérez, 2006).

And last month, Gella and my sons ganged up on me. I had resisted, I had said, 'No, no, no.' And then I figured, you know, if it means so much to people that I love, why shouldn't I do it? So they convinced me I should do a book of my Yiddish papers, not necessarily on Yiddish, but in Yiddish. And I'll send you a copy, each of you, because I don't know who needs it. No one will buy it. It will cost me money to publish it. And then I'll have to send it out to potential readers and plead, 'Please accept this as a gift with my best regards.'

**MP:** But you're going to do it?

**JAF:** Yes, if it means that much to Gella. I've already picked the papers.

One thing I think I've accomplished is that all my colleagues realize that Yiddish is not just some wretched or funny mishmash, as its opponents claim.

**MP:** What's the estimated number of Yiddish speakers nowadays in the world, approximately?

**JAF:** It's a very hard question to really answer – I'm the one who makes the estimates year by year. You have to estimate things like, what would the figure be if all the countries that have censuses were asking the same question because they're not asking the same questions.

**MP:** It has to be standardized.

**JAF:** So we don't know what speakers means. Do you mean speakers day by day, everyday, or as only language speakers, or as most common language speakers, or as if the need arises they can speak it? What does *Umgangssprache* mean really?

**MP:** Vernacular.

**JAF:** Does it mean the only vernacular? People can have several vernaculars.

**MP:** An informal variety.

**JAF:** The only informal variety? Does it mean a separate language?

**MP:** In other words, there's no answer to the question.

**JAF:** It's very hard to give a real answer to the question. Now the next problem is that no one asks the hard-to-ask people. For example, to get into the ultra-orthodox communities to ask census questions is impossible. First of all, it's impossible because they don't believe in censuses by a foreign government, a *goyish* government.

In Israel, the Israeli government doesn't count them. I once found more Yiddish speakers in Jerusalem by myself than they had reported in the census. And I figured there must have been twice as many. I said, 'How could that be?' Oh, they agreed with me. They said, 'You know we can't count them.' The government can't count them or estimate them? They said, 'Look, they don't recognize us, we don't recognize them.' That's the census department talking to you: we only count people that recognize us.

So, the most recent article written in Yiddish that I've sent off to the Yiddish weekly that publishes one article by me every month happens to be on this topic, 'Language censuses in Yiddish.' I figure about two million, including everyone who is uncounted and if we adopt a minimal definition of speakers – that is people who could speak if they had to and not just if they wanted to, people who could make themselves understood. But when you add any conditions to that, grammatically correct or native or near-native or something like that, the number would be different. You know, many Jews have it now as a second or third language. And most people have it as a childhood memory.

**MP:** And you consider it to be your mother tongue? Yiddish, not English.

**JAF:** It is my mother tongue. Does it come through in my English? I imagine it does.

**NHH:** Well, and your children speak Yiddish. And your grandchildren?

**JAF:** The two older ones, in whose education and upbringing we were greatly involved, when they meet us, they do speak Yiddish to us. The younger ones, however, understand when I ask them a question. So yes, we've succeeded in getting it into the third generation – actually, they're the fourth generation because I'm the second generation, my children are the third, my grandchildren are the fourth. A little language lives on such shaky ground, but it constitutes a most creative tension for its community and dedicated defenders and users.

**MP:** Joshua, thank you very much for four hours of a most inspiring conversation.

**NHH:** Thank you.

**JAF:** You've been very kind.

## Notes

1. The interview was recorded with the kind permission of Joshua Fishman. We are grateful to Shannon Sauro, PhD candidate in Educational Linguistics at the Graduate School of Education, University of Pennsylvania, for her transcription of the original four-hour recorded interview.
2. Transliterations of Yiddish words throughout are in accord with the system adopted over 50 years ago by the US Library of Congress and the Yivo.
3. The check is framed and hung on Fishman's main study wall as a  souvenir.
4. Ferguson has also edited highly influential volumes with Fishman: Fishman *et al.* (1968) and Rubin *et al.* (1977).

## References

Blom, J. and Gumperz, J. (1972) Social meaning in linguistic structure: Code-switching in Norway. In J.J. Gumperz and D. Hymes (eds) *Directions in Sociolinguistics* (pp. 407–434). New York: Holt, Rinehart, and Winston.

Edwards, J. (2004) Ecolinguistic ideologies: A critical perspective. In M. Pütz, J. Neff-van Aertselaer and T.A. van Dijk (eds) *Communicating Ideologies: Multidisciplinary Perspectives on Language, Discourse, and Social Practice* (pp. 273–290). Frankfurt: Peter Lang.

Ferguson, C.A. (1996) *Sociolinguistic Perspectives: Papers on Language in Society, 1959-1994.* Oxford & New York: Oxford University Press.

— and Heath, S.B. (eds) (1981) *Language in the USA*. Cambridge: Cambridge University Press.

Fishman, J.A. (1960) A systematization of the Whorfian hypothesis. *Behavioral Science* 8, 323–339.

—. (ed.) (1966) *Language Loyalty in the United States*. The Hague, London & Paris: Mouton de Gruyter.

—. (1985) Whorfianism of the third kind. In J.A. Fishman *et al.* (eds) *The Rise and Fall of the Ethnic Revival* (pp. 473–488). Berlin/New York: Mouton de Gruyter.

—. (1991) *Reversing Language Shift*. Clevedon: Multilingual Matters.

—. (2006) *Do Not Leave Your Language Alone: The Hidden Status Agendas Within Corpus Planning in Language Policy*. Mahwah, NJ: Lawrence Erlbaum.

—. (forthcoming) Sociolinguistics: More powers to you (on the explicit study of power in sociolinguistic research). In M. Pütz, J.A. Fishman and J. Neff-van Aertselaer (eds) *'Along the Routes to Power'. Explorations of Empowerment through Language*. Berlin/New York: Mouton de Gruyter.

— Ferguson, C.A. and das Gupta, J. (eds) (1968) *Language Problems of Developing Nations*. New York: Wiley and Sons.

Haugen, E. (1953) *The Norwegian Language in America: A Study in Bilingual Behavior.* Philadelphia: University of Pennsylvania Press.

Hertzler, J.O. (1965) *A Sociology of Language*. Doubleday: Random House.

Herzl, T. (1896) *Der Judenstaat*. Leipzig: M. Breitenstein.

Kloss, H. (1966) German-American language maintenance efforts. In J.A. Fishman (ed.) *Language Loyalty in the US*. (pp. 206–252).

Lehrer, L. (1934) *Azoy zenen Mentshn*. New York: Matone's.

Lehrer, L. (1959) *Azoy zenen Yidn*. New York: Matone's.

Pütz, M., Fishman, J. and Neff-van Aertselaer, J. (eds) (forthcoming) *'Along the Routes to Power'. Explorations of Empowerment through Language*. Berlin/New York: Mouton de Gruyter.

Rubin, J., Fishman, J., Jernudd, J., Das Gupta, J. and Ferguson, C.A. (eds) (1977) *Language Planning Processes*. The Hague: Mouton.

Skutnabb-Kangas, T. and Phillipson, R. (eds) (1994) *Linguistic Human Rights: Overcoming Linguistic Discrimination*. Berlin/New York: Mouton de Gruyter.

Valdés, G., Fishman, J.A., Chávez, R. and Pérez, W. (2006) *Developing Minority Language Resources: The Case of Spanish in California*. Clevedon: Multilingual Matters.

Williams, G. (1992) *Sociolinguistics. A Sociological Critique*. London and New York: Routledge.

*Part 1*

# Personal Perspectives on Sociolinguistics

# Chapter 1

# *My Life Through My Work; My Work Through My Life*

I have lived a rather uneventful Jewish-American life and the chronology of that life is in no way unusual. It is about as 'newsworthy' to say that I graduated high-school at age 18 and to say that I celebrated my Jewish coming of age ('bar-mitsve') at age 13. These are the usual or obligatory ages for such experiences and they provide no particular insights into anything that came before or later. At any rate, the date of my birth and the dates of my various academic degrees and major publications are all recorded, together with other rather uninspired information, in the usual standard references in which major American academicians are listed, and, therefore, only a few of them need be mentioned in this account.

Rather than adopting a chronological approach to my life, a topical approach is much more appealing to me. The topics that mean most to me, of course, are the topics of my writings as well as the methodological and philosophical preferences that have informed them. Nevertheless, certain early experiences were undoubtedly foundational to everything that followed and, accordingly, I will start at or near the beginning and go on from there.

## Childhood and Youth: A Second-Generation Language Activist

I grew up in Philadelphia, a very WASP-dominated town at the time, the elder child of Yiddish speaking immigrants from Czarist Russia. The neighborhoods in which I lived, up to the time of my leaving in 1948 for graduate work at Columbia University, were all middle-class Jewish neighborhoods populated largely by Yiddish speaking immigrant parents and grandparents, on the one hand, and by their proudly and demonstratively Yiddish-ignorant children and grandchildren, on the other hand. This was a rather typical sociolinguistic setting for that time and the only distinctive aspect of it was the fact that my parents were conscious and conscientious Yiddish language activists and that their children, my younger sister Rukhl and I, happily and eagerly followed in their footsteps. In all truth, there were a few other 'Yiddishists' like my parents, both in Philadelphia as a whole and even in our own immediate neighborhood, and there were even also a few other young people, like my sister and I, who willingly dreamed and pursued the impossible dream of Yiddish language maintenance among the younger generation. Nevertheless, this was a relatively atypical preoccupation even in the immigrant generation and doubly so among the second generation. Atypical too, the overriding seriousness with which the defense and propagation of Yiddish were pursued and the degree of success encountered in that connection within the Fishman household *per se*.

The non-definitive nature of autobiographies is clearly demonstrated by the fact that I have never been able to fully account for my parents' success in transferring to my sister and me their dedication to Yiddish. Their intelligence and devotion 'to the cause' were clearly exemplary, but I can more fully differentiate between them and the other, less successful members of the small and tireless band of Philadelphia Yiddishists only on the dimension of selfless activism. Our home and my parents' laboratory (my father was a dental mechanic, a profession he acquired, along with his American citizenship, while serving in the American Army during World War I) were unofficial ministries of culture and education. My father worked with his hands on dental-plates and bridges, but the telephone was always cocked to his ear as he incessantly conversed with other activists, teachers, writers and actors throughout the country. My mother kept the accounting-books and sent out the bills, but between one billing period and the next she addressed masses of envelopes and post cards pertaining to forthcoming conferences, readings, poetry recitals, theater performances, school meetings, etc. Every Yiddish book and journal published anywhere in the world arrived at the laboratory and all Yiddish writers stopped off there, if only to obtain assistance in selling their books, when coming to Philadelphia. Every Yiddish cultural event that transpired in Philadelphia was conceived there and was subjected there to a critical 'after the fact' evaluation. In addition, there seems to have been a fortunate if random co-occurrence of language-focused interests between the Fishman generations, because although my sister (later to become a highly regarded Yiddish poetess in Israel) and I both went through the usual stages of adolescent revolt in many respects, and although our relations with our parents were sometimes far from harmonious, Yiddish always remained an unquestioned verity for us and a link between us. Many of the topics to which I have devoted several years of professional sociolinguistic attention, e.g. language maintenance and language shift, language and nationalism, bilingual education, the spread of English, language and ethnicity, language planning and reversing language shift, can be traced back to concrete concerns, topics, involvements and even specific discussions of my childhood and adolescence within the very unusual home and family which gave me my first perspective on language in society.

## Other Formative Early Influences

Three other aspects of my growing up have constantly remained with me: an early emphasis on writing and publishing, an early stress on multidisciplinary perspective and an early fascination with the nations, cultures and languages of the world.

As a child, I began writing for Yiddish youth journals. The earliest such publication of which I have any record today is a short story published in 1938, when I was 12, although I began to write Yiddish poetry (blessedly unpublished) as early as age seven or eight (and, in the five-generational archives that Gella has set up in our home, I have the notebook by which to prove it). In 1940, a year after my bar-mitsve, I became the founding editor and 'publisher' of (as well as constant contributor to) a Yiddish youth journal (originally called Ilpik [acronym of Y.L. Perets Yugntklub], later Yugntruf). This activity provided me with my first experiences of contacting potential contributors and subscribers, as well as with my first exposure to the technical problems of the publishing 'industry'. These efforts continued for the next dozen years and even the first 'date' that I had with Gella Schweid, who was to become my wife in 1951, was ostensibly for the purpose of discussing the possible renewal of a Yugntruf (the journal had lapsed in 1950, after transferring its editorial offices to New York, in the mid-40s, when Uriel Weinreich and several other New Yorkers were added to its editorial board). My writing and editing always had to be 'fit in' during after-school-hours ('school' also included attendance at Yiddish counterpart 'supplementary' institutions, from the elementary through to the post-secondary levels; later, during college and graduate school, I also taught at such institutions), often going on late into the night and throughout weekends and holidays or vacations. Later, as a faculty member, I found it 'perfectly natural' to constantly be engaged in professional sociolinguistic writing and editing and to find the time for doing so at 'odd hours' and at 'off hours', when others were accustomed to sleeping or to taking it easy. To this very day I find that writing is relaxing, rather than tiring, and stimulating, rather than exhausting.

I attribute my multidisciplinary predilections to the early realization that matters often looked remarkably different to Yiddishists and non-Yiddishists and to Jews and non-Jews. By extension, I was not surprised later to find that they also looked different to historians, psychologists and anthropologists. I also came very early to the realization that a point of view held by few people need not be wrong and, indeed, that in matters of value-laden 'social reality', it was very hard to conclusively prove or disprove propositions of any kind and, therefore, that following a variety of perspectives was the best approach one could take for arriving reasonably close to the truth. I think I was better prepared to take each approach seriously as a result of my neighborhood high school (Olney [pronounced: AHLney] H.S) experience which required 'academic students' (coming from a pretty evenly balanced mixture of Irish, German and Jewish extractions, who had to learn to get along with each other, a lesson clinched only by America's entry into World War II when we were in out junior year) to take five majors every semester and every day of the school week. English included a book of the Bible, a work of Shakespeare and the works of a more modern British or American author every semester for four years. History included a year of world history, a year of ancient history, a year of English history and a year of American history. Science included a year of earth sciences, a year of biology, a year of chemistry and a year of physics. Mathematics consisted of two years of geometry (including solid geometry) and two years of algebra (including trigonometry). My foreign language was Spanish, probably because my mother had studied Latin, my father, German, and 'only girls took French'. These subjects were all taught at a demanding and stimulating level and made me realize that every discipline had its assets and its debits, its limitations and its unique perspective and conribution. The only sound preparation for all contingencies was a preparation that required mastery of them all. Like every other student, I had a 'favorite subject' (history/social studies, taught by an exceptionally provocative faculty), but I could not really imagine a good historian who had not prepared well in the other subjects as well, because all of them (including science and mathematics) potentially contributed to historical documentation, verification and appreciation.

My fascination with countries, cultures and languages began with stamp-collecting. When I was eight years old, Ivory Soap gave away a stamp album and foreign postage stamps to anyone who sent in a stipulated number of wrappers of its products. I soon learned the names of all of the countries, where they were on the map and the crucial words or non-Latin letters that identified their stamps, by devoting untold hours to these tasks. As time went by, I also learned a little of the history of each country and wrote letters to American ambassadors all over the world asking them for stamps of the countries where they were stationed. Their positive replies were among the major joys of my childhood, above and beyond the joys of Yiddish. The world of many peoples, cultures and languages, Jews, Jewishness and Yiddish among them, became the stage on which my particularistic and my generalized interests and appreciations co-existed harmoniously and reenforced one another. As a childhood stamp collector I vowed I would some day visit as many countries as I possibly could. That vow came to be realized and my fascination with the multinational, multicultural and multilingual nature of mankind has continued unabated to this very day.

## Finding the Sociology of Language/Sociolinguistics

I didn't really come into full contact with the world of 'official sociolinguistics' until 1963 (and it was a very small world indeed then), when I was already 37 and a fellow at the Center for Advanced Study in the Behavioral Sciences (Stanford, California). As I now reconstruct my life, I had been a sociolinguist unwittingly for at least 30 years by then and had already taught a semester of 'Sociology of Language' at the University of Pennsylvania in the spring of 1960. The appearance of Osgood and Sebeok's *Psycholinguistics* (1954), even as far back as my post-doctoral fellowship at Columbia University in 1953–1954, had made me quite aware of the need for the term 'sociolinguistics' to parallel the already available term 'psycholinguistics', but when I expressed this need to Roger Brown (whose *Words and Things* [1958] made almost as powerful an impression on me during my two years on the Penn faculty as did Einar Haugen's *The Norwegian Language in America* [1953]), he replied that such a word was 'unscannable' in English. As a result, I generally continued referring to what I was doing and to what I wanted to do by the name 'sociology of language'. My intellectual route to working in this field, inevitable though it might now seem, was a more indirect one than might be expected.

I had gone through the University of Pennsylvania (earning both a B.S. and M.S. in four years [1944–1948] so that my four year Mayor's Competitive Scholarship would pay for both), starting first as a 'pre-dental' major for one semester, to placate my father's request that I at least 'try it', and then continuing as a history major and a Spanish minor. My father had fond hopes of our working together if I became a dentist, but I soon switched majors, my intention being to ultimately go on to graduate school in New York, to specialize either in Jewish history (with Salo W. Baron) or in linguistics (with André Marinet). I had heard about both of these giants from the Weinreichs, whose home in Manhattan I had begun to frequent in the fall of 1943, after their younger son, Gabriel, had been my assistant at a Yiddish summercamp ('Nayvelt') the summer just before. Max Weinreich quickly became and long remained my major academic advisor and my model of academic excellence and of Yiddish scholarly-plus-societal involvement.

However, although he gave me Baron's and Martinet's names, he also discouraged me from specializing either in Jewish history or in linguistics. 'We already have enough historians and linguists' he told me solemnly, the 'we' not being a 'royal we' at all, but rather a 'Yiddish societal we', from the perspective of the Yiddish Scientific Institute-Yivo (later: YIVO Institute for Jewish Research) of which Weinreich was the director. The YIVO, originally founded in Vilna (Lithuania, 1925), was then the academic 'crown jewel' of what remained of modern Yiddish secular culture after the Holocaust. Weinreich had been among its co-founders and the prime force behind its full-blown reemergence in the USA after his arrival here in 1940. I, on the other hand, had discovered its journal (*YIVO-bleter*) in my parents' library in Philadelphia, during my college years, and kept in my wallet a list of issues that were missing in that little collection, just in case I might come across any of them at the used book shops that I frequented on my regular (undergraduate) visits to New York.

The first time that I met Weinreich he immediately invited me to come to the YIVO's Annual Conference and sent me his personal check for the train-fare, so that there would be no monetary excuse for my not coming. From that day, to the day of his death in early 1969, Weinreich continued to involve me in the Yivo's committees, conferences and publications, an involvement which continued until 1976 when it was sundered by the Yivo's attempt to censor the issue of *YIVO-bleter* which I was then preparing in the capacity of General Editor. But, to return to my college days, it was unthinkable either to me or to my parents that I would enter graduate school (1948) without consulting with Max Weinreich, and as a result of that consultation, I entered Columbia as a psychology major (a field in which 'we' did not have enough specialists). My first furnished apartment in New York was on West 123 Street in Manhattan, just a few blocks from Columbia University and right across the street from the YIVO. As on many other subsequent occasions in my life, I had succeeded in leaving home and yet, simultaneously, in not leaving it completely.

At Columbia I gravitated inexorably toward social psychology, although I remember telling my advisor, Irving Lorge, that I ultimately hoped to concentrate on language-related research. Lorge, himself a specialist in word-counts and in other language-related pursuits within educational psychology, was not unsympathetic. However, he quickly pointed out that there was as yet little call for such specialization and that my first priority should be to complete my doctorate, a goal which I attained under his direction in 1953, writing my dissertation on the negative stereotypes of 'Americans' held by the different groups of Jewish youngsters who attended the very varied spectrum of Jewish schools in New York City. Thereafter, he felt, I would be able to teach and research 'anything' I wanted to. In this prediction he was not mistaken. After completing a post-doctoral SSRC fellowship of quantitative methods in the social sciences, I taught social psychology every semester (three times per year, counting summer sessions) at City College (now City College of the City University of New York) for three years (1955–1958) using Bram's *Language and Society* (1955) as my text. Mine was the only such social psychology course in the Psychology Department, or in the history of the department, but, as Lorge had predicted, the sanctity of the classroom was inviolate and I could teach 'anything' I wanted to as social psychology, as long as it was not subversive of morality or polity. I mention 'subversive' because those were the McCarthy years and I expressed my outrage at his terrorization of American intellectual life via a witch-hunt against communists by editing an issue of the Society for the Psychological Study of Social Issues' *Journal of Social Issues* (whose editor I was later to become [1965–1968]) on 'Witness Perform-ance Under Stress' [1957]).

My degree in psychology has given me a unique slant on the sociolin-guistic enterprise, as unique a slant, indeed, as my Yiddishist origins. Different research designs, often more quantitative and more experimen-tal than those that occur to linguists, language scholars, anthropologists, sociologists, political scientists, historians or educationists, have fre-quently turned up in my work, as has an abiding interest in attitudes and a concern for measurement and issues of reliability and validity. All in all, however, starting off from psychology in my pilgrimage to soci-ology of language has merely assured me of continuing and intensifying the same multidisciplinary perspective as my early years at a fine high school in Philadelphia had initially provided. It was not long before I was grateful for having had the incredible good luck not to have gone directly into either linguistics, history or sociology. Exploring them all later and indirectly assured me of a much richer and more unique intel-lectual experience, although perhaps a less thorough one, than might otherwise have been the case.

When I returned as a faculty member to the University of Pennsylvania in 1958, 10 years after having received my M.S. there, my rank and title were Associate Professor of Psychology and Human Relations. The Human Relations affiliation stemmed from my being the Research Direc-tor of The Albert M. Greenfield Center for Human Relations, an academic unit that focused on intergroup relations. It was through that unit, and with my joint appointment in psychology, that I began to offer a year-long course called 'Human Relations and Language' (rather than 'Language and Human Relations' as I had initially suggested, because the Linguistics Department insisted that any course starting with the word 'language' could be offered only and exclusively by its own members), comprising one semester of 'Psychology of Language' and one semester of 'Sociology of Language'.

It was at the close of my second year at Penn that I was awarded a very substantial, long-term research grant by the Language Research Section of the Office of Education, a grant which – in our eagerness to return to New York – I immediately (1960) took with me to Yeshiva University. The purpose of this grant was to determine the 'Non-English Language Resources of the United States', but for me personally, at a supra-rational level, it was also an opportunity to find out if any of the other immigrant languages were in a better state of health than Yiddish and, if so, why. This grant resulted in my first major sociolinguistic publication, *Language Loyalty in the United States* (1966), the manuscript of which I completed during a fellowship year (1963–1964) at the Center for Advanced Study in the Behavioral Sciences, Stanford, California.

Coming, as I did from psychology, it was the 1959–1960 course in 'Human Relations and Language', the 1960–1964 grant to do research on the 'Non-English Language Resources of the United States' and my 1963–1964 year at CASBS, a year which was concluded with a Faculty Seminar in Sociolinguistics at Indiana University, conducted by Charles A. Ferguson (incidentally, also a Philadelphian and a Penn graduate, who was to remain a life-long friend), that finally led me, after a very long detour, into more than a quarter century of full-time sociolinguistic endeavor. Ultimately, no one knew, remembered or cared that I had come to my interests in language in society from within the unlikely borders of psychology and Yiddish. Indeed, whenever I mention these facts to my students and colleagues, they are surprised. For them I am a sociolinguist, or, better yet, just a linguist 'like everyone else'. I have taught in linguistics departments all over the world during the past quarter century and my untroubled acceptance there is a major source of gratification to me. Nevertheless, it is quite clear to me that in very many ways I am not really a 'linguist like everyone else' at all.

## Centralizing the Periphery

Perhaps I feel myself to be at the periphery of linguistics because I have always specialized in being at the periphery of establishments. The children of immigrants could not doubt that they were at the periphery of cultural and intellectual life in Philadelphia as a whole, and at the University of Pennsylvania in particular, during my years there. They had to struggle to convert that periphery, as viewed from the centers of power and status, into a meaningful center for their own lives. Yiddishists, a minority within a minority, have long been at the periphery of the American Jewish establishment but have struggled to gain recognition and legitimacy for the much maligned object of their affection.

Within the sociolinguistic enterprise, I have specialized in marginal groups, neglected languages, forgotten individuals, overlooked possibilities and outmoded or societally downgraded concerns. My goal has been to utilize the peripheries to which I am attracted in order to provide fresh perspective on the recognized or fashionably 'central topics' and, indeed, to demonstrate that these peripheries are far more illuminating and stimulating – i.e. more centrally important – than is usually appreciated.

The general principles derived from the study of minority societies and their threatened languages are widely applicable, if correctly delineated, to sociolinguistic contexts the world over. Minority efforts to foster language maintenance and to reverse language shift processes reveal language and identity phenomena, as well as boundary issues, with respect to social situations and functions that are merely different in degree rather than in kind from such phenomena, issues and allocations *vis-à-vis* English or French. Indeed, the sensitivity of most sociolinguistic issues in the contexts of threatened languages has probably increased my sensitivity to the importance of minor changes and small differences which might otherwise easily be lost sight of under more sanguine circumstances. The periphery magnifies and clarifies. Above all, it refuses to take matters for granted. It refuses to confuse peripherality with unimportance, or weakness in numbers or in power, with weakness *vis-à-vis* equity, justice, law and morality.

My methodological proclivities have also tended to set me apart from the mainstream of American (socio)linguistics. Not only is the bulk of my work either macro-sociological, historical or quantitative, but it resolutely refuses to be restricted to corpus (phonology, syntax, discourse, etc.) concerns or even to manifest any interest in such concerns at all. For a long time many linguists were puzzled by my topics and by my levels of analysis. One early reviewer put it roughly this way: 'Fishman presents us with data and findings which are tantamount to cracking an egg, pouring out its contents and concentrating on its outer shell'. I have never argued with this implication of peripherality, although it made me sad for the future of a human-studies discipline in which a concern with history, society and culture would be so regarded; I have merely insisted that the shell too is part of the egg and that without it the so-called 'contents' would soon be little more than an intellectually trivial, formless and lifeless mess.

In comparison with the foregoing, one aspect of peripherality has always been much on my mind, but, strangely enough, it has not resulted in outspoken criticism on the part of my colleagues. The wellspring of many of my ideas and, even more, the source of much of my intellectual and motivational unrest, continues to be the world of Yiddish (perhaps I should say the 'worlds of Yiddish' since both ultra-Orthodox society and modern, secular society intrigue me). The danger in drawing incessantly from that well is that I will, unknowingly and unsuspectingly, foster a Yiddish-centric view of the sociolinguistic enterprise. I have endeavored to guard against this danger by testing my theories and findings against Spanish, French and German in the USA, against Irish, Frisian and Basque in Europe, against Maori, Australian Aboriginal languages and Australian immigrant languages in the Pacific, and against such 'success cases' of minority revivals and reversals as Hebrew, French in Quebec, and Catalan. I have criticized others for not differentiating sufficiently between what was unique and what was of general significance in a particular context. I often wonder whether I am skating on thin ice myself in this connection, but I continue to try to extrapolate validly and provocatively from the supra-rational concerns, sensitivities, responsibilities, insights, fervent wishes and moral principles that I most frequently derive from 'listening to Yiddish with the third ear'.

Of course, that is not my only source of insight. I have always read widely, ever since childhood, and I have traveled widely for over a quarter century, the latter to such an extent that my children, noticing my frequent visits to countries with serious minority-language problems, often wondered whether their 'poppy was a spy for the CIA'. My family and I have lived for extensive periods abroad (where Gella and I always gave daily lessons in Yiddish language, literature and Jewish history and customs to our three sons) and I have learned to understand and even to speak languages that were totally foreign to me during my childhood and adolescence (including Spanish, Hebrew, Dutch and Hausa). Nevertheless, hardly a day has passed during the past half-century that I have not re-examined the world of Yiddish in order to help me formulate a hypothesis or scrutinize an idea, even if the material I was working on was Irish, Hausa or a highly general theoretical issue. I don't think I am the only one who derives the general from the specific, by any means, but I don't notice anyone else admitting to a similar unconscious or semi-conscious orienting tendency and I think we would all be better off if we spoke more openly about what it is that moves and motivates us. Our pretense at complete rationality is a subterfuge, at best, and, at worst, it keeps us from appreciating the emotional side of our subject matter in the real world of affairs.

The cultivation of marginality has also made me more than mildly interested in the combination of opposites and in undertaking the contradiction of accepted assumptions (whether popular or professional). Language shift cannot be appreciated, it seems to me, without realizing the existence of counter-currents devoted to reversing language shift. Similarly, modernization cannot really be fathomed by anyone not deeply interested in tradition. When seen from the periphery, these processes are not contradictory, as is usually assumed, but, actually, complementary and even interdependent in nature. New hypotheses often flow from combinations of old assumptions.

## Yiddish as an Object of Scholarship

It took me almost 20 years from the time I began concentrating on sociolinguistic matters to the time I began researching Yiddish topics *per se* with any frequency. During all those years, I had probably derived innumerable hunches and hypotheses from my intellectual-emotional-applied immersion in Yiddish concerns. However, the number of papers that I wrote directly about Yiddish in all of those years was actually rather negligible. The major reason for this disparity was that I had not trained explicitly in the Yiddish field, primarily as a result of Weinreich's injunction, and, as a result, I required both additional time and assurance before I felt comfortably confident as to my mastery of the social and cultural history covering a thousand years of Yiddish language and literature, on the one hand, and of about four centuries of prior research by other scholars, Jewish and non-Jewish, in that connection. I finally fully crossed the continental divide in this respect in 1973, after spending part of the prior three years (the very years when my family and I resided in Jerusalem, which was my headquarters during the time I directed the Ford Foundation sponsored International Research Project on Language Planning Processes in Israel, India, Indonesia and Sweden) assisting Shlomo Noble in rendering into English the first two volumes of Max Weinreich's incomparable four volume *Geshikhte fun der yidisher shprakh* (1973). The opportunity to study this splendid work in all of its detail more than made up for the detour and delay that Weinreich's original advice had occasioned. By the time I entered the field of Yiddish sociolinguistics, I was already a recognized scholar in various general sociolinguistic areas and the expertise and reputation that I had already acquired there provided my Yiddish publications with a wider audience and a broader, more general theoretical framework than would otherwise have been the case, had I started with Yiddish first. My *Never Say Die!* (1981), *Ideology, Society and Language* (1987), *Readings in the Sociology of Jewish Languages* (1985) and *Yiddish: Turning to Life* (in press) are all testimony to my recent and ongoing work in this area.

## Topical Clusters and Concentrations

I see my work as concentrating on a handful of interrelated topics. The most highly-developed cluster includes such works as *Language Loyalty in the United States* (1966), *Rise and Fall of the Ethnic Revival* (1985) and *Reversing Language Shift* (in progress). These works argue for a better appreciation for the resilience of minority community life and against the widespread (and particularly American) intellectual assumption that a monotonic, downward progression and ultimate eclipse are the inevitable prognoses for minority life in reasonably open, modern societies. My findings and hypotheses have consistently pointed to other possibilities as well, namely revitalizations, revivals and reversals of various magnitudes, including a fairly endless array of mutual influences between the sidestreams and the mainstream. The worldwide ethnic revivals of the mid-sixties have provided significant support for my findings and views, the latter constantly focusing on the language counterparts of larger and more encompassing sociocultural processes in a relatively small number of well-documented settings. True to my initial training, each of these works also seeks to combine considerable historical depth with quantitative data analyses. Ultimately, I refuse to grant either the superiority, the inevitability or the desirability of large-scale or modern econotechnical and ethnocultural establishments and I consider the ability of smaller systems to survive, to adapt and to create to be testimony to the human spirit. The ability of smaller systems (and often of non-modern or folk-systems) to contribute significantly to human health and happiness has also been one of the main themes in the Medical Anthropology courses which I have taught to students of Clinical Psychology and Health Psychology at Yeshiva University's Ferkauf Graduate School beginning in 1981.

Another major theme in my work is that represented by such titles as *Language and Nationalism* (1972), *Ideology, Society and Language* (1987) and *Language and Ethnicity* (1989). This concentration seeks to plumb the ideological, emotional and political efforts on behalf of particular ethnolinguistic linkages. My oft repeated interest in Whorf and in Herder also pertains to this same theme. The frequently encountered view that a particular ethnocultural identity is impossible without its historical 'dynamic' linkage to the language with which it has been traditionally and intimately associated, is obviously empirically disconfirmable. Ethnocultural identities frequently outlast their linguistic counterparts and constituents – nowhere more so than among Jews. Nevertheless, the recurring sense of reciprocity and fated co-occurrence between them is testimony to the emotional and cognitive power of the particular historical congruencies that constantly arise between languages and their associated cultures. Obviously, the major symbol system of any culture is a very likely one to become symbolic of that culture for its members (and for outsiders as well). Although these congruencies are disconfirmable in any ultimate or necessary and sufficient sense, such disconfirmation is achieved at a tremendous price of cultural dislocation and will, therefore, be adamantly and understandably resisted by those who labor on behalf of cultural authenticity. Thus, I am by no means the 'primordialist' that those who are quick to label others have claimed me to be (labeling is so much easier than careful reading), but that does not blind me to the very strong primordialist sentiments that sometimes control the lives of ordinary folk, for good as well as for bad.

My language planning interests stem from the realization (going as far back as early adolescence) that language maintenance processes and language ideologies commonly have their applied counterparts, whether pro or con. *Language Problems of Developing Nations* (1968), *Language Planning Processes* (1977) and *Progress in Language Planning* (1983) have all sought to contribute to the greater historical and sociocultural contextualization of efforts on behalf of particular languages. Of course, my *Reversing Language Shift* (in process of completion and already mentioned in the first topical focus, above) is also essentially a study in status planning, albeit one that focuses entirely on threatened languages. Other sociolinguists have understandably focused on corpus planning, 'understandably' particularly because corpus planning is governed by a far smaller and more manageable set of considerations than is status planning, an effort which is totally at the mercy of a wide array of social, cultural and political factors and opportunities.

Finally, I come to my methodological interests. These are evident from several of my studies which seek to utilize a large array of diverse and possibly complementary methods, rather than remain fixated on one method and one type of data alone. *Bilingualism in the Barrio* (1972) was primarily a methodological expedition and represented the first use of various types of factor analysis and of cumulative multiple correlation methods within sociolinguistics. My efforts to utilize more advanced quantitative methods have continued to this very date, as have my efforts (which began as far back as *Language Loyalty* [1966]) to combine quantification with ethnography. The courses that I have repeatedly given in social science research methods and in social science measurement theory and measurement practicum, the byproducts of my own graduate training in psychology, have enabled me to remain at the forefront of work in this area and to more easily and fully infuse it into my sociolinguistic research and writing.

## Pedagogical Interests

As a result of my '(co-)founding father' role in the sociolinguistic enterprise, I have had the opportunity to prepare textbooks and 'readers' that have helped shape the field by contributing to the training of students. My introductory texts (*Sociolinguistics* [1970, subsequently also in French and in Dutch], *The Sociology of Language* [1972, subsequently also in German, Japanese, Spanish, Italian and Serbo-Croatian]) and my collective volumes (*Readings in the Sociology of Language* [1968, reprinted three times], *Advances in the Sociology of Language* [vol. I, 1971, reprinted; vol. II, 1972], *Creation and Revision of Writing Systems* [1978], *Societal Multilingualism* [1978], *Bilingual Education* [1976, subsequently also in Italian], *Bilingual Education for Hispanic Students* [1982] and *Readings in the Sociology of Jewish Languages* [1985]) are ample indications of my devotion to the process of training students in the sociology of language and in several neighboring areas of specialization. My constant guiding principle in these volumes has been to introduce more sociology and political science into the training of the next generation of sociolinguists.

The present generation of 'founding fathers' has frequently made up its sociology as it went along, certain that (unlike linguistics) this was an area in which all reasonably sensible folk could rely on their own wits and ingenuity. Accordingly, many sociological 'wheels' have been reinvented time and again, whereas most major theories and schools of sociology really remain literally unknown in sociolinguistics to this very day, to its own detriment and to its further impoverished isolation from the social science mainstream. I have struggled against such provincialism and amateurism, but much (indeed, very much) remains to be done along these lines. Without such efforts, sociolinguistics must remain a backwater, relative to the social sciences more generally, regardless of the enrichment that it may represent *vis-à-vis* linguistics proper. Little wonder then that, as of now, sociologists *per se* have generally shown little interest in the sociology of language. The nourishment of such interest remains an unmet interdisciplinary challenge almost to the same degree that it was a quarter century ago.

## Outer Success and Inner Success

I rather quickly acquired all of the outer trappings of professional success. I became a full professor after only two years in full time academic life and after only five years of academic teaching and affiliation. I have been a Fellow at several prestigious 'think tanks' on four different continents (at Stanford, Honolulu, Princeton, Wassenaar and Jerusalem). I have founded and edited a major book-series in the sociology of language (*Contributions to the Sociology of Language*) since 1971, a series in which some 60 books have appeared at the rate of over three per year. I have founded and edited a major scholarly journal in the sociology of language (*IJSL = The International Journal of the Sociology of Language*) since 1973, the 100th issue of which will appear in 1993. I became 'Distinguished Research Professor of Social Sciences' at Yeshiva University in 1966 (i.e. only six years after moving there from Penn), 'Linguistic Society of America Professor' at the Summer Linguistics Institute of 1980, an honorary 'Doctor of Letters' from the Free University of Brussels in 1986, and

'Emeritus Distinguished Research Professor of Social Sciences' in 1988, upon opting for early-early 'retirement', at age 62, so that I could devote myself completely to research and writing. Nevertheless, notwithstanding all of these recognized marks of success, I am well aware of the fact that my professional contribution will be judged to have been a significant one only if my ideas will continue to be of interest to future generations.

My first very widely read paper was 'A systematization of the Whorfian hypothesis' (1960), for which I must have received a thousand requests for offprints. Its claim to fame is that it is systematic, as its title suggests, distinguishing between verbal and other cognitive behaviors, on the one hand, and between the lexical and grammatical language levels, on the other. These two distinctions lead to a double dichotomy when they are related to each other and the overall tight structure of the presentation then facilitated a very powerful and parsimonious analysis of the intriguing findings and conclusions of Whorf himself and of those who subsequently sought to test his hypotheses. Such tightly structured theory is relatively rare in the social and behavioral sciences and I have been able to approach it again only in a few other instances. My distinction between bilingualism (an individual variable) and diglossia (a societal variable), on the one hand, and my demonstration of the relationship existing between the two, on the other hand, have also proved to be extremely fruitful ones, both in my own work and in the work of others. My seemingly simple notion of the functional complementarity of the varieties within a speech repertoire, has come to be not only a sociolinguistic axiom but a very powerful notion in the analysis of language shift pressures the world over. My heuristic typology of bilingual education (transitional, maintenance and enrichment, first expressed in a talk to TESOL in 1968) has become a truism and a mainstay of that field, just as the distinction between ethnicity and nationality, on the one hand, and between nationalism and nationism, on the other hand, have introduced a set of much needed basic clarifications into the study of ethnolinguistic mobilization. My proposition that post-exilic Jewish vernaculars have arisen out of language-shift processes during periods of relative Jewish acceptance among non-Jewish neighbors, rather than out of fission due to Jewish ethnoreligious lacunae in the languages of those neighbors, has also proved to be a provocative one.

These few parsimonious and integrative insights, attained by dint of much hard work throughout a quarter century's labor, make me feel humble, indeed, both because they reveal how little I have accomplished that meets the standards that I have set for myself and because they also give testimony to the continued theoretical amorphousness of much of the sociolingustic enterprise and to the difficulties that must yet be overcome before it can become a rigorous area of theoretical consolidation. Now, more than ever before, when the number of researchers and students associated with the field is both sizable and growing, the need for theoretical parsimony and conceptual integration, rather than merely the proliferation of findings, strikes me as one of the primary needs of the field, a need by which my own work, as well as the work of all other co-founders, will be judged increasingly as time goes by.

## Concluding Sentiments

My long-term, studied, peripherality, fruitful though it may have been intellectually, has also brought with it (or, perhaps it proceeds out of), as its counterpart at the level of personality, an excessive shyness and stubbornness, as well as a strong preference for working alone. I am grateful to Yeshiva University, a university without a department of linguistics, without any graduate work in sociology and even without a strong commitment to the graduate social and behavioral sciences *per se*, for its benevolent neglect over a period of many years. Other than during my three brief stints of administrative work there (Dean, Graduate School of Education, 1960–1963; Dean, Ferkauf Graduate School of Humanities and Social Sciences, 1964–1966; Vice-President for Academic Affairs, 1973–1975) Yeshiva paid very little attention to what I was doing and left me almost completely to my own devices, allowing me to easily avoid excessive teaching (or even teaching at all) by obtaining research grants, unpaid leaves of absence and paid sabbaticals. Probably only under such circumstances of liberated peripherality could I, as a member of a graduate department of psychology, find the time and the freedom to become a co-founding father of the sociology of language and an honorary linguist to boot. The major price that I paid for staying at Yeshiva (1960–1988, seven of these years being spent on leaves or sabbaticals) was not to be surrounded by many sociolinguistic majors among my students nor by many sociolinguistics co-workers among my colleagues. In addition, I could teach sociology of language only infrequently there, and generally only to non-majors. I compensated for these lacks by immersing myself in research projects at Yeshiva, while depending heavily on visiting appointments elsewhere (usually at Stanford University but also at Harvard University, Columbia University and Hebrew University) and on the Linguistic Society of America Summer Institute courses (at University of Illinois, University of Hawaii, University of New Mexico and Stanford University) and NEH institutes (at Yeshiva University and Stanford University) that I conducted for linguistics majors and for junior faculty members, in order to provide me with those very stimulants that Yeshiva lacked. I am particularly proud that many of the students who studied with me at other institutions have gone on to be outstanding researchers in their own right.

Having published a full-blown biography of a 'language leader' and having now on my work-schedule the preparation of several other (but probably shorter) such biographies, I am the first to admit that such studies, fascinating and informative though they may be, are far from being fully balanced and unbiased. Many, if not most, of the crucial decisions in one's life cannot really be pinned down factually or explained motivationally. I am similarly, if not more, dubious about autobiographies. I have changed substantially during the quarter century of my full-time involvement in and dedication to the sociology of language. In many ways, I am no longer 'now' the same person that I was 'then', even though I have maintained many of the same traits and interests throughout almost my entire conscious life. However, though even I cannot really fully remember how I was 'then', nevertheless, I am still convinced that I remember more and know more about my life than does anyone else. If my recollections, above, are not entirely accurate or insightful, they are still possibly more so than would be anyone else's, based as those would necessarily have to be on the bare bones of 'the documentary record' and the incidental recollections of others. Accordingly, I am happy for the opportunity to put my own recollections and interpretations on paper.

The fact that my wife, some of my children and even some of my grandchildren are Yiddish speakers (and even pro-Yiddish 'doers') is a matter of great pride and satisfaction to me, as is my awareness that the language will survive for untold generations and develop further in its ultra-Orthodox environment. During the three years in which my family and I resided in Jerusalem (1970–1973), Gella and I 'took the plunge' and moved from our former 'secular traditionalism' to ('modern-' or neo-) Orthodox Jewish traditionism (although primarily in an overt-behavioral sense rather than in cognitive style or in terms of accepting the complete belief-system). This has added a previously missing dimension to my understanding of much of human life worldwide (in which ethnoreligious traditions are much stronger than they are in the West), of the Jewish experience throughout the ages, as well of the role of Yiddish *per se*. I am, probably best described, at this stage, as a 'positive agnostic', i.e. as one who is too deeply involved in scientific inquiry, and in the hope that the results of such inquiry can be of use in the betterment of human affairs, to be able to rely on faith alone as a way of attaining either understanding or amelioration. On the other hand, I am sceptical about human ability to understand the ultimate natural and human mysteries only on the bases of those material and overt manifestations that science can fathom. I suppose I have more scepticism about understanding my own life-experience (e.g. my own love for Yiddish and for my grandchildren) on the basis of what science can teach, than I have faith in faith as an answer to human problems and as a route to intergroup understanding and mutual acceptance. I feel strongly that there is more 'out there' (even more to the sociology of language) than science can grasp and I have a personal need for poets, artists, mystics and philosophers too for a deeper understanding of all that puzzles me. So I rely on all of the foregoing, and on intuitions too, even while being somewhat sceptical of them all, hoping that they will all admit to their own peculiar limitations and that they will all become more reasonable about the role of reasonableness *per se* as a necessary and desirable ingredient in the quest for wisdom and happiness.

The sociology of language too has a definite contribution to make to that quest, I am convinced, and the fact that I have made a contribution to this field of endeavor is, therefore, an increasing consolation to me as the number of 'years that cannot return' becomes greater and greater. I have never seen any social science benefit from puristically separating theory from application. Instead, I have viewed the probable connection between them both as a valuable reciprocal stimulant and as a provocative natural test, even though I consider my own work to be only marginally 'applied'. I have also often gone back and forth between launching into brand new topics and replowing old ones once again, but more deeply and broadly, hopefully with newer conceptual and methodological tools. I have seen both types of projects yield unexpected (and gratifying) results. In Isaiah Berlin's terms, I consider myself a somewhat foxy hedgehog.

I am particularly grateful that I have developed the stamina to stay away from Annual Meetings. Indeed, in my entire career I have only been to three meetings that have been substantively worthwhile: a meeting at Evian in 1966 (at which I launched the Research Committee on Sociolinguistics of the International Sociological Association), a meeting at Airlee House in 1966 sponsored by the Social Science Research Council (which resulted in the volume *Language Problems of Developing Nations*), and the Invitational Meeting on Language Planning at the East-West Center, Honolulu, in 1969 (at which the groundwork was laid for the subsequent International Research Project on Language Planning Process). Although I have delivered many (probably too many) keynote addresses, I invariably prefer solitude – and I am very grateful when I am able to find it – when I am in the midst of creative work, whether reading or writing). This preference also makes me a hard person to get on the telephone, although I do answer my mail quickly.

I am grateful, above all, to Gella (and also to my children and grand-children) for having provided me with the constant affection and family stability that have made it possible for me to work happily, quietly and productively for so many years in a field that mirrors and informs so much of my cognitive and emotional life. The riches that I have had to share with my family are mostly the riches of the mind and of the heart, but these are really the greatest riches that there are.

## References

Bram, J. (1955) *Language and Society.* New York: Random House.

Brown, R.W. (1958) *Words and Things.* Glencoe, IL: Free Press.

Fishman, J.A. (1960) A Systematization of the Whorfian Hypothesis. *Behavioral Science* 5, 323–339.

——. (1970) *Sociolinguistics: A brief introduction.* Rowley, MA: Newbury House.

——. (1972) *Language in Sociological Change: Essays.* Selected and introduced by Anwar S. Dil. Stanford, CA: Stanford Univ. Press.

——. (1984) The sociology of Jewish languages from a general sociolinguistic point of view. In W. Downes (ed.) *Language and Society* (pp. 3–21). London: Fontana.

——. (1991) *Yiddish: Turning to Life.* Amsterdam & Philadelphia: John Benjamins.

—— [*et al.*]. (1985) *The Rise and Fall of the Ethnic Revival: Perspectives on Language and Ethnicity.* Berlin & New York: Mouton de Gruyter.

Haugen, E.I. (1953) *The Norwegian Language in America.* 2. vols. Philadelphia: University of Pennsylvania Press.

Osgood, Charles E. and Thomas A. Sebeok, (eds) (1954) *Psycholinguistics: A Survey of Theory and Research.* (Supplement to *Journal of Abnormal and Social Psychology,* 49.) Baltimore, MD: Waverly Press.

Weinreich, M. (1974) *Geshikhte fun der yidisher shprakh.* 4 vols. New York: YIVO Institute for Jewish Research.

——. (1980) *History of the Yiddish Language.* Chicago & London: University of Chicago Press.

## Chapter 2

# Bloomington, Summer 1964:
# The Birth of American Sociolinguistics

Joshua A. Fishman is Distinguished University Research Professor, Social Sciences, Emeritus, at Yeshiva University and Visiting Scholar, Linguistics, at Stanford University. He is General Editor of the *International Journal of the Sociology of Language* and of the book-series *Contributions to the Sociology of Language*.

Having always derived generalizations from empirical data and having a preference for initially studying even my empirical data at a lower rather than at a higher level of abstraction, I propose to reflect on the past third of a century of American sociolinguistics in that fashion as well, using the summer of 1964 as my point of departure. I was at the Center for Advanced Study in the Behavioral Sciences (Stanford, CA) during the 1963–1964 academic year, rewriting my *Language Loyalty in the United States* for publication, when I came across a notice in the *LSA Bulletin* (or was it in the *SSRC Items?*) inviting applications from those interested in participating in a Seminar on sociolinguistics that was to be part of the 1964 Summer Linguistic Institute at Bloomington, Illinois. I asked Einar Haugen, who was also at CASBS that year, and to whom I had shown several of my *Language Loyalty* chapters, whether he thought I should apply. He told me that he would be on the faculty of the Linguistic Institute that summer and would also be participating in the Seminar and he encouraged me to apply. It was already late, either very close to or even a little after the announced deadline, so he advised me to call Charles Ferguson at the Center of Applied Linguistics, rather than lose the few extra days that a letter would require. I knew Ferguson's name from his 'Diglossia' article and from his paper on 'Myths about Arabic', but I had no reason to believe that he would know me since my only noteworthy publication at that time was my 'Systematization of the Whorfian Hypothesis' (1960). I did call him and although he seemed a little cool on the phone, he accepted my application.

Even though I applied, I really did not know whether to hope I would be selected or not. Leaving Palo Alto for Bloomington in the summer, two months before the scheduled completion of my precious year at the

CASBS, could be interpreted as being doubly intrapunitive. I (and Gella and our three boys) would be exchanging one of the world's loveliest summer climates for one of the more oppressive ones, and after Bloomington we would be going back to New York, and who knew if we would ever see the Bay Area and the Peninsula again. Gella and I decided not to tell the children until we would know for sure whether my application had been accepted. It did not take long before a positive answer arrived and I spent my last month at CASBS feverishly completing a paper on 'The Differences between Monolingual and Multilingual Polities' (to be published in 1966 in a collection edited by another participant in the Seminar, Stanley Lieberson). A very perceptive friend commented at the time, 'Going to Bloomington must be awfully important to you if you are willing to give up two months at CASBS for it'. It was important for me. I did not know what to expect intellectually (that would depend on who else had gotten selected, but with Ferguson and Haugen there, how much of a risk could *that* be?), but I did know that I did not want to continue to be without a community of like-minded scholars, as had been my lot till then.

## The Make-Up of the Seminar

When I finally met the other 'seminarists' (technically we were all considered to be faculty members of the LSI and, therefore, of the University), I realized that I knew only Haugen and Leonard Savitz from before. I had met Savitz during my two years as Associate Professor of Psychology and Human Relations at the University of Pennsylvania (1958–1960). He was primarily interested in criminology and in social disorganization more generally, but he was also interested in social problems very broadly, including social problems involving language. I was always on the lookout for sociologists with language interests of any kind, so I began corresponding with Savitz, after my leaving Pennsylvania, about putting out together a set of 'sociological readings' pertaining to language. Because language was my first priority and Savitz's third, I finally went ahead with this idea on my own during the year at CASBS (and, in its final and unconscionably delayed version, my *Readings in the Sociology of Language* 1968 included several papers by 'seminarists' as well). I had also corresponded quite a bit with the German sociologist of language Heinz Kloss, in connection with his chapter on German in the United States for my *Language Loyalty* book (indeed, Ferguson had called me to get Kloss's address, in order to invite him to join the seminar, since, seemingly, very few other Americans were in touch with him at that time). Finally, I had at least met John Gumperz, because he used to come up from Berkeley to the weekly 'linguistics seminar' at CASBS. He had let me read his manuscript on code-switching in Hemnesberget (1964) and had begun to educate me as to the manifold differences between ethnographic and survey research (even though I had already done some of the former and much of the latter). Let me add that I also knew three other seminarists at least by name: William Bright (from his spring 1964 conference on sociolinguistics, several of the preprints of which I had read), William Labov (because he had been a student of my friend Uriel Weinreich, from whom I had gotten copies of some of Labov's early papers) and William Stewart (because of his 1962 paper on typology of multilingual settings). I had neither any prior contact whatsoever with nor knowledge of Jack Berry, Paul Friedrich, Chester Hung or Stanley Lieberson.[1]

Even if we count Ferguson as a sort of 'impartial chairman', there were only five sociologists (Hunt, Kloss, Lieberson, Savitz and myself – a refurbished social psychologist) and seven anthropologists/linguists (Berry, Bright, Friedrich, Gumperz, Haugen, Labov and Stewart). The standing of the two groups, from the point of view of making immediate contributions to an emerging sociolinguistics, was even more unequal than their numbers alone would imply, and their interactions with one another were qualitatively quite different.[2] The sociologists, with the exception of Kloss, had published little that could be immediately co-opted into sociolinguistics, although both Lieberson and I were about to publish several germane items within the next few years. Also, the sociologists did not know one another well (or even at all) prior to Bloomington, given that most of them had never interacted, directly or vicariously, before. As it turned out, they generally also had neither strong methodological nor substantive (not even language) interests in common, except for Hunt and Savitz who were both 'language as a social problem' oriented. The anthropologists/linguists, on the other hand, had mostly at least rubbed shoulders before, had all read some of each other's work, and, in some cases, had a number of substantive and methodological interests in common (Ferguson and Gumperz, e.g. had worked on India-related material together and Bright too had worked in India), and their interest in language and/or society did not make them 'odd balls' in their own professional circles. Accordingly, they were much more active in the seminar than were the sociologists, and the contributions that they made at that time have been more lasting *vis-à-vis* sociolinguistics as a field of specialization.

## The Anthropological/Linguistic Advantage

Several of the anthropologists/linguists came to the Seminar with a very tangible head start, so to speak. The Hymes/Gumperz symposium at the 1963 American Anthropological Association meeting in San Francisco (on the very day that John F. Kennedy was assassinated!)[3] – with papers by Hymes, Gumperz, Ferguson, as well as by Labov and

Ervin, to mention only those who later were associated in one way or another with the Seminar – was entitled, 'The Ethnography of Communication'. The papers put together by Lieberson, appearing some two years later, nine of whose 13 papers are by members of the Seminar, still carried the less focused title, 'Explorations in Sociolinguistics'. Gumperz and Hymes started off their issue by pointing to 'the good fortune of copresence in the same area over several years' of many of their contributors, something which enabled them 'to have frequent discussions and to discover the common interests that link their work'. Lieberson, on the other hand, started off his issue with the admission that, 'there is no systematic collective effort on the part of sociologists to investigate the linguistic correlates of social behavior and, on the other hand, the influence of society on the nature of language'.[4] The Gumperz and Hymes papers had a shared theme and many had a shared methodology. The Lieberson papers had neither. The Gumperz and Hymes papers were addressed to anthropologists/linguists who were already convinced of the importance of language but who may have needed to be convinced that the 'ethnography of speaking' was a promising way to study and understand language in society. The Lieberman papers were addressed to sociologists who were not (and still are not) by any means convinced of the importance of language and the papers themselves provide no unifying theme or methodology by means of which they could become convinced.

## The 'Two Cultures' Problem in Sociolinguistics

The Seminar itself reflected and foretold many of the differences between these two publications. Some of the anthropologists/linguists at the Seminar were already familiar with or sold on the ethnography of communication; indeed, to some of them 'sociolinguistics' was little more than a more interdisciplinary label (or an opportunity for interdisciplinary expansion) for the ethnography of communication. The sociologists at the Seminar were (with the exception of Grimshaw) quite distant from ethnography and, at best, considered it to be just another method and one with severe validational and public scrutiny problems of its own. Of course, the anthropologists/linguists were fully familiar with linguistic theory and with the collection and analysis of field data and most of them gravitated markedly toward the types of topics that could be coordinated with selected snippets of corpus. None of the sociologists at the Seminar was trained in linguistics (neither then nor since) and, indeed, their work gravitated markedly toward macro-sociological concerns and methods. The result was a distinct lack of full acceptance of one another's work on the part of some of the members of each of the two subgroups of seminarists. When I presented my paper on the

'Differences between Multilingual and Monolingual Polities' I was asked by one of the linguists where my 'corpus' was. It was, partially, in order to avoid this kind of irrelevant question in the future (at the Seminar I asked my questioner whether he felt it was 'necessary to explain the causes of World War II at the phonological level, too, merely because the subsequent combatants had initially engaged in negotiations'), that I soon returned to my earlier preference for 'sociology of language' as the name of my field; no one would expect a linguistic corpus in the sociology of anything. When Gumperz presented his Hemnesberget paper, he was asked by a sociologist why his 'hard data' was not presented in tabular form, and why he had performed no statistical tests to 'substantiate his impressions'.[5]

## Problem-Driven Versus Theory-Driven? Or Something in Between?

There were many underlying reasons why sociolinguistics appeared on the scene in the early sixties. The reason that the seminar itself most fully represented was the ample availability of financial resources to support novel intellectual undertakings. The Seminar was supported by the SSRC, an agency whose *raison d'être* is to provide research and training grants for just such purposes. Let us remember what 1964 was like, and not confuse it with, subsequent years. The Vietnam war was still a relatively minor affair, entirely lacking any indication of its subsequent escalation into a full-fledged military campaign, on the one hand, or protest movement, on the other hand. Neither bilingual education nor any other minority language-related issue had yet been highlighted, either by adherents or opponents. There *was* a war on poverty and Head Start was already fully underway, but only a few advocates of Black English and William Labov's Lower East Side study realized the language potential in that connection. The Ford Foundation's International Division was not yet supporting far-flung language policy related research and its Education Division was concerned with language (under Marge Martus' aegis), but as a purely cognitive (teaching/learning) tool rather than as a societal indicator and constituent. There was still little if any outside support for a social problems-driven sociolinguistics. As for the Seminar and its participants, social problems were similarly deemphasized there. Although I had definitely included the social problem and social policy components of the lamentably still ongoing attrition of U.S.A. language resources in my *Language Loyalty*, I do not remember this perspective ever coming up for discussion during the entire eight weeks in Bloomington. I had quickly learned my lesson and avoided bringing up a topic that I had tackled with so little ethnography (there *was* one ethnographic chapter however, generally overlooked, devoted to a Polish mining town in Pennsylvania) and no corpus whatsoever. If Savitz and Hunt were unhappy about this deemphasis of 'language problems', they were very relaxed and nonvocal about it. All in all, I do not think that the Seminar was social-problems driven or that the subsequent work of the Social Science Research Council's 'Committee on Sociolinguistics' was in any way motivated along these lines. When I once quietly mentioned to Sue Ervin, who was seated next to me at a particular Committee meeting, that we were attending to language in such theoretical terms that 'the fact that people were willing to kill and be killed for their beloved language was being completely overlooked', she stopped the deliberations and quoted me. However, nothing but looks of annoyance greeted my observation. Linguicide was not on the proper level of abstraction for our Committee, just as it had not been for the Seminar.

But the Seminar was not theory driven either. Gumperz may have seen ethnography as a means of capturing basic reality and he may have looked forward to seeing it become the dominant method for the study of language behavior, but I do not think even he viewed it as anything but the best, most scientific way of arriving at a theory of such behavior. Labov was convinced that his techniques for studying linguistic variables, across formality levels and across social classes, were part and parcel of linguistics pure and simple, and that no separate field of inquiry such as sociolinguistics was either implied, necessary or desirable. His Black English work was still ahead of him, but when he finally tackled it, he did not do so in order to come up with social policy findings but in order to derive very basic language change and language variation formulations. He may have later come to think of his findings and methods as encompassing much or most of sociolinguistics, but that was not clearly the case at the Seminar and, had it been, it would hardly have carried the day in either camp. Ferguson certainly had no grand scale theory in mind and even middle range theory did not seem to preoccupy him. Ferguson was obviously disappointed with sociology by the end of the Seminar. It did not seem to have anything solid to offer, and in a disciplinary way, neither by way of substance nor methodology. That may still be a valid criticism of sociology today, but Ferguson himself worked (and still works) on a very large array of fields and topics, and, in *this* sense, at least, he came (and comes) very close to sociology. Actually, Ferguson comes pretty close to epitomizing the level of abstraction that was most common at the Seminar, i.e. a focus on topics (and on whatever method or methods they may have required, including the method of history), rather than on social problems, on the one hand, or on theory construction and testing on the other hand. Theoretical generalizations may be derivable from many such studies, but that is a long way off and remains 'iffy' at best. I have not been too disturbed by that.

Sociolinguistics, notwithstanding its constantly disorganized state, has contributed handsomely and lastingly to linguistics, and the sociology of language has done likewise *vis-à-vis* sociology, during the very same third of a century in which a very much 'tighter' and grander linguistic theory both rose (noisily) and fell (silently).

## Accomplishments of the Seminar

None of the above is meant to imply that the Seminar did not accomplish much, let alone that I ever regretted giving up two months at CASBS in order to attend it. Quite the contrary. It was extremely worthwhile and shaped a good bit of the rest of my career, and continues to do so to this very day, more than 30 years later. A very considerable number of publications, courses and conferences flowed directly from the Seminar and from the SSRC Committee on Sociolinguistics which had sponsored the Seminar and which continued to meet for the next decade or more. The membership of the Committee was constantly drawn primarily from those who were in (or 'almost in' or who visited) the Seminar during the summer of 1964. The Research Group on Sociolinguistics of the World Congress of Sociology was a direct spin-off from the Committee, since it was founded as a result of the Committee's having sent me to the WCS's Evian meeting (late August 1966) to organize a group that would help guarantee that sociolinguistics did not become a strictly American affair.

But it was not only in immediate and long-term professional recognition, organizational activity and funding terms that the Seminar was eminently worthwhile. From the point of view of sociology, it launched or confirmed several sociologists on language-related pursuits which (have) lasted for essentially their entire academic lives. This might not otherwise have been the case had they not made the personal and intellectual connections which the Seminar facilitated. When I did a census-type study after the Seminar, I always reviewed Lieberson's recommendations in that connection. These recommendations were essentially hammered out with a group of sociologists at the Seminar.[6] I made sure to include an ethnography of speaking as well as Labovian variables in my *Bilingualism in the Barrio* (1971). This required me to work with linguists (Gumperz the chief one among them for one of the two years of that project), and after the seminar I was much readier to do so than before. I worked with linguists once more on my (our!) *Language Planning Processes* (Rubin *et al.*, 1977). I had never been a number-cruncher pure and simple, but after the seminar it was clearer to me than ever before that the historical, cultural and micro-level aspects of any topic needed to be explored at their own levels and with their own appropriate methods and data. My *Language Loyalty* (1966) was already conceived as interdisciplinary, well before the Seminar, but after the Seminar I became incurably sensitized to the contribution that a corpus might make to an appropriate investigation. And, lo and behold, I am finally working on a corpus-related study now! I have done historical/biographical research in my *Ideology, Society and Language* (1987) and have repeatedly returned to the same field-sites for my *Reversing Language Shift* (1991). My very close friendship with Ferguson, and my continued friendship with several of the seminarists and visitors to the Seminar, has continued to this very day, and they represent an important segment of my social and intellectual interaction network. Several of the linguists/anthropologists formed equally important (and perhaps substantively even more interactive) linkages as a result of the Seminar. To this very day, sociolinguists usually tend to be very few in number on any one campus, and therefore they tend to rely on phone, mail, conferences and personal visits even more than do other academicians. The Seminar provided me with a network for feedback, assistance and even moral support that has lasted for a third of a century. These are not things to be sneezed at. From my early interactions with the Weinreichs (particularly during my graduate school years) through today I have thought of myself as a bridge between linguistics and the social sciences. The Seminar helped me immeasurably to see this as a worthy and a challenging (as well as stimulating) role.

But the above positive 'bottom line' should not hide the fact that the absence of consensual theory and methodology, or even a consensual definition of whether sociolinguistics is a field and, if so, what it includes, the gulf between its 'socio' and its 'linguistic' subgroupings, the absence of linguistic training among the former and of sociological training among the latter, the far lesser tie of the field as a whole to sociology than to anthropology/linguistics ... all of which the Seminar itself revealed, have all remained hurdles that need to be overcome by future generations of sociolinguists. The 'founding fathers' did their best, but they did not, by any means, do everything that needed (let alone everything that still needs) to be done in and for sociolinguistics.

## Notes

1. I should also mention a few of the scholars each of whom visited the Seminar, separately, for a few days at a time, throughout the summer. I had met Susan Ervin (today Ervin-Tripp, ed. comment) in the same way that I met John Gumperz. She too used to come up from Berkeley, from time to time, to participate in the CASBS 'linguistics seminar' and I had read (and assigned) several of her papers on bilingualism for my 1959–1960 courses on 'Psychology of Language' and 'Sociology of Language' at Penn. I knew Joan Rubin from her 1962 paper on 'Bilingualism in Paraguay'. Wallace Lambert was also a 'known entity' for me because of several of his psycholinguistic studies of bilingualism. I also knew Dell Hymes from his 1962 'Ethnography of Speaking' paper (I believe that his 1964 volume of readings on *Language in Culture and Society* had either already just appeared or, at least, that its table

of contents was known to most of us by then). Braj Kachru was just a young newcomer at that time. He spent some time at the LSI that summer and came to tell me about his research at that time (on Indian English), but I do not remember him coming to the Seminar *per se*. Allen Grimshaw was in a category all by himself. He was not an official member of the Seminar, but he was not exactly an outside visitor either. He was then already at Indiana University and came to some of the Seminar discussions and even to some of its social gatherings. I knew him from his graduate student days at Penn.

2. Bright left the Seminar after only a week or two, due to a sudden death in his family. As a result, the bulk of the eight-week seminar consisted of 11, rather than 12, members (plus the chairman).

3. Although published in December 1964, as Part 2, vol. 66, no. 6 of the *American Anthropologist*, most of the papers were available as typescripts either by the time of the seminar or even before that.

4. Although not published until 1966, as vol. 36, no. 2 of *Sociological Inquiry*, most of the papers by sociologists were actually presented, discussed, written and/or revised at the Seminar.

5. For more recent commentary concerning this paper, see Brit Maehlum. 1990. Codeswitching in Hemnesberget – myth or reality? *Tromsö Studies in Linguistics*, vol. 11, 338–355 (Tromsö Linguistics in the Eighties). Oslo: Novus Press.

6. See his 'Language Questions in Censuses', *Sociological Inquiry* 36, 262–279.

## References

Fishman, J.A. (1960) Systematization of the Whorfian hypothesis. *Behavioral Science* 5, 323–339.

——. (1966) *Language Loyalty in the United States: The Maintenance and Perpetuation of non-English Mother-tongues by American Ethnic and Religiuous Groups*. The Hague: Mouton.

——. (1987) *Ideology, Society, and Language: The Odyssey of Nathan Birnbaum*. Ann Arbor: Karoma.

——. (1991) *Reversing Language Shift: Theoretical and Empirical Foundations of Assistance to Threatened Languages*. Clevedon, UK: Multilingual Matters.

—— Cooper, R.C. and Ma, R. (1971) *Bilingualism in the Barrio*. Bloomington: Indiana University Press.

Gumperz, J.J. (1964) Linguistic and social interaction in two communities. *American Anthropogist* 66(6), 137–153.

Hymes, D.H. (1962) The ethnography of speaking. In T. Gladwin and W.C. Sturtevant (eds) *Anthropology and Human Behavior* (pp. 13–53). Washington DC: Anthropological Society of America.

——. (ed.) (1964) *Language in Culture and Society: A Reader in Linguistics and Anthropology*. New York: Harper & Row.

—— and Gumperz, J.J. (eds) (1964) The ethnography of communication. *American Anthropologist* 66(6), entire.

Lieberson, S. (1966) Language questions in censuses. *Sociological Inquiry* 36(2), 262–279.

Maehlum, B. (1990) Codeswitching in Hemnesberget – myth or reality? *Trömso Studies in Linguistics* 11, 338–355. Oslo: Novus Press.

Rubin, J., Fishman, J.A., Jernudd, B., Das Gupta, J. and Ferguson, C.A. (1977) *Language Planning Processes*. The Hague: Mouton.

Stewart, W.A. (1962) Outline of a linguistic typology for describing multilingualism. In F.A. Rice (ed.) *Study of the Role of Second Languages in Asia, Africa, and Latin America* (pp. 15–25). Washington, DC: Center for Applied Linguistics.

## Chapter 3

# Putting the 'Socio' Back into the Sociolinguistic Enterprise

To my way of thinking, there is a mid-life crisis today in the sociolinguistic enterprise, particularly among those engaged in its more 'macro' aspects (as most of us are at least some of the time and as some of us are most of the time), and one of the reasons for that crisis is that instead of progressing firmly on its two legs (one propelled by matters 'linguistic' and the other propelled by matters 'socio'), macro-sociolinguistics is trying to move ahead primarily on the former while merely shuffling along or muddling through on the latter.

The above diagnosis is not intended to be interpreted as a commentary on the work of Professor X or Professor Y, i.e. it does not flow from a consideration of the work of this or that specific protagonist in the unfolding drama of modern sociolinguistics but, rather, from a consideration of the sociolinguistic enterprise more generally, particularly from its more 'macro-socio' efforts, as I have come to know them, both from my own involvement and via more than a quarter century's perusal of the world-wide literature devoted to this field.

### Genesis: In the Beginning

Starting at the 1964 Summer Linguistic Institute at which American sociolinguistics was 'born' (thanks to an eight week faculty Seminar sponsored by the Social Science Research Council and conducted *primus inter pares* by Charles A. Ferguson) and at which 10 scholars who claimed to be crucially interested in that field-to-be convened, studied and argued in order to give it shape, American sociolinguistics has been quantitatively and qualitatively the brainchild of anthropological linguistics. While it is true that roughly half of its initial grandfathers or godfathers were sociologists, in the formation of the field and in its rapid worldwide development via publications, conferences and courses, the anthropological linguistic half clearly and constantly outweighed the sociological half. I do not subscribe to conspiracy theories of history and, therefore, I do not suspect that this outcome was due to any malicious or even consciously 'discipline-centric' bias among the linguists present. Nevertheless, I do think that a convincing case can be made that for the anthropologists and linguists at the Seminar, sociology was low man on the social science totem-pole even before the Seminar got underway and that it remained such thereafter. Linguists in general, and perhaps anthropological linguists in particular, often enjoy looking down on sociology. In the pecking order among academic disciplines, it would seem that sociology is so close to the bottom of the list that it can clearly look down only on 'education', i.e. on teacher preparation and pedagogy. About which discipline is the joke told relaying the advice of an old dean to a new one at a college just about to be launched: 'It's the cheapest area to get underway. All that its faculty needs is some desks, some blackboards and some chairs. They don't need any computers and they don't even need any waste paper baskets. They recycle their garbage themselves!' Obviously, that's sociology to most American and British academicians. The only sociology that obviously made very good sense to some linguists, even then, was that at the far-micro end (ethnography and ethnomethodology), but even that contribution was quickly neutralized by being so absorbed and naturalized into the ethnographic heartland of anthropology proper that its interdisciplinary intellectual origins were quickly and conveniently forgotten.

Although I freely and fully admit that the boundaries between the social science disciplines are often quite arbitrary (I, for example, see no good substantive or methodological sense for the departmental division that currently exists between sociology and political science, and Seymour Lipset's recent election to the presidency of the American Sociological Association, after having served as president of the American Political Science Association merely serves to confirm me in this view), I still think that the *raison d'être* of an interdisciplinary discipline is to be exactly such, interdisciplinary, and that it is, therefore, not an idle question to ask 'Why did sociology so quickly become and remain such a junior (or even silent) partner in the formation of sociolinguistics?' There are probably many reasons why that was (and still is) so. To my way of thinking, this was primarily the result of over two hundred years of modern, Western sociology in which the notions of 'language' and language-focused or language-directed social or societal processes received very little attention. Accordingly, modern sociolinguistics was 'born' (or, more accurately – considering its pre-World War II German origins – 'reborn') already imprinted with the topics, theories and methods that 'societally sympathetic' linguists, particularly anthropological linguists, were familiar with and these definitely did not include disciplinary sociology. In addition, anthropology and sociology had long had (and to some extent still have) their intra-departmental and their inter-departmental 'dificulties', to say the least, in both the USA and England, and sociolinguistics inherited the aftermath of the long-simmering family dispute between them.

Every new beginning has to take off from what came before it and anthropological linguistics, from Sapir on, was simply what had come before for most linguists interested (then as now) in sociolinguistics. Anthropological linguistics immediately and unreflectingly became both the conscious and the unconscious point of departure for sociolinguistics and the 'socio'-side of sociolinguistics has been paying the inevitable price of that point of departure ever since, particularly in English and in German sociolinguistic circles which have long been intellectually and methodologically aligned or attuned to each other.

## The Linguistic Weltanschauung of Early Sociolinguistics

We usually refer to Whorfianism when we use the expression 'Linguistic Weltanschauung'. However, at present, although I *am* referring to a kind of Whorfianism – i.e. to the blinders and biases that all ethnolinguistic traditions force upon their members – I am referring to (anthropological) linguistics *per se* as an ethnolinguistic tradition, one that has, willy-nilly, forced blinders on its own definition of sociolinguistics, particularly with respect to any recognition of the need for the new field's immersion in the theoretical and methodological sociological literature.

From the point of view of anthropological linguistics there *was*, of course, a distinction between ethnolinguistics and sociolinguistics but the distinction was a rather trivial one (primarily locus of study and level of abstraction). Methodologically, theoretically and even bibliographically no real distinction was intended. While the more innovative term '*socio*linguistics' was preferred to the then practically dormant alternative '*ethno*linguistics' (the new term did, after all, draw a few new faces and emphases into the total enterprise), there never was any interest in coming to know or even to recognize sociology in any disciplined or disciplinary sense, i.e. treating it in the same way that the sociologists among the 'founding fathers' of sociolinguistics quickly realized that they would have to treat linguistics in order to 'do' at least a major chunk of sociolinguistics.

In the lion's share of sociolinguistics, 'sociology' was, and has largely remained, a code-word for the type of familiarity with social stratification (by age, sex, class, religion and/or ethnicity) that any intelligent person could glean from the *New York Times*, at most, if not just from informal personal observation of the world immediately around him or her. As a result of this self-imposed underexposure to serious sociological stimulation, sociology was rarely explicitly asked or encouraged to contribute anything crucial to sociolinguistic research or theory. And sociology, being what it is, namely a loose congeries of theories, methods and data-sets (and, therefore, in many ways harder to learn than tight-structured linguistics), was particularly ill-prepared to speak up on its own behalf. Indeed, it was willing to be called, anything (including being called a 'weak-sister') as long as it was called, and it *was* called, initially, e.g. to assist in the intra-linguistic struggle with Chomsky's 'native speaker intuition'. That was an intuition that was simultaneously situation-free, fatigue-free, emotion-free, conflict-free, value-free, identity-free, purpose-free and thoroughly monolingual as well, and a recognition of sociology within the total 'non-Chomskian coalition' could provide endless additional examples of how totally removed from the real world any such linguistic intuition would necessarily and obviously have to be.

## Exodus: Mutual Ignorance Breeds Mutual Contempt

Nevertheless, although the name of sociology was 'called' very early, its substance was never studied. Indeed, the wheels of a self-confirming hypothesis were thus set in motion very early and, by end large, they have remained in motion ever since. The initial thinly disguised contempt for sociology (obviously not hard to come by, given sociology's reputation as an academic 'Johnny come lately', its lack of topical implicationality and its lack of the same methodological uniqueness – or even central tendency – that characterizes such human sciences as psychology or anthropology, not to mention linguistics) has resulted in an imperviousness to disciplined sociological thinking which has now lasted for two academic generations and threatens to yet stretch into a third. Sociology was and is often still either quietly or audibly sneered at as 'non-rigorous', 'speculative' and 'merely intuitive', but these widely recognized shortcomings were also quickly seized upon to excuse uninformed approaches to the socio-side of the sociolinguistic enterprise on the part of linguists too busy to study sociology. They even seemed to appreciate the opportunity to be non-rigorous in *this* connection, not realizing that they were often being non-rigorous in some of the very sociological areas in which rigorous work long had been and was being done.

On the other hand, sociology has fully returned the compliment. Discovering only sociological ignorance in the brunt of the sociolinguistic literature, it is hard to find references to sociolinguistics or sociolinguistic findings in most sociology textbooks or integrative compendia. A careful examination of the past dozen years' worth of the *Annual Review of Sociology* reveals only half a handful of sociolinguistic review-articles out of the roughly 300 published during this period. *Sociological Abstracts* regularly publishes about 150 sociolinguistic abstracts per year, but here too the proportion remains roughly the same as in the *Annual Review*, i.e. roughly between 1% and 2%, and even this small proportion may be partially attributed to the fact that *Sociological Abstracts* owns the *Linguistics and Language Behavior Abstracts* bibliographic-retrieval bank and may merely be saving itself money by including more *LLBA* abstracts in *SA* than it might otherwise do.

Obviously, only a very small proportion of the worldwide sociolinguistic literature is getting through to sociology. That may or may not be a pity. Were sociologists to take the time needed in order to become better informed with respect to the sociolinguistic literature they would have to castigate it seriously for its usual lack of well-formulated and internally-consistent theories, not to mention its utter unfamiliarity with Comte and Durkheim, with Weber and Marx, with Parsons and Eisenstadt, with the eighteenth and early nineteenth century social theorists and with the methodological strictures of sociology insofar as societal data collection and analysis are concerned.

Given the foregoing state of affairs, it should be totally unsurprising that whereas almost all American linguistics departments (and a good many elsewhere as well, of course) include courses in sociolinguistics today (not a mean accomplishment for an area of specialization which began barely three decades ago), almost no sociology departments do so. Indeed, the two fields are as remote from each other now as they were in the early 1960s. Linguistics majors do not generally take graduate courses in sociology, not even if they are sociolinguistics majors, and sociology majors generally do not take graduate courses in linguistics or even in sociolinguistics, not even if they are symbolic interactionists or mass-communications specialists. While I do remember Max Garfinkel telling me in the mid-60s that he required his graduate sociology majors to 'take linguistics to disabuse them of their naive assumption that they know about language just because they talk, read, write and understand it' (that striking me even then as a very minor use of linguistics, although it indicated at least a recognized need for it), I do not remember any linguistics chairman or director of a sociolinguistics program telling me that sociolinguistics majors are required to take graduate course-work in sociology in order to disabuse them of their impression that they know about society because they live in it, have already taken some anthropology and keep up with the *New York Times*. After three decades, sociolinguistics has remained just as it was: a province of linguistics and anthropology, and a rather provincial province at that.

## Leviticus: The Costs of Provincialism

The greatest loser by far in this 'reciprocal ignorance pact' is the socio-linguistic enterprise. Most students of language policy and language planning, language and ethnicity, language maintenance and reversing language shift, bilingual education and language spread, have quite simply 'created' their sociology as they went along, without investigating the sociological literature on intergroup conflict and conflict resolution, on political organization and political processes, on governmental operations viewed from the perspective of organization theory, on social deviance and social disorganization, on mass communication and nationalism, on neighborhood dynamics and family dynamics, on ideology and multiple group membership, on ethnicity and childhood socialization, and even without really learning the methods that have been perfected in sociology for the study of any of the above.

Sociological blind-spots such as these have become part of the culture of sociolinguistics and they remain, therefore, to be handed over to a third generation by the second generation who acquired them from the founding fathers of the field some 20 to 30 years ago. Robert Merton and Paul Lazersfeld, George Homans and Milton Yinger and James Coleman, none of these figure in sociolinguistic training today, nor does the design of experiments, the construction of questionnaires or attitude scales, the proper implementation of survey methodology and sample selection or the multidimensional analysis of data. Note that I am not really advocating any particular brand or school of sociology or any particular 'all purpose' research methodology or data collection and analysis technique; to accuse me of that on the basis of referring to the particular readings and methods that I am citing here or that I myself have utilized and cited most often is to miss my point today and to do so only because one ostensibly favors a different kind of sociology than the kind(s) that I utilize. On some other occasion I may decide to defend my own selection from the sociological treasure-trove, since it has been far from accidental or unreflective. What I am advocating here and now is a disciplined, hard-nosed grounding in *any* major substantive segment and data-collecting and analyzing method among all those that sociology has to offer, so that one can both criticize it and select from it knowingly.

Naturally, I am also disappointed by the meager sociolinguistic impact on sociology. The sociological study of many of the above mentioned areas could profit from informed sociolinguistic input. However, since sociolinguistics is the smaller and the newer field, I am frankly more disturbed by its ignorance of sociology than by sociology's ignorance of sociolinguistics. By way of contrast, the interdependence and inter-stimulation characterizing linguistics, psycholinguistics and psychology must be viewed as simultaneously obvious and mutually gratifying to all three. The result is, predictably, that psycholinguistics is taught in psychology departments as often as in linguistics departments and that psycholinguists often have joint appointments in both departments that pertain to their area's joint-patrimony, something virtually unheard of among sociolinguists.

Of course, modern psycholinguistics is a full decade older than modern sociolinguistics, but endless major disciplinary (rather than merely impressionistic) contributions to psycholinguistics also flowed from psychology far before the mid-fifties-flowering that finally turned psychology of language into psycholinguistics. From its early scientific beginnings, branching out from philosophy, psychology has evinced a continual interest in language and in speech and in their contributions to higher mental processes (memory, thinking, imagination, problem solving, intelligence, goal-directed behavior, etc.) as well as in their reflection of emotion, personality and interpersonal relations. One of the major German founders of scientific psychology was Wilhelm Wundt and one of his major interests, represented by several tomes, was Sprachpsychologie. That interest was never dropped when psychology made the transition from being a German-dominated science to being an American-dominated science, not even during the heyday of behaviorism, after World War I. Compare that to the total scrapping of German Sprachsoziologie (and not only the Nazified Auslandsdeutsche Volksforschung) in connection with the development of American and Western sociolinguistics. Psychology and linguistics have both been 'winners' as a result of their healthy two-way relationship in the area of psycholinguistics, just as sociology and linguistics have both been 'losers' as a result of the two-way indifference between them, and sociolinguistics, the presumed hybrid derived from both of them, has been the major loser of all.

## Numbers: Some Fruits of Dialog

In my own work, I have repeatedly tried to break out of both of these reciprocal and self-confirming provincialisms. I do not want to present myself to you as entirely innocent *vis-à-vis* the critique that I have presented above. I was trained in psychology myself and I have had to work hard in my mature years to learn whatever sociology I have learned. Nevertheless, while realizing fully that I must leave any evaluation of the success of my efforts to others, I do want to present some very brief indication of what I believe I have gained from (and perhaps even contributed to) sociology by picking my examples from my most recent explorations into the ongoing reversing language shift (RLS) efforts on behalf of a dozen different threatened languages throughout the world. The *New York Times* and even some linguists have accustomed us either to the demise or to an 'unreasonable clinging to life' of such languages. Perhaps that is why no one had hitherto attempted a comparative analysis of just how the struggles on their behalf have rendered meaningful and provided direction to the lives of millions the world over.

My prior 'sociological immersion' provided a perspective that made it clear to me, e.g. that RLS efforts did not fit into any of the established types of 'social movements' that sociology had documented since the rise of the Chicago School nearly three quarters of a century ago. They were neither as ephemeral as 'collective behaviors' (crowds, mobs, riots, panics) nor as establishment-oriented as the more enduring, organized and goal-oriented 'movements'. Although RLS movements are necessarily oppositional to the mainstream, they nevertheless differ from other 'oppositional movements' whose critiques of the mainstream also lead them to set up alternative social institutions of their own (political parties, schools, coops, mutual assistance societies, etc.). In some ways RLS efforts are like the nativistic, revivalistic and even messianic movements that altruistically disregard 'least effort' solutions to social problems and that stress affect-laden 'identity recovery' or 'identity reconstruction'. However, unlike the latter, RLS movements are not typically non-Western in preferred lifestyle, not change resistant, not past-oriented, not hopeless outbursts of simple societies in the last gasps of resistance to triumphant, technically superior, complex Western modernity. Indeed, although mesmerized by putative kinship myths and their derivative 'Xmen via Xish' obligations and commitments, RLS movements are highly rational in the most modern 'resource mobilization' sense, certainly every bit as rational as is the modern Western pursuit of such goals unrelated to 'market productivity' as religious liberty and equality of the sexes.

Finally, however, RLS movements are also not necessarily like ethnicity-en-route-to nationalism movements more generally. The latter movements are inherently political in nature, working directly toward attaining self-regulatory control in various modern-power-related spheres of life. RLS movements, however, precisely because they are so substantially language-focused, have a crucial intergenerational mother tongue continuity focus, a cultural focus if you like. This unique focus makes it necessary for them and them alone to relate everything that they do to the home-family-neighborhood nexus, the nexus in which mother tongues are passed along during a very brief – almost fleeting – period of normal socialization and enculturation. Certainly, in their early or weak stages, RLS movements must consider all their other 'ultimate aspirations' as reinforcements and expansions of the nexus of intergenerational mother tongue transmission rather than as ethnonational goals in their own right, regardless of the power that may ultimately flow from them. Nationalist movements strive for political power; RLS movements, however, rightly strive to keep the language going even without a state and even without cultural autonomy arrangements, mass media, Xish in the worksphere and, yes, even without schools-in-lieu-of-public-education in which Xish is the medium of instruction. A knowledge of the sociology of nationalist movements *per se* is necessary in order to see RLS movements in terms of their unique similarities and differences to other organized ethnicity-linked phenomena.

Note that familiarity with the dialectic *within* sociology, i.e. with its attempt to define different types of social movements, helped me recognize the distinctive features of RLS movements, but that the dialectic *with* sociology, i.e. confronting sociology with a given sociolinguistic reality, helped me go beyond the prior sociological alternatives. But this brings me to the question of why modern, Western sociological thinking relative to ethnicity-linked phenomena such as RLS movements, is as limited as it is. An acquaintence with two centuries' worth of social and political theory reveals its equation of 'modernization' with the maximization of individuality, i.e. with liberation *from* groupness rather than, as RLS movements see modernization, as liberation *for* groupness. Of the classic thinkers, e.g. Burke, Rousseau, Montesquieu, Mill, only Rousseau had a change of heart toward the end of his days in this connection, being the first to recognize the emptiness and alienation of the totally free and, also, the first to recognize that such societal maladies as aimlessness and social atomization could be alleviated only by those very same communal bonds that interfered with complete individual freedom. These two directions were integrated, as balancing and equally necessary forces, in Rousseau's 'Utopia', but most social theorists since Rousseau, up until the belated appearance of the post-industrial left, have opted either for the one or for the other. Most of the current RLS movements that I have reviewed are typically continuations of Rousseau's pursuit of utopia, seeking to accommodate both modernity's enchantment with individualistic happiness and ethnicity's enchantment with commitment to kinship and affiliation, with a particular language often being viewed as the obligatory key to both.

Most mainstream social theoreticians prefer to err on the side of the claims of individuality, risking social alienation rather than subjugation and disruptive intergroup hostility. The popular press usually panders to this bias in the bulk of its accounts of Soviet and Yugoslav post-perestroika affairs. Even Herder has been downgraded for his 'romanticism' with respect to language groups far and wide, and certainly Gumplowitz with his theories of 'racial' (which then meant roughly what ethnic means today) conflict and 'racial' creativity and his even more obviously rightwing to fascist counterparts in French social theory, did nothing to make mainstream American or British sociology more sympathetic to the modernity-plus-continuity strivings of minority societies within their own national establishments and the world over. Perhaps sociolinguistics' sympathetic sensitivity to the affiliative and inte-grative role of language and its recognition of social movements that stress this role, a sensitivity and recognition that seem to have come to the modern sociolinguistic enterprise almost from its very outset, may also have contributed to some of the unnecessary and self-punitive tensions between mainstream or establishment sociology and the relatively radical sociolinguistic enterprise.

The ultimate theoretical contribution of (macro-)sociolinguistic theory to sociology may lie precisely in the former's rich potential for stimulating the empirical and theoretical rethinking of affiliative societal phenomena as both normal and basic social processes rather than as peripheral aberrations. A sociologically informed sociology of language can engage sociology in a variety of mutually fruitful dialogs. One of these dialogs, I am sure, will deal with the relevance of communal affiliation in the search for gratifications that the mainstream and its social theories have not recognized sufficiently, namely the search for commitment and the search for affiliation in modern social life, a modern life in which the gratifications of individuality are not lost sight of either. But in order to engage in such a dialog, in order to learn from each other, the two parties must first be persuaded to take each other seriously. Sociolinguists, and those linguists who are sociolinguistics some of the time (as so many are), must study sociology in order to obtain a disciplined (even if only introductory) familiarity with its theories and methods. They will find no powerful formulas there, no open sesames, no all-purpose shibboleths, but, rather, 200 or more years' worth of ongoing and painfully cumulative and self-corrective struggle to freely think through the basic societal processes, processes that it is foolhardy for sociolinguistics to be ignorant of or, even worse, to re-invent on their own.

## Deuteronomy: The Sociolinguistics of the Twenty-First Century

There must not be a third and yet a fourth sociologically innocent and ignorant generation of sociolinguists! There must be a multi-theoretical and multi-methodological effort to keep that from happening, an effort which will inevitably broaden the sociological contributions to sociolin-guistics, transforming sociolinguistics (at least in its macro-realizations) into an area that is as informed about sociology and society as it is about linguistics and language. The Summer Linguistic Institutes have a role to play in pursuit of this rapprochement and so does the Social

Science Research Council and NEH and, indeed, every linguistics department offering graduate work in sociolinguistics. The requirement of 12 credits of sociology for graduate students in sociolinguistics (I had originally twice suggested 24 credits in 1978 publications) is not an outlandish one and, together with various steps on behalf of faculty retraining, will go a long way toward putting the socio back into the sociolinguistic enterprise. After these efforts will have been in place for a generation our descendents will look back upon our time with puzzlement, wondering why it took so long for such an obviously desired state of affairs to come into being.

Perhaps, as in so many other respects, California will start the ball rolling in this new or revised campus-focused direction. Off campus, there have already been a few other voices. Like mine. Glyn Williams, a young Welsh sociologist of language, is about to publish a volume with Routledge entitled *Sociolinguistics: A Sociological Critique.* I have just written a brief introduction to it, even though my work is also subjected to an analytic critique there, as is that of all of my generation. In addition, the Research Committee for Sociolinguistics of the International Sociological Association (a Committee which I sparked as far back as 1965) has just sent out a call for papers for a 1992 conference on 'the interface between sociology and linguistics'. Two swallows do not a summer make, but my hopes are high.

In the Jewish mystical tradition the Messiah is waiting, chained somewhere (various diaspora sites are mentioned in the very specialized literature on this topic), chained and waiting due to the continuing and prevailing iniquity of humanity, waiting to be released so that he or she can usher in an eternal age of happiness and enlightenment. Sociology too, although far less messianic in its promise, is chained and waiting, somewhere in our own disciplinary provincialism, waiting to come to sociolinguistics, to broaden and deepen it somewhat and to enable it to live up to its name. Events like those of the past few days here in Santa Cruz (a four day 'Symposium on the Sociology of Language and Speakers of Other Languages') have made me hopeful that it may not be too long now before the two, sociology and sociolinguistics, will finally get together.

For me, part of the joy of living and the joy of working is that I feel so keenly (and pleasurefully) that there are still many unknown sociolinguistic continents to explore. They are significant continents, still waiting for the Columbus who will finally put them on the sociolinguistic map. It is my very firm belief these *new* continents, as well as the old ones that have already been at least partially explored, will get to be known ever so much better, ever so much more fully and ever so much more provocatively if our explorations are accompanied by sociological insights and skills, than if they are attempted, as hitherto, largely without them.

## Note

1. 'Forum Lecture', Summer Linguistic Institute (Linguistic Society of America), University of California, Santa Cruz, July 10, 1991. An earlier and much briefer version of this paper was presented, in part, at Sociolinguistic Symposium #8, March 28, 1991, Roehampton Institute, London.

## Chapter 4

# Diglossia and Societal Multilingualism: Dimensions of Similarity and Difference

There is no sociolinguist whose name and whose work mean more to me than Charles A. Ferguson. Similarly, among all of my students in a lifetime of teaching, there is none of whom I am fonder or prouder than Alan Hudson. As the one who may well have introduced him to 'diglossia', more than a quarter-century ago, I have been particularly proud to note the tenacity he has brought to the task of clarifying this concept, which was one of Ferguson's greatest contributions to our field (and to Arabic and Southeast Asian studies as well). Although this concept has played a central role in my own work, and although Ferguson was and Hudson is too gentlemanly to have said so in as many words, others have quite openly told me that I have overextended and overgeneralized the term to be synonymous with societal multilingualism more generally. Since I have long taught a course called 'Varieties of societal multilingualism' (indeed, since 1978 when my *Advances in the Study of Societal Multilingualism* appeared) and have taught it far and wide throughout the world (without being aware of anyone else doing so), I would like to use this discussion both to deny any such charge of overextension or synonymity and yet to clarify why it is that I take diglossia to be one kind (N.B. just *one* kind, of many) of societal multilingualism. The pursuit of the manifold differences and similarities between the various types of societal multilingualism is an honorable, valuable and provocative undertaking within sociolinguistic theory more generally, and I, in particular, want to thank Alan Hudson and will long remain indebted to him for having stimulated me to explicate these similarities and differences again, in partial response to his own understanding of how societal multilingualism differs from diglossia.

## Genetic and Nongenetic Diglossia

Hudson goes beyond Ferguson in recognizing that both genetically related and unrelated codes may stand in a diglossic relationship to one another. From my point of view, this is a considerable and a very welcome loosening of the reins and one which I and a few others have advocated during the past nearly 30 years. Nevertheless, Hudson still considers the genetically related cases as more representative of the truer etiology of diglossia (the development of a restricted-access H variety, which is, and always remains, no one's mother tongue, out of a universally shared mother tongue L, which is 'forever' consensually allocated only for vernacular/informal purposes). It is precisely because this monocultural etiology of H and L does not apply to the Haitian case that Hudson cannot comfortably accommodate it within his model, although it is manifestly of the genetic-diglossia type. Similarly, since the Paraguayan Guarani/Spanish case is also obviously not monocultural in etiology, it is not as quintessentially diglossic in Hudson's view as is the Arabic case, for example. Thus, for all 'practical' intents and purposes, the genetic case and the monocultural etiology case are generally conflated in Hudson's discussion and constitute the preferred cooccurring and defining phenomena of diglossia as a whole.

## Imbalance of Power

Furthermore, Hudson agrees with and attributes to Schiffman (1996) a conflation of 'imbalance of power' and nongenetic diglossia. The scenario is a simple one, namely $B \rightarrow A = \frac{B}{a}$, that is, external $B$ enters the cultural space of $A$ and three generations later ('and for a long, long time thereafter') the entire population is $a$-speaking but the formerly vernacular $b$-speakers are predominantly in control of ('have cultural access to') the code and the functions requiring formal $B$. However, I am not at all convinced that the conflation attributed to Schiffman is justified as an across-the-board definition of nongenetic diglossia. Schiffman's work itself provides many contrary examples in South Asia and I myself have spent many years studying a case that was both *nongenetic* and *monocultural* in etiology (namely the Hebrew/Yiddish case in pre-nineteenth-century Ashkenaz). In such cases, the 'superposed H' (to use Ferguson's locution) was not super*im*posed by an outside culture or borrowed from one, but, rather, was 'endogenously' arrived at and continuously maintained, whereas the population's L changed due to dependency contacts and migrations. Thus, there are examples of monocultural and nongenetic etiologies, just as there are of genetic and heterocultural etiologies. 'Imbalance of power' does not apply well to the former, because the class structure that obtains (as one does in any and all human cultures) does not reflect or grow out of an underlying ethnic difference. Even were it to do so, it would still be erroneous to confuse etiology with the operating circumstances 'on the ground' half a millennium later (as, e.g. in Paraguay).

## A Two-by-Two Table Plus Time

Obviously, the sociologically beloved 'two-by-two' table that can be constructed out of any two cross-tabulated dichotomized variables applies also to the genetic/nongenetic and monocultural/multicultural etiological (i.e. historical) reconstruction. Such a cross-tabulation leaves us with four subtypes of diglossia; however, if we add the dimension of time depth then we must prepare for the possibility of transformations from one subtype to another. The etiological type $\frac{B}{b} \rightarrow \frac{A}{a}$ can pass through several centuries of $B + \frac{A}{b}$, a before resolving into the common $\frac{B}{a}$ pattern mentioned earlier, even passing through a $B + \frac{A}{a} + b$ stage en route, in view of the generally slower rate of change in formal literary and governmental functions than in informal vernacular ones (as, e.g. the spread of Hindi into non-Hindi mother-tongue areas in Southern India, each with their very own written varieties that have long been mutually noncomprehensible from the perspective of vernacular speech). In such cases, we may even find the upper classes switching the H languages of power, whereas the vernaculars, the only varieties fully available to the lower class, remain everyone's L vernaculars throughout half a millennium or longer. The spread of English during the past (twentieth) century may also have shown examples of the former type of diglossia genesis, and even more varieties may become evident as English also continues to spread into areas of prior literacy. In such cases, obviously, it is H that is unstable rather than, as was the case in the Jewish-vernaculars fold, where L is unstable. Thus, it is not etiology but time depth and the dynamics and course of social change that enable us to locate cases of diglossia stabilization, destabilization and restabilization, both of H and of L (and even more than once in the 'same' cultural area if sufficient time depth is scrutinized). Clearly, then, there are more than four kinds of diglossia 'out there', if the world is our oyster, and their recognition requires (a) that our dichotomies be recognized as merely conceptual conveniences and (b) that there be some consensus as to how long a period of time to require in order to suggest that diglossia obtains in a particular instance of societal multilingualism.

I may have adopted a too permissive rule of thumb, but I was following one that had previously been suggested by Heinz Kloss, namely, that 'more than three generations' qualifies as the lower limit of 'a long time' insofar as the stability of societal arrangements is concerned. Perhaps five generations should have been required, because then almost *no one alive could claim to have witnessed when a particular H/L consensual functional convention had come into being.* A manageable stability convention permits the recognition of more variance *vis-à-vis* diglossia, just as does the recognition of variance with respect to presence/absence of genetic relationship and variance with respect to presence/absence of monocultural etiology. Greater variance with respect to degree of stability permits greater interaction between diglossia and other phenomena of prime sociolinguistic importance, namely such aspects of theoretical and applied sociolinguistics as either (a) reversing language shift or (b) language planning more generally. Michael Clyne has clearly documented (1997) that much of language planning involves both planning and unplanning previous planning (i.e. 'doing, undoing, and redoing'). The same may be said of diglossia, once we recognize that it can be an object of organized social consciousness. If we merely dichotomize time, then our four-celled table immediately becomes an eight-celled table, now including proto- or 'virtual' diglossias as well as long-established diglossias with differing degrees of separation, functionally and linguistically.

## Diglossia and Reversing Language Shift

The modern Political Zionist movement was an instance of undoing a traditional diglossia that had lasted some 2000 years, between Jewish vernaculars and the Holy Tongue, Hebrew. The ultra-Orthodox Jews in Israel, however, opposed the undoing of long-term Ashkenazic Hebrew/Yiddish nongenetic diglossia and either fostered its retention by establishing schools and communities of their own (Glinert & Isaacs, 1999) or fostered its replacement by a newly recognized genetic diglossia in which centuries-old traditional Hebrew plus Judeo-Aramaic served as H and modern Israeli vernacular Hebrew (intraculturally reinterpreted as *'a totally different language than the Holy Tongue'*) served as L (i.e. as one of the 'Jewish languages other than Hebrew', as these are collectively referred to in Fishman, 2000b). At early stages in their pursuit of the sheltering harbor of functional diglossia, threatened vernaculars may argue for language-planning policies that will protect them in vernacular or L functions. Once such functions have been sufficiently attained, bolstered and accepted for all 'insiders', the stages of undoing and redoing may yet arrive, when the formerly threatened 'language of everyday life' (Fishman, 1980) comes to be championed for H functions as well (and possibly for all H functions bar none). Diglossia is, therefore, a 'fighting term' in real life. It is not only a concept in sociolinguistic discourse; it is a concept in political discourse as well, wherever RLS is a man-in-the-street issue. It may be opposed and defended sequentially, depending on the fortunes of the hitherto threatened L, being advocated at various stages of its advocacy in terms of different notions of 'long enough' and even of 'genetically related enough'. Genetic etiology too is far from an open and shut case, regardless of whether lay or professional expertise is resorted to.

## Diglossia and Language Planning

Fully one-half of all eight theoretically available 'directional programs' of language planning consist of distancing efforts *vis-à-vis* a locally and temporally intrusive language of greater advantage (Fishman, 2000a). The greater advantage *vis-à-vis* ultimate diglossia obtains, at least in principle, for local linguistic contenders rather than for outsiders. The total array of status planning (via political, religious, cultural and econotechnical means) that goes into planning, unplanning and replanning the diglossia aspirations of constituencies is referred to as language-status planning. However, language planning also obtains when the constituencies are politically exclusive ones. Polities interact ('communicate') too and they may do so diglossically with respect to certain functions (e.g. negotiations may be conducted in *a*, but treaties *per se* may be in *B* alone or even in *B* and *C*). It is in this connection that the difference between bilingualism and diglossia becomes quite striking, since both polities may be overwhelmingly monolingual and yet the interpolity communications, given that they are conducted by a special class of interlocutors called diplomats, may be and remain for centuries entirely diglossic. This realization, not one that should be foreign to or too strained for sociolinguists, provides for diglossia as a between-group rather than only as a within-group convention, indeed it recognizes a convention reaching at least from biblical antiquity into our most modern times. As long as we recognize that language planning and communicational reality as a whole pertain to the conventions of intergroup communication, our diglossia model becomes enriched. Indeed, our model must permit ever more enrichment as additional dimensions of *diglossic variance* are successively recognized. Nevertheless, not every instance of societal multilingualism is diglossic. Far from it.

## Societal Multilingualism

If there are so many different types of diglossia, what then is societal multilingualism over and above just the contrastive analysis of each of the foregoing (which would be no mean accomplishment, at any rate)? A cover term to summate and/or to highlight the differences between various parameters of variance is no mean achievement and one that should be hailed rather than regretted. What is social science about, other than the partitioning, comparison and evaluation of the variance encompassed by the phenomena it recognizes? Such recognition leads to the realization that societal multilingualism is even more variable than diglossia. Its study includes the various types of diglossia but also the various types of nondiglossic interaction: For example, each 'side' sending and receiving in its own preferred language (as among some

Amazonian cultures and within the Parliament of the EU; see Fishman, 1993), or the huge variety of *ad-hoc* arrangements (e.g. the perhaps temporary reciprocal use of non-native German in post-World War II Eastern Europe, the traditional lingua francas of Mediterranean commerce and sailing, the rise and spread of new pidgins in already-multilingual Africa, etc.). All in all, the field of societal multilingualism is far from a one-concept field and diglossia is merely one of its many central parameters of interest (still others being language attitudes, the intergenerational transmission of classical languages and their functions, both secular and religious, writing systems, and, certainly worthy of mention, digraphia; see Grivelet, 2001).

## A Vote of Thanks and a Demurral

All in all, although I may have major doubts and differences *vis-à-vis* some of the positions that Hudson takes on diglossia, I move that we proffer him a vote of thanks for requiring us to sharpen up our thinking about the matter, as well as about matters related to it. I do not think I have ever before stressed the greater importance of long-term cultural continuity, rather than linguistic etiology, in matters diglossic. Given such continuity, originally exogenous language-contact settings can turn into fully fused sociocultural entities with a totally ubiquitous H and L. The various cultures in which Latin served as H alongside different Romance-language Ls (from Portuguese and Gallego in the west to Romanian in the east) may all seem to the linguist to be instances of genetic diglossia during the nearly two millennia of their existence, but the differing contexts of the original historical conquest ('power imbalance') and occupation of the conquered by the conquering is obvious from the historical record. The long-term stability and yet fluidity that is required for the relationship between nonliterate (or less literate) and literate (or more literate) cultures to meld, be they Roman soldiers and the local Celtic, Germanic or Slavic populations of the far-flung European empire, or the subsequent Teutonic, Mongol and other Asian hordes and the by-then already romanized local populations that demographically swallowed up these unlettered scourges, illustrate the possibility of stable cultural arrangements to meld populations and to create long-lasting diglossic conditions that are neither respecters of nor dependent upon the 'degree of relatedness between the [original] constituent codes'. Nor do their outcomes today derive from the original absence or presence of power differentials. Every case of diglossia has its history but in no case is that history predetermined by its etiology, linguistic or sociocultural, and decreasingly so as we move closer to modern times and further away from the origin scenarios (both linguistic and societal).

Initial imbalances of brute power between two melding populations may come and go ('go' to the extent that one can ultimately no longer even talk of two populations), or they may transform into prolonged differences of access to the life of literacy and of literacy-permeated speech, or, and this is the final transformation, into full-scale functional access to the appropriateness of H and L, permeating the entire phenomenologically unitary society, so that very much the same individuals utilize H and L in their different rounds of life. Clearly, these are but different realizations of the same functional repertoire, so that, finally, it is not etiology, linguistic distance, or power imbalances nor anything but the long-term stability of a very distinctive and fully incorporated intracultural arrangement that makes for diglossia. Hudson is correct, in my view, in suspecting the rarity of this specific cultural arrangement within the entire gamut of societally multilingual arrangements, but he is incorrect in so narrowly limiting the more manifold sociocultural circumstances out of which diglossia can and does arise and in underappreciating the long-term stability that is basically required to maintain it regardless of the particular route that it takes at the outset or even for centuries thereafter.

## Sociolinguistic Theory

Instead of fearing, as does Hudson, the various treatments of the variety of societal multilingualisms because they seem to imply manifold 'surface manifestations of the same underlying phenomenon', it might be more appropriate to view diglossia in more variegated fashion, so as not to fail to see its underlying relationship (i.e. its patterned differences and similarities) to the other varieties of societal multilingualism with which it cooccurs. Our allegiance to Occam's Razor promotes parsimony only where essentials are not overlooked. Neither parsimony nor good sociolinguistic theory require (nor do they benefit from) separating related phenomena so that they have nothing to do with each other. Quite the contrary. A unified theory of societal multilingualism (or of any other societal phenomenon) not only lays bare the few systematic underlying dimensions in accord with which many seemingly different phenomena can be seen in varying relationship with each other (rather than merely being either 'entirely the same' or 'entirely different' from one another), but such a theory also ties in with other macrosystems as well. True enough, those macrosystems (e.g. positive/negative ethnolinguistic consciousness, language planning and reversing language shift, language education, etc.) have their own major axes and satellites, but they must also utilize and interact with the basic principles and processes of societal multilingualism, if for no other reason than that they are so commonly processes that reflect individual and societal purpose with respect to the management of varieties of societal multilingualisms.

## References

Clyne, M. (1997) *Undoing and Redoing Corpus Planning*. Berlin: Mouton de Gruyter.

Fishman, J.A. (1967) Bilingualism with and without diglossia; diglossia with and without bilingualism. *Journal of Social Issues* 23 (2), 29–38.

——. (1978) *Advances in the Study of Societal Multilingualism*. The Hague: Mouton.

——. (1980) Attracting a following to high-culture functions for a language of everyday life. *International Journal of the Sociology of Language* 24, 43–73.

——. (1993) Ethnolinguistic democracy: varieties, degrees, limits. *Language International* 5 (1), 11–17.

——. (2000a) The status agenda in corpus planning. In *Language Policy and Pedagogy; Essays in Honor of A. Ronald Walton*, R.D. Lambert and E. Shohamy (eds) (pp. 43–53). Amsterdam: Benjamins.

——. (2000b) Language planning for the 'other Jewish languages' in Israel: An agenda for the beginning of the 21st century. *Language Problems and Language Planning* 24, 215–232.

Glinert, L. and Isaacs, M. (eds) (1999) Pious Voices: Languages Among Ultra-Orthodox Jews (special issue). *International Journal of the Sociology of Language* 138.

Grivilet, S. (ed.) (2001) Digraphia. *International Journal of the Sociology of Language* 150.

Schiffman, H.F. (1996) *Linguistic Culture and Language Policy*. London: Routledge.

*Part 2*
# Loyalty, Shift and Revitalization

## Chapter 5

# *What is Reversing Language Shift (RLS) and How Can It Succeed?*[1]

It is no exaggeration to say that millions of people throughout the world are consciously engaged in efforts to reverse language shift and that many hundreds of thousands do so as members of movements whose explicit goal is RLS. Yet the efforts of these millions and the goals of these hundreds of thousands have been relatively little mentioned in the social science literature and have remained only infrequently referred to, even in the sociolinguistic literature. Part of the reason for this ethically unjustified and intellectually as well as practically disappointing state of affairs, it seems to me, is that both the social sciences as a whole and sociolinguistics in its own right have sliced up their treatments of social movements in general, and reformatory or protest social movements in particular, in such a way that RLS never clearly appears as the distinctive phenomenon that it is.

This is not terribly surprising. The modern, Western social sciences have only very recently come to recognise socially patterned language use and socially manifested behaviour towards language as topics to be reckoned with. Sociolinguistics itself, on the other hand, even in its more RLS-sympathetic (although less intensively cultivated) 'macro' or 'sociology of language' pursuits, has not yet arrived at a sufficiently refined taxonomy of language status planning to explicitly provide for the consideration of RLS activity. As a result, very refined terminological and conceptual distinctions are made with respect to the 'minus' side of the ledger (we speak of language attrition-shift-endangerment-loss-death and can itemise many studies of each way-station along this increasingly negative progression), while the 'plus' side remains rather gross and undifferentiated and studies of revival, restoration, revitalisation and restabilisation remain proportionately few and far between. At the same time, language 'status planning', of which RLS is a sub-category, is overly identified with central government efforts, hardly the most likely or the most sympathetic auspices for minority RLS efforts.

The most general reason for the neglect of RLS is probably the fact that RLS is an activity of minorities, frequently powerless, unpopular with outsiders and querulous amongst themselves; it is an activity that is very often unsuccessful and that strikes many intelligent laymen and otherwise intelligent social scientists as 'unnatural', i.e. as counter to some supposedly natural drift of historical events or the obvious direction of social change. It is hard for self-serving mainstream intellectual spokesmen and institutions to be sympathetic to the lingering, cantankerous, neither fully alive nor fully dead quality of many (perhaps most) efforts on behalf of receding minority languages (and the majority of sidestream scholars, too, are ultimately dependent on the mainstream for their perspectives if not for their very livelihoods). Indeed, RLS efforts are often like the 'gomers' or 'crocks' that constantly reappear in the emergency rooms of major metropolitan hospitals – elderly, complaining individuals who neither die nor get better and for whom nothing effective can seemingly ever be done. Most young doctors, like most majority spokesmen in other fields, learn to 'meet'em, greet'em and street'em', i.e. to make light of the complaints of these embarrassing unfortunates and to turn to other, more tractable cases as expeditiously as possible. Crocks take up scarce resources (staff time, energy, funds, supplies, equipment) and contribute disproportionately to staff burnout. They are no more than obviously 'suspect' and unpopular reminders of the failure of modern medicine to be able to cope with chronic social and individual health problems, particularly those that are characterised by a goodly overlay of social pathology, on the one hand, and that are seemingly irreversible, on the other. Minorities that are struggling for their very lives, for dignity, attention and affirmative action are inevitably suspect and unpopular. Both RLS efforts and gomers are unwelcome testimony to shortcomings of the mainstream and to the tremendous will of the neglected and the 'different' to lead their own lives and to find their own satisfactions, regardless of outside pronouncements that nothing can or should be done for them.

## RLS Among the 'Social Movements'

RLS efforts may very well be an individual activity, even the activity of an isolated individual, but they are much more characteristically a socially patterned and organised activity of the type that sociologists refer to as 'social movements'. But where, exactly, do RLS efforts belong in the long array of types of social movements studied by social scientists? RLS movements not only differ in many respects from the 'collective behaviour' phenomena (crowds, mobs, panic scenes, riots, etc.) that sociologists of an earlier generation so frequently studied, but they also differ interestingly from the types of bona fide social movements that have elicited more recent sociological attention. Like the latter, RLS efforts have definite goals, they are enduring and organised, and like some of them, too, they are commonly enacted outside of 'normal' institutional channels (e.g. mainsteam political parties, voluntary organisations, schools, media, etc.) and, indeed, are often oppositional to such institutions and tend to set up alternative social institutions, organisations and structures of their own.

However, there is often about RLS efforts a very palpable degree of affect, a sentimental (rather than merely an instrumental) bonding, a stress on real or putative ethnokinship, an aspiration towards conscious-ness and identity (re)formation, a heightened degree of altruistic self-sacri-fice and a disregard, for 'least effort' advantages, to the degree that RLS behaviours often impress outsiders as bordering on the 'irrational' and the 'mystic'. It is perhaps the latter characteristics that have tended to elicit fear, suspicion and rejection in the mainstream and that have led to frequent charges that RLS efforts are a species of 'collective behaviour' after all, rather than manifestations of the 'social movement behaviours' of the comfortably rational and familiarly materialistic mainstream or mainstream-proximate types. These fears and suspicions have raised a series of road-blocks to the appreciation of RLS and other ethnic 'beha-viour-and-identity' movements during the past century and a half.

## 'Irrational' Ethnocultural Behaviour-and-Identity Movements

There is, of course, a long history to the charges of 'irrationality' by those who are in control of secure ethnocultural establishments of their own against those who are without such control and seeking to attain it. Lord Acton criticised the 'preposterous' ethnocultural claims aroused by Herder and fostered by the French Revolution among the peoples without states and 'therefore without histories' throughout Europe. Sub-sequently, many of these claims were sufficiently powerful to be attacked from below (rather than from above as was the case with Lord Acton), by Marx and Engels, in their efforts to foster a new and presumably more rational proletarian identity. Again and again, ethnicity has been delegitimised in the West (by both secular and Church spokesmen) as anti-modern, anti-intellectual, irrational, anti-progressive and anti-civil. Little wonder, then, that modern social science should also be heir to this tradition,[2] particularly given the fact that so much of modern social science is American and America views itself (and its identity) as univer-salistically supra-ethnic rather than parochially ethnic in the deeply traditional (and self-styled deeply historical) Old World sense.

One of the earliest social science attempts to understand the seemingly non-modern and anti-modern identity re-establishment efforts of small peoples was Ralph Linton's (1943) analysis of 'nativistic movements' among small, overrun, indigenous peoples in the colonial empires established by the modern West. Linton described as 'nativistic' any conscious, organised attempt on the part of a society's members to revive or perpetuate selected aspects of their severely dislocated culture. Although Linton differentiated between 'revivalistic' and 'perpetuative' nativism, as well as between 'magical' and 'rational' efforts on behalf of either, he devoted major attention to the revivalistic-magical quadrant in his four-fold table and considered nativism as a whole to be a reaction to the unbearable oppression, dislocation and domination of Western rule. Implicitly, therefore, there is a non-Western flavour to the entire phenomenon, such that the cultural self-protective efforts of small Western populations at the mercy of non-Westerners would not only be deemed 'perpetuative' and 'rational' but might be said *not* to be nativistic at all, but, rather, protective of Western civilisation. Clearly, Linton did not anticipate either 'revivalistic' or 'perpetuative' RLS efforts within the very West itself (where, indeed, the lion's share of such efforts have occurred) and his conceptualisation of cultural behaviours is excessively dichotomous; it is either X or Y, Western or non-Western, whereas most RLS efforts envisage more complex, more contextual and situational repertoires composed of ingredients of X and Xishness and Y and Yishness.

Anthony Wallace (1956), writing a dozen years after Linton, as well as Bernard Barber (1941), writing just a few years before Linton, contributed an interest in 'Messianism' to the discussion of nativistic efforts. For Barber, such Messianism is the mystic solution to a cultural impasse; it is an attempt to find supernaturally derived stability and hope in a culture which is otherwise in realistic shreds and tatters. For Wallace, Messianism, nativism and millenarism are all types of 'revitalisation', i.e. movements which emphasise the elimination of alien persons, customs, values and/or artifacts. Thus, both Barber and Wallace focus essentially on irrational and backward-looking solutions, and, as a result, would not have much to say about the bulk of RLS efforts which are really attempts to arrive *at self-regulated modernisation*, i.e. at Xish modernisation that is in the spirit of and under the aegis of Xishness as defined by 'Xmen-with-Xish'. Western social science seems to be primarily telling us that modernisation and authenticity preoccupations cannot go together, just as authenticity preoccupations and rationality cannot go together. The seeming anomaly of modernisation, rationality, affectivity and authenticity, the cornerstones of RLS, are theoretically unprovided for because such a complex combination strikes modern social science as perversely contradictory, as 'so near and yet so far' from the mainstream ethos. The true complexity of modern minority movements is elusive, doubly so since such movements are contraindicated given the simplistic theories according to which mainstream processes and virtues are considered simultaneously prototypical, normal and inescapable.

In many ways, Russell Thornton's (1986) retrospective analysis of the Amerindian Ghost Dance movements of 1870 and 1890 hews close to the irrational and backward-looking characterisations encountered in Wallace's discussion of revitalisation movements, as one might expect from a consideration of manifestations that predicted demographic/ cultural recovery as a byproduct of dances that would bring the dead back to life. Nevertheless, Thornton does add one crucial new twist to the discussion thus far: a realisation that such movements are at least phenomenologically rational and that they may be sufficiently motivating to be productive 'resource mobilisation' as well. However, Thornton's magnanimous admission that the ghost dances 'were deliberate responses ... that probably made sense to the Indians involved ... (and) in terms of their culture ... (were) essentially rational acts' is not only a condescending tautology but implies that no such rationality would obtain from the point of view of modern, Western culture.

Setting aside the fact that Thornton overlooks the frequency with which modern Western populations engage in efforts to protect *their* sanctities (sanctities that are obviously above and beyond the rational), the rationality of goals and the rationality of means must always be analytically separated. RLS is usually a thoroughly modern enterprise in terms of the rationality of its means (any implied equation between RLS and ghost dances being totally out of order), while its goals admittedly partake of the rationality of modern religious and ideological verities that a major portion of mankind considers to be worth struggling toward, regardless of price in time, effort and resources. Still provocatively interesting for us today, however, more so than any of Thornton's judgemental comments, are his conclusions that the Amerindian efforts to which he refers were most extensively and rewardingly engaged in by those very cultures that had been most dislocated and that, *in toto*, these efforts were basically attempts to re-establish group boundaries. Neither of these considerations requires notions of 'irrationality' but rather, as Thornton fully realised, are fully consistent with 'resource mobilisation' and 'relative deprivation' theories within the social sciences.

A further step along the path of re-rationalising and de-mystifying revitalisation movements was recently taken by Duane Champagne (1983). He realises that there are basic similarities between the revitalisation movements that occur in structurally less differentiated societies and the reform or guided cultural change movements that occur in structurally more differentiated (= more modern) ones. Both types of efforts utilise the most effective means available to their societies, those of the latter societies being organisationally, institutionally, materially and conceptually more advanced and, therefore, more capable of accepting the inevitability of cultural change and able to influence its outcome via political and economic means. Champagne's analysis should once and for all remove the penumbra of backwardness and irrationality from efforts of the RLS types. Such efforts may fail or prevail, depending on rationally analysable factors (i.e. they do so on the basis of means and circumstances totally like those that govern the success and failure of the other social movements with which they must compete), differing from their contemporary competitors more with respect to ends than to means. Indeed, given the scarcity of means that most RLS efforts have at their disposition, a good case can be made that they often *attempt to be more rational* with respect to their deployment than is frequently the case for movements that are socially ascendent.[3] All in all, attempts to convince the modern mind of the rationality of ethnocultural behaviour-and-identity re-intensification movements have experienced some success during the past half century, but much movement in this direction is still necessary before RLS efforts will be commonly viewed as the natural, thoughtful and constructive undertakings that their participants take them to be.

## RLS, 'Backward Looking' Resistance to Change, and Cultural Conservatism

Another oft-repeated stereotypic charge is that RLS and related re-ethnification or ethnic re-intensification movements are backward-looking ('past oriented'), conservative, change resistant dinosaurs. Of course, most basic philosophical values tend to have their origins in the past and small cultures that are now in particular danger of erosion naturally recognise a past when that was not (or not as much) the case. RLS efforts are very sensitive, due to their very goal-consciousness *per se*, to the constant diminution in the numbers or proportions of speakers/users of the language-in-culture on behalf of which they struggle, to the incursions of time, to the fact that things were better 'then' than they are 'now'. But this does not need to make them more 'backward looking' (if by that we mean: seriously pursuing a return to and a preservation of the past) than are most other opponents of present evils, injustices and dislocations. Shall we designate as 'backward looking' all those who remember when urban neighbourhoods were much safer cleaner and far less polluted than they are today, merely because they strive towards a closer approximation towards past superior standards in these respects? Many others, besides RLSers, yearn for social and cultural arrangements that will foster stronger family bonds of affection, mutual care and concern, respect, ethical behaviour and commitment.

Many others, outside the RLSers, realise that local communities must be more fully involved in their schools, health agencies, playgrounds, zoning regulations and child care services, if they are to overcome the problems and inefficiencies of the growing massification and bureaucratisation of modern society. One does not need to be a member of either the Old Order Amish or the Institute for Cultural Conservatism to bemoan the general lack of intellectual concern for the moral and spiritual dimensions of modern life and, accordingly, it is unfounded to accuse those RLSers who have any or all of the above concerns of displaying a stultifying opposition to modernity. As some social scientists have already recognised, 'defenders' of the core values of modern democratic systems are apt to perceive and point out real threats to the well-being of that system. Such defence should really be viewed as part of the process of change, part of the direction-finding or direction-setting field of forces that we call change, otherwise the empty cycle of 'change for the sake of change alone' will be upon us.[4] RLSers have sometimes been accused of goal fixation to the point of forgetting why the goal is being pursued to begin with. But certainly this charge also applies to those who are 'modernists in principle' while forgetting the humanistic religious, philosophical and ideological goals that make life human, purposeful and worthwhile.

But in reality, RLSers are not merely _not_ defenders of some mystical, mythical and bygone past; they are actually 'change-agents on behalf of persistence'. Very few social scientists indeed have been inclined to conceptualise and analyse the relationship between change and persistence, probably because of our modern fascination with the dynamics of change _per se_. But all change is interspersed with persistence as well, just as all persistence is interspersed with ongoing change. Persistence no more means equilibrium than change means chaos. The forces and processes of change coexist, _in a single process_, with the forces and processes of persistence, and what most social scientists mistakenly call 'change' is really the by-product of the _interaction_ of persistence and change. Actually, the power of persistence helps provide the direction and generate the resultant of the total dynamics that are operative at any time and place. Ethnolinguistic persistence involves a basic continuity in the meaning of symbols. For RLSers a given language is the first and foremost of these symbols, as is their interpretation of that language as being truly fundamental to identity and continuity. Although RLS is rendered difficult by the values, movements and processes opposed to it, it is also rendered difficult by its inevitable interweaving with ongoing sociocultural change. Experienced RLSers realise that all cultures are constantly changing and that their goal is merely to regulate and direct this change, so that it will not contradict or overpower the core of their cultural system, rather than legislate change out of existence.

Identity persistence and ethnocultural persistence are not synonymous, of course. The former is purely phenomenological and is no basic criterion of RLS, i.e. it can be attained without RLS, while the latter involves a studied persistence of behaviours, i.e. *commitments to implemented interpretations* (of life, of relationships, of history, of symbols). RLS requires societal boundary maintenance, rather than merely being the result of such boundary maintenance. Language is a prime boundary-marker and protector, because it not only implies and reflects core boundaries but because it constantly creates and legitimises them as well. RLS seeks to avoid the dislocations that inevitably result from the destruction and substitution of core symbols, behaviours, boundaries and values, possible though it may be to come through such destruction and substitution with one's phenomenological social identity intact. It is not change *per se* that is opposed by RLSers but changes in a core behavioural complex in which the language is generatively and regeneratively linked to the protected cultural core.

For the persisters, language is both corpus and message and the authentic message without the authentic corpus is as empty as the authentic corpus without the authentic message. Nevertheless, a corpus can and must generate endless novel messages too, since the novel ones not only enable the authentic ones to achieve their contrastive sanctity but assure that sanctity of a new life, timeliness and vigour as well. As Spicer (1980) recognised ever so long ago, 'a people that endures ... embodies the most important kind of social unit which men can create: a living, cumulative interpretation (and here I would add: enactment) of human life ... collective purpose and destiny'. Only by persisting in the midst of change, only by indigenising change, only by taming and refashioning change (thereby taming and refashioning persistence too) does RLS reflect a creative guarantee as to its living potential, rather than degenerate into some totally lifeless, antiquarian oddity. It is not the return of the past that RLS seeks, but the mining of the past so that the core that animated it can continue to be implemented.[5] For all of its fascination with change, much of the thoughtful West is also 'past appreciative'. For all of their use of the past, most RLS movements and efforts are future-oriented.

## The Oppressiveness of Tradition and the Pursuit of 'Authenticity'

Although RLS is a type of sociocultural change, it is not of the type that the social science literature has classically and generally attended to. There is, of course, some recognition of a 'cultural paradigm' in mainstream social science discussion of social change, a paradigm that views innovation as an ongoing process that is literally impossible without continuity of beliefs, values, behaviours and symbol systems. However, social theory knows much more about fostering change (the 'structural paradigm') and advancing individual authenticity via liberation from repressive societal regulation than it knows about fostering continuity. Indeed, change for change's sake has come to occupy a somewhat hallowed position in social theory and has influenced the social sciences as well. John Stuart Mill, well before the mid-nineteenth century, equated tradition with unhappiness. Thereafter, the view that humans can be themselves ('authentic') only if they live without any imposed social structure at all has occupied a central niche among Western social thinkers. Even earlier, Edmund Burke had proclaimed that repression was a basic fact of social life (power for some and obedience for the rest) and Montesquieu and Rousseau had anticipated him by declaring that to maximise one's happiness each individual required freedom to shape a happiness that would be completely of his own design. If the need for group liberation was acknowledged at all (as it was by Montesquieu, who, nevertheless, concentrated on sexual, religious and political groups but was strangely oblivious to ethnocultural groups) such liberation was justified on the basis of the happiness that would be derived from being freed from ties to groupness, i.e. authenticity was viewed as liberation *from* groupness rather than as liberation *of* groupness or *for* groupness.

Only Rousseau vacillated, late in life, recognising that the emptiness and alienation of the totally free required for their alleviation those very communal bonds that decreased individual freedom. He reconciled the two, individual happiness and communal affiliation, only in utopian terms and recognised, even so, that utopias themselves were, therefore, at odds with the openness and the constant changeability of urban modernity. Among the more or less systematic schools of social thought only the Herderians, the nationalists, the racists and the Marxists defended carefully selected (and very different) affiliative ideals for any length of time after the flawed and failed spring of '48, and none of these were ever really taken seriously by the mainstream of Western social science. Furthermore, before the recent appearance of the new, post-industrial left, the Marxists themselves were as classically anti-ethnic as were the bourgeois thinkers.[6]

Perhaps of greater import for recent theoretical opposition to planned ethnicity-fostering culture change, such as RLS, is the 'alternative society' or 'commune movement' of the 1960s and 1970s. It harks back to Montesquieu in its abhorrence of mechanistic, dehumanising, competitive and materialistic societal ties and by emphasising individualistic and counterculture, rather than mainstream or traditional cultural definitions of 'success'. The new 'life-style', studiously supra-ethnic in nature, stressed openness, intimacy, flexibility, co-operation and altruistic sacrifice, Gemeinschaft features that theoreticians had once ascribed to the ethnically integrated, small community but which the communes derived independently from their anti-establishment vantage point.[7] Many RLS efforts reveal a close similarity to the anti-establishment and anti-materialistic Gemeinschaft strivings of the 'communes', thereby underscoring even more the void that so often (and so needlessly) separates the ethnic dimension and the radical dimensions of modern social criticism. Clearly, 'traditionless authenticity' and 're-ethnifying authenticity' are poles apart, regardless of the term 'authenticity' that they share. Their common stress on achieving self-regulatory status is often overlooked, primarily because the former is individualistic and the latter is group-cultural in orientation *vis-à-vis* the attainment of happiness. The perfect combination of both might well be optimal, but requires as much acceptance of the claims of (minority) ethnoculture as of the claims of individuality. Modern Western thought has generally been more willing to suffer the pains of the latter rather than grant the legitimacy of the former.

## Growth in Theory Pertaining to Ethnicity

A final area of attempted *rapprochement* and accommodation between Western social theory and ethnic re-intensification efforts pertains more directly to an understanding of ethnicity *per se.* The ethnic revival of the mid-1960s to the mid-1970s roused both bourgeois and leftist thinkers from the stupor that had clouded their thinking about ethnicity for over a century. It came to be belatedly recognised by those who sought to grapple with the far-flung (although not overly deep) ethnic stirrings in most parts of the First and Second Worlds, that many of the myths and biases that had previously coloured their views of ethnicity (irrationality, backward-looking focus, conservatism, oppression of individual 'authenticity' culminating in sociocultural/political oppression) were substantially erroneous or unfounded. Ethnicity did not involve attempts to preserve the traits of either static or pre-modern cultures. The transitions between and the combinations of traditional and modern behaviours and sentiments were actually exceedingly varied and constantly ongoing in all populations, including those that were non-state forming. States and non-states differed not only in market articulation and in power but in social organisation and in historically deep cultural manifestations. The greater power of the state ('the most successful predatory form of social organisation') might force irreversible changes upon non-state societies, but this was not as predictable an outcome towards the end of the twentieth century as it had been in the nineteenth, given the relative increase in non-state resources and the use of modern methods in all spheres of life (including non-state spheres), while the finite nature of state resources became ever more apparent. Indeed, the influences of non-state entities on their surrounding 'host' states came to be increasingly evident.

Resource mobilisation theory, important though it continued to be for the study of social movements, seemed to provide less new insight into the persistence of indigenous sidestream ('peripheral') ethnicity than had initially been hoped. Sidestream ethnicity resists reduction to the level of grievances (and manipulable, largely specious grievances at that) and the ethnic revival requires for its explanation additional factors, above and beyond the combination of minority grievances (old or new) and increased minority resources. Declining status inequalities between 'central' and indigenous 'peripheral' populations became quite noticeable – due both to the growing ethnic middle class which, nevertheless, did not forego its cultural identity as a means of social mobility, and the growing competitiveness of the latter *vis-à-vis* social rewards (including the reward of acknowledged cultural legitimacy). Indeed, the unexpected versatility of re-invigorated ethnic movements clearly highlighted their ability not only to maintain an indigenous leadership but to tap and activate indigenous resources of dedication as well.

The ability of universality and particularism to develop and coexist simultaneously within the very same populations was a rude awakening for both Marxist and non-Marxist theorists who had assumed that industrialisation, urbanisation, modernisation and the spread of education would inevitably reduce ethnic consciousness and lead to the demise of narrower loyalties in favour of broader ones. This prediction was not confirmed, narrower and broader loyalties being far more syncretistic than theory-conscious intellectuals had imagined, and the post-industrial Left was forced to identify with rather than continue to reject the cultural self-regulatory aspirations of ethnic minorities in the West itself. Bourgeois thinkers too went through much soul-searching and reformulation in the light of the evident significance of ethnicity within mainstream academia itself. Ethnicity efforts came to be viewed as reformist of mainstream insensitivity, much like pro-environmental, anti-sexist and anti-bigness or anti-industrial-growth efforts. However, even this is not the entire story, since ethnicity efforts *are* sometimes allied with conservative political, religious and moral reform efforts as well. Ultimately, however, although much has changed in mainstream thought concerning ethnicity since Lord Acton, most recent developments in ethnicity theory still treat ethnicity as *reactive to* or as *transformational of* other, 'more basic' material circumstances and aspirations.

This evident disinclination (even after 150 years of painful and reluctant theoretical change) towards accepting ethnicity in its own right, as a permeable, changeable but ultimately also quite robust and recurring identity–values–behaviour complex, a complex that situationally influences aspects of mainstream as well as sidestream life, even under the most modern circumstances, remains a blind spot in social theory that only further 'rethinking' can overcome. The ultimate theoretical contribution of RLS research to general social science theory is its rich potential for providing further empirical and theoretical perspective contributory towards exactly such rethinking.[8] Rather than being viewed as threats to the state or as byproducts of split labour markets or even of boundary maintenance processes *per se*[9] (none of which, by the way, give signs of disappearing from the horizon in the foreseeable future), ethnicity and ethnicity movements must come to be appreciated more ethnographically and phenomenologically, i.e. more from the point of view of the insider who experiences them rather than from the point of view of the outsider who views them, telescopically or microscopically, from afar without appreciating, therefore, their affective significance. So terrified are most Western thinkers of the charge of 'primordialism' that they refuse to understand the recurring appeal of primordialism to common folk the world over. Like physicians who refuse to appreciate the common man's dread of cancer or AIDS, they therefore, unknowingly but intra-punitively limit their own ability to understand the condition they are presumably treating.

The ethnic rejection of the mainstream-identity as representing one's sole and complete identity (and, indeed, the growing search for sidestream roots) implies an acceptance of self and one's origins that is also rich in potential for better understanding of others, and of inevitable links to others, as well. If the simplistic ethnic myth of fixed, homogeneous and completely bounded cultures must give way to a more realistic sense of the changeability and intersectedness of all cultures, the awareness of this myth, on the one hand, and, on the other hand, the absolute necessity of undertaking attempts to cultivate the threads of intimacy, involvement and historical relevance, so that meaningful, unalienated social existence remains possible, are often better realised by minorities than by the majorities that smugly disregard, abuse or regulate them. The real question for modern life and for RLS is not whether this is a discrete or interacting world, but, rather, given an incredibly complex field of interacting forces, how one (not just minority ethnics but any social movement) can build a home that one can still call one's own and, by cultivating it, find community, comfort, companionship and meaning in a world whose mainstreams are increasingly unable to provide these basic ingredients for their own members.

## RLS Theory: A Perspective for Rational Effort to Build and Safeguard Gemeinschaft Aspirations So That They Will Be In Touch With But Not Inundated by the World at Large

The eight stage analysis of and prescription for RLS that is presented here is an alternative planning theory in the sense that it attempts to bridge the gap between social science and societal reform. Planning scientists and planning practitioners tend to look down on one another, trading charges of conceptual poverty and lack of realism (and, therefore, lack of validity). Most of the explanatory theories advanced in language planning, for example, do not reveal, and, therefore, cannot provide, insight into the struggle of some societies towards intergenerational linguistic continuity. Appropriate RLS-status planning can only occur if the societal link between generations is constantly kept in mind and if every putative RLS effort is tested by the question 'how will this effort reach into and reinforce the intergenerational link?' – a link that must take place early, affectively and verbally if RLS is to come about. This does not mean that well-grounded RLS theory can provide us with a blueprint for the future. The future cannot be reduced to a series of technical applications of theoretically formulated steps, neither in economic planning, in agricultural planning, in educational planning, in family planning nor in RLS planning. The best that RLS theory can do is to provide greater societal perspective for negotiating the difficult priorities that any RLS effort inevitably involves. As with all other types of social planning, RLS planning will inevitably be accompanied by unexpected side-effects and even negative consequences. However, there is no alternative modern route to social problem-solving than the route via planning. For the advocates of RLS there is, therefore, no dilemma as to whether RLS planning should occur. If there is a dilemma, it deals with the how of RLS, i.e. with a systematic overall approach that can guide the efforts that must be undertaken.

To begin with, even before concrete efforts are undertaken, RLS involves 'consciousness heightening and reformation'. The importance of ideological clarification and awareness for the process of directed cultural change can easily be exaggerated but it cannot be denied. RLS behaviours cannot challenge conventional institutions and mainstream-derived ideas as to the role of Xish without fully clarifying the ideal of 'Xmen-with-Xish'. It is hard enough to row against the current; it is virtually impossible to do so without knowing where one would like to get to. Any organised activity, particularly ethnically related organised activity, immediately raises questions of right and wrong, desirability and undesirability, legitimacy and illegitimacy, possibility and impossibility. RLS advocates must explore these issues as frankly and as openly as their surrounding political culture permits, i.e. not only with each other, but also with those who are RLS-uninterested and with those who are RLS-opposed. It is always easier to communicate only with those who are already converted, however, those who do so inevitably face the danger of ceasing to explain basic premises even to themselves.

The premises that Xmen are not Ymen and that Xish culture (daily and life-cycle traditional observances, distinctive artifacts, beliefs and values, exemplary literature, art, music, dance, etc.) is not Yish culture must not be skipped over, no more than the premises that Xish culture is worth maintaining, that it can be maintained only if it becomes more self-regulatory, that one of its main props and creations is its own language and that the latter must be fostered in as many domains of individual and social life as are intra-culturally acceptable and feasible. Any such exploration will inevitably be difficult and initially 'touchy'. It forces to the confrontational surface hitherto quiescent assumptions of what being a good Xman entails. Unless these assumptions are clarified and consensualised, at or soon after the outset, all RLS efforts coming thereafter will be conflicted and contested from within. The goal of fostering commitment to and implementation of a society of authentic 'Xmen-with-Xish' is a difficult one to attain, all the more so if language shift is already far along and the phenomenon of 'Xmen-via-Yish' has already spread, taken root and proved itself to be rewarding. The hoped-for benefits of RLS must be clearly spelled out and its implied, suspected or alleged debits must be openly faced. People cannot be tricked into supporting RLS. They must be convinced to accept a definition of their 'best interest' and 'most positive future' that depends upon and derives from RLS and from the rewards and self-regulatory capacity of the 'Xmen-with-Xish' stance. The first ones to do so will obviously be pioneers and must be particularly ready to work hard in order to attain very sparse results. All this becomes possible only when the RLS enterprise can count on the participation of maximally dedicated and ideologically oriented individuals. The crucial importance of self-aware ideological communities for the process of cultural change is well-documented[10] ('solidarity' is the currently fashionable codeword for this state of affairs, but it is much better that this be spelled out in terms of social domains and directed efforts than that another codeword be bandied about), even though it is quite clear, and will become even clearer in what I still have to say, below, that consciousness and ideology are not enough. They are merely the first of many concerns, all of which, taken together, constitute a theory and a model of the intergenerational transmission of language, culture, society and identity.

## Stages 8 to 5: RLS on the 'Weak Side'

The notion of a graded series of RLS priorities is offered here as a heuristic device more than as a proven fact. Real life is always full of more complexities and irregularities than theory can provide for. As a result, there may be less implicationality or reproduceability in real life than the theory implies.[11] Nevertheless, the notion of graded priorities in RLS efforts, even if it is less than perfectly validated, has two virtues: (a) the virtue of more parsimoniously and forcefully directing attention to crucial issues or 'first things first', and (b) the virtue of constantly directing attention to the absolutely crucial question of the link to intergenerational continuity. The first virtue is a significant one, because RLS, like all minority-based efforts, is more likely than not to be characterised by a serious shortage of resources. Accordingly, it is important to focus the meagre resources that *are* available in as judicious a way as possible. The second virtue constitutes a reminder that RLS must not be carried away by the most fashionable technologies or the most glamorous institutions that are so very much 'in the public eye'. When all is said and done, any and all seriously intended RLS effort must still stand the acid test of fostering demonstrable transmissibility across the intergenerational link. It is the achievement of that transmissibility, rather than the modernity and glamour of the means employed, that characterises a good investment of RLS time and effort. Of the eight post-ideological steps that I have in mind, four are particularly urgent and germane to RLS efforts at their earliest and weakest stages, when political conflict and power goals cannot be afforded, allies are few and far between, and self-help is, therefore, the only dependable approach.

### Stage 8

The reassembly of the Xish language-model *per se*, is an obviously rock-bottom stage at which RLS can begin, once adequate ideological clarification has been attained. This stage applies not only for total language communities, as Australian Aboriginal examples indicate, but also for particularly dislocated networks of languages that are possibly still in good repair elsewhere, although often inaccessible; indeed, wherever fluent native speakers are no longer available and where even second language speakers command dubious fluency and correctness, a prior stage of re-establishing community norms of Xish grammar, phonology, intonation and prosody, ideomaticity and semantic typologies is highly desirable. This may call for the importation of outside specialists and teaching–learning materials that can provide models of the variety or varieties of Xish that are to be 'oralised' and/or 'litericised'. The alternative is to indigenise a new, non-native local variety of Xish. This is no sin, of course, and has occurred in many places (e.g. in Ireland and among

Amerindian as well as Aboriginal language advocates), but it obviously exposes an ethnolinguistic authenticity movement, such as RLS, to the particularly difficult-to-rebut or embarrassing charge of inauthenticity. Although such charges are ultimately answerable (precisely because mainstream authenticity also has about it a goodly proportion of conscious and unconscious innovation), it is probably better if one can avoid this issue to begin with and, thereby, to be free to turn RLS-attention to code implementation rather than to remain preoccupied with issues of code definition and specification.

The role of linguists is most obvious at this stage, although not linguists alone. Linguists are notoriously poor at motivating and organising the societal devotion that is required if stage 8 is to be transcended and if RLS is to become a social movement rather than merely a monograph, a textbook or an X-as-a-second-language-course.

### Stage 7

This is a remarkably gratifying stage on the one hand, and a remarkably misleading one on the other, in so far as the true stage of RLS affairs is concerned. The fact that there is a large, still active, elderly population ('elderly' being defined as 'past childbearing age') that organises and partakes of endless Xish public events, rituals, ceremonies, concerts, lectures, courses, contests, readings, songfests, theatrical presentations, radio and television programmes and publications is, of course, a tremendous societal achievement and a great joy to those individuals who are personally involved in and enriched by these activities. However, from the point of view of RLS, all of these activities are merely rallies of the 'last Mohicans'. They serve to enthuse the already enthusiastic, to convince the already convinced. At best, they may be said to keep motivation high among the already committed and, in that way, to keep open the possibility that other means of RLS, via efforts that are linked to and involve the younger generations, may still be devised, adopted, implemented and emphasised.

It is hard for a thousand 'old-timers' who attend an absolutely first rate 'pageant for Xish' to believe that on the morning after Xish is still no better off than it was on the night before. However, that is really the case, quite regardless of how many 'young guests' were also present on any one such particular occasion or another, because 'special events' of this kind are just that; as such they are simply not linked into the ongoing, normal, daily family-socialisation pattern. Their audiences disperse and there is no carryover from the ideological and aesthetic highs that these events often attain, to the concrete rounds of daily life and, most particularly, to the child socialisation nexus on which RLS ultimately really depends. This is not to say that stage 7 is useless; it is merely to say that it is ultimately useless if it too, like stage 8, cannot be transcended.

## Stage 6

This stage consists of family-, neighbourhood-, community-reinforcement (and of organised RLS activity squarely aimed at each of the foregoing) and constitutes the heart of the entire RLS venture. It may be merely metaphorically enlightening to believe, as Kenneth Burke claimed (1954: 136), that 'men build their cultures by huddling together, nervously loquacious, at the edge of an abyss', but it is inescapably true that the bulk of language socialisation, identity socialisation and commitment socialisation generally takes place through intergenerationally proximate, face-to-face interaction and generally takes place relatively early at that. Spicer (1980), one of the few social scientists to have invested a professional lifetime in the study of 'persistent (though stateless) peoples', put it this way in his final summary:

> ...[T]he persistence of configurations of identity symbols depends on the kind of communication possible in local community organizations, uniting household groups. It is in the milieu of the effective local community ... that the basis for choosing to identify with an enduring people becomes established. (Spicer, 1980: 358)

Unfortunately, knowing that RLS must always feed into and connect up with real, natural, daily community life if intergenerational transmissibility is to be attained, is no guarantee at all that such linkages can be brought about. In modern, democratic contexts it is not at all easy to plan or engineer RLS efforts that focus directly on family-, neighbourhood-, community-building. Although many Jewish settlements and kibbutzim in Ottoman Palestine became bastions of Hebrew language revernacularisation, they functioned in this fashion at the tremendous price of tearing themselves away both from the Jewish life round about them and from the Jewish life, primarily Yiddish-speaking Eastern European, from which most of the RLSers and their followers had come. That they could make a virtue out of this double alienation is merely a testimony to the self-sufficient life-style that they were able to establish and the robustness of the sociocultural boundaries that they long maintained between themselves and other Jews (whom they obviously viewed as 'Xmen-via-Yish'). Even so, many of the Hebrew-revernacularising townlets and kibbutzim failed, as have almost all of the experimental communities established too expressly for language maintenance or RLS purposes. We will examine some of the difficulties and solutions that pertain to this stage below, after we have reviewed all of the stages. At this point, it must suffice to say that *if this stage is not satisfied, all else can amount to little more than biding time*, at best generation by generation, without a natural, self-priming social mechanism having been engendered thereby. For a language that has shrunk to 10% of its former 'realm', remaining at 10% may seem like an accomplishment of sorts, but it is also a confirmation to 90% of the population that the ideal of 'Xmen-via-Yish' is really the more viable alternative. This is why simply maintaining the stage 7 status-quo-ante is an undesirable long-term 'solution' for endangered languages. Attaining stage 6 is a necessary, even if not a sufficient, desideratum of RLS. Unlike other stages, when stage 6 is transcended it is not merely 'left behind'; quite the contrary: all subsequent stages must be diligently tied back to and connected with stage 6 if they are to contribute to the living reality of RLS rather than merely to its propagandistic hoopla or one-upmanship.

## Stage 5

This stage entails formal linguistic socialisation. Although such socialisation does not need to be restricted to literacy and literacy alone, that indeed is by far the lion's share of what this stage entails in modern settings. Whether restricted to literacy or not, this stage adds additional varieties to the learner's repertoire, above and beyond those that can be acquired in the largely oral and familiar interaction within most family-, neighbourhood- and community-intergenerational situations. The availability of more formal varieties (and, in modern life, reading/writing essentially involves more formal varieties than does most of speech) gives Xish a range which enables it to be more comfortable *vis-à-vis* the greater range that is normally available in Yish and Zish, due to the governmental and econotechnical functions of the latter. Xish religious, legal and oral traditions can all be tapped for the elaboration of such more formal varieties and the attainment of literacy in one or another of these varieties contributes to the solidification of wider intercommunal bonds and the cultivation of additional support opportunities for RLS. Clearly, stage 5 entails a kind of schooling, one that may initially be open and attractive to adults as well as to children. However, it does not involve schooling in lieu of compulsory Yish administered education, and, as a result, can avoid many of the expenses and most of the Yish control-and-approval requirements that such education generally entails.

Stages 8 to 5 constitute the 'programme minimum' of RLS. These stages do not involve major costs and they do not crucially depend on Yish cooperation. They are generally of the 'do-it-yourself' variety and, as such, can be approximated in most types of political and economic climates. They are particularly appropriate for numerically and politically weak language-in-culture settings and are not restricted in applicability to permissive democratic settings, although the latter are always more facilitative in so far as overt organisation efforts are concerned. RLS concentration on these four initial steps, particularly *on any subgrouping of them that also includes step 6*, generally presumes a bilingual model of Xish society in which Y/X diglossia is attained and maintained by surrendering to Yish all effective control over the more modern and interactive media and pursuits. Such diglossia is not a rare or impossible goal, nor is it a goal which inevitably consigns its adherents or practitioners to poverty, backwardness, non-participationism or isolation from the mainstream. Compulsory and higher education, economic opportunity and governmental service may still be entirely open to those who espouse and maintain the lower level 'Xmen-via-Xish' position, but, except for presumably minor and voluntary Yish accommodations via translation, usually in connection with absolutely crucial public welfare services and whatever media and public visibility Xish can obtain by means of the numbers and funds at its own disposal, the bulk of such opportunities will clearly be available to them only in Yish. That being the case, the future of Xish rests squarely on the relative impermeability of the intergroup boundaries and on the non-negotiability of the 'Xmen-via-Xish' position at stages 6 and 5.

This being the case, a case which is often described and experienced, justly or unjustly, as 'second-class citizenship', it is clear why RLS movements often seek to push on beyond these stages into the upper reaches of sociosymbolic life. However, it should be clear that just as not to do so constitutes an unjustified foreclosing of RLS opportunity and sociolinguistic potential, so the premature crossing over of RLS efforts into the arena of the second four stages runs the risk of burdens and challenges that may be excessive, non-productive and even dangerous for the entire RLS enterprise. The choice between these two types of risk is a fateful one, indeed.

## Stages 4 to 1: RLS on the 'Strong Side'

Education in lieu of compulsory schooling involves an intrusion of the state into the life of the family, neighbourhood and community. Most democratic states provide for the possibility of substantially curtailing or substantively modifying (or pro-RLS orienting) this intrusion by means of private, parochial or proprietary schools. Such schools must still follow the minimal essentials of the approved general curriculum, employ state certified teachers in conjunction with teaching those minimal essentials and maintain facilities and schedules that meet state specifications pertaining to fire, safety, health and attendance standards. Otherwise, however, they are free to lengthen the school day and the school year to facilitate the addition of courses and experiences that are particularly desirable to them. The maintenance of such relatively independent schools (type 4a schools in our complete typology) obviously entails major costs for RLS-advocates and their supporters. These costs can sometimes be avoided if Xish speaking parents and actually or potentially Xish speaking children are sufficiently concentrated and if the Yish authorities are sufficiently co-operatively inclined to justify and to permit special RLS public school programmes for minority language children. Generally, such programmes are reluctantly and unreliably offered, are really compensatory in nature and orientation and inferior in educational quality. They do not foster either the image or the reality of Xish cultural self-regulation. They are particularly unsuited to the attainment of the goals of weak and inexperienced RLS movements, and the more centralised the Yish educational establishment is, the more unsatisfactory such schools are if the local attainment of RLS success *per se* is utilised as the criterion of 'success'.

Even where schools of the latter type (type 4b schools we have called them in our case by case reviews) do not suffer from outright or hidden sabotage by the governmental authorities on whose personnel, funds and approval they depend, they present the danger of leading away from the Xish community of orientation and can yield positive results only if sufficiently surrounded by and embedded within an RLS oriented family–neighbourhood–community field of forces. Several localised examples of RLS-oriented type 4b schools exist to indicate that this goal is not impossible of attainment, but, on the whole, it is very rarely attained and its attainment often depends on the prior or concurrent establishment in nearby areas of cultural autonomy arrangements that transcend schooling *per se*. In essence, they represent the conversion of compensatory 4b programmes into self-regulatory 4a programmes via the attainment of a political accommodation at a governmental level higher than the local school authority. In the absence of such higher and transcendent considerations, which obviously aim at dovetailing schooling with stage 6 institutions and processes, there is absolutely no reason to assume that schooling (even type 4a schooling) is either a guarantee of or even a prop for successful RLS. We must guard against allowing our academic affiliations and general biases (which tend to make us view education as the universal panacea for any and all problems) to lead us prematurely to assume that schooling is 'the solution' to RLS problems more specifically. The Irish experience alone should disabuse us of that fallacy.

Unreconstructed schools of type 4b, even more so than schools of type 4a, are a bridge between the immediate and the larger, less Xish, less controllable environment. Only the demographically and economically strong can cross this bridge with relative safety by providing the societal support that schools themselves need in order to successfully extend RLS efforts out-wards into the larger community. No such extension can succeed before the basic family–neighbourhood–community support of Xish is in place. We will return to this point below.

## Stage 3

This stage pertains to the worksphere in general, but it is at its most powerful in connection with the higher, more influential worksphere which cannot be contained within Xish neighbourhood/community limits. This is a tremendously influential setting for RLS efforts and, indeed, one which pervades and colours all of social life, particularly in modern, secular contexts. With its necessary implications for social status and mobility the worksphere has become the most fully rational-ised and cross-nationally, cross-ethnically and cross-linguistically con-nected domain of modern functioning. As such, it is a particularly difficult area for RLS to penetrate, influence and control. The growing predominance of multinational firms and the frequent rotation of their office incumbents, plus the fact that services or products are provided to an ethnolinguistically very heterogeneous clientele and that there is a constant growth and change of technology, products and services, are all features that prove to be linguistically problematic for all but the largest 'establishment languages'. The insuperable road-blocks which they frequently represent in so far as RLS is concerned must be realisti-cally viewed in that perspective, although opportunities for RLS will necessarily vary depending on the overall degree of modernisation that the Xish and Yish economies have attained.[12]

However, even when aspects of everyday higher-worksphere oper-ations *can* be altered to accommodate local RLS pressures, the link between the worksphere (higher or lower) and intergenerational language transmission is far from direct or obvious. Individual or group economic circumstances certainly influence such RLS concerns as the rate of selection of own-group and own-language marriage partners, the rate of childbearing, the neighbourhood of residence, the language of family-life, of child-socialisation and of the medium of instruction selected for one's children. These are all 'lower order' (i.e. more funda-mental) concerns than the worksphere itself and must also be tackled directly, as indicated earlier, rather than only indirectly via RLS efforts pertaining to the worksphere *per se.* Thus, while it is true that the work-sphere must be 'captured', particularly for those seeking a maximum of cultural autonomy (rather than a diglossic H/L arrangement), it is also true that it is quite difficult to do so and that in doing so the forging of links to stage 6 must be constantly kept in mind. The formation of 'contract groups' that work together in Xish (in the lower worksphere) and of service centres or counters operating in Xish, or of Xish 'cells', 'branches', 'floors' or 'networks' in large firms, these are all possible tactics for introducing and maintaining Xish at work, but it is the indirectness of any positive link between work and stage 6 that must constantly be kept in mind and innovatively tackled and reinforced in a pro-RLS fashion.

## Stage 2

Stage 2 is concerned with lower governmental services i.e. those that have direct contact with the citizenry, including the local mass media. As with the worksphere, these must be viewed as more than merely factors in the 'creation of a climate' for RLS (many language movements pay far too much attention to such symbolic goals) and even as more than the creation of contexts for Xish use. The services and media entailed at this stage reach into the very neighbourhoods and, indeed, into the very homes that constitute the nuclei of RLS and of Xish life itself. The importance of Xishising these services and influences is beyond question, but only to the extent that their links to stage 6 are focused upon. Without such links the Xishisation of these services and influences constitute no more than a holding pattern; they buy time but they do not become self-priming RLS devices. The location and staffing of these services and the content and orientation of their programmes cannot themselves function as intergenerational transmission linkages. Such linkages must be there, maintained by far more direct family-, neighbourhood- and community-building processes, before governmental services and lower mass media can make transmissible contributions to RLS. It is doubtlessly harder to build Xish neighbourhoods and to assist Xish-speaking families than to broadcast in Xish on the television. The former, however, are immediate building-blocks of intergenerational transmission whereas the latter obviously is not.

## Stage 1

Finally, stage 1 may be reached, the stage at which cultural autonomy is recognised and implemented, even in the upper reaches of education, media and government operations, and particularly within the region (or regions) of Xish concentration. Once again, it must be clear that it is not some very general, unfocused, amorphous 'atmosphere effect' or process of osmosis that is of primary RLS concern in this connection, but, rather, what it is that stage 1 can do for stage 6 that really counts. The communications, rewards and opportunity structures emanating from 'on high' influence family, neighbourhood and community processes via a very long, involved and impersonal chain of indirect influences and, therefore, their contributions to RLS are, ultimately, equally indirect and uncertain. While stage 1 can make a definite contribution to RLS, this contribution must be successfully translated into intergenerationally transmissible stage 6 processes and interactions before it will have more than bureaucracy-building and élite-building effects. Stages 3 to 1 are not only difficult for Xish to penetrate (due to their Yish locus of control and their Yish-dominated, even if heterogeneous, clienteles), but they all link back to mother tongue acquisition only in a roundabout fashion and with considerable time lapse, if at all. They may help shape adult identity and language use, much more so than they help implant basic identity and mother tongue use in the young. Were this not so, much of the indigenous non-English mother tongue world, so dependent on English-speaking jobs, English-speaking media and English-speaking governmental functioning, would be of English mother tongue and of Anglo-American ethnicity by now, whereas this is obviously not the case in any part of that world.

## Problems of Focusing on 'Lower Order' Neighbourhood and Community Organisation

The stagewise discussion, above, clearly implies that there are weaknesses to RLS efforts on the 'strong side', just as there are undeniable strengths to RLS efforts on the 'weak side'. Clearly, the 'strong side', with its stress on the institutions of modernity and on the structures of cultural autonomy (control of education, the worksphere, media, governmental services) is more than most RLS movements can realistically aspire to in the foreseeable future. Equally clear is the fact that even when such props for RLS *are* attained, *they must still be translated into the lower order processes of stage 6* if a self-priming intergenerational transmissibility system is to be constituted and set into motion. The 'strong side' itself is not such a system, although it may adequately trickle down to that system once that system is in operation. Thus, the key to RLS is stage 6 and it is to some of the problems of stage 6-building that we now turn.

Stage 6 may be viewed as an arena for 'collective action' and, therefore, as politically encumbered and, in accord with the theory of such action, as subdivisible into interest articulation, organisation, mobilisation and opportunity utilisation. Adopting the 'collective action' approach to step 6 would help alert us to the fact that beliefs, resources and actions do not always come together in unproblematic ways. Particularly when it is at its early stages, RLS efforts find it difficult to convince others that sociocultural change is needed and that established power and interest can be influenced and modified by minorities with clearly focused views and a stagewise programme of goals and priorities. Another early difficulty is the over-reliance on voluntary and part-time leadership and on part-time leisuretime activists. One route that has been much used to temper such over-reliance is the involvement of individuals whose normal work-responsibilities include participation in or attention to social action, e.g. teachers, professors, social workers, lawyers, etc. However, these too can rarely offer full-time commitment and are usually establishment regulated and establishment dependent in many ways. Moreover, much of the literature on collective action and social action is too general in its orientation to be of direct relevance to RLS efforts or to early RLS efforts in particular. In the latter connection, the accumulated body of theory and data pertaining to organisational functioning, to neighbourhood organisation and to interest-group processes may be more helpful.

Those who believe that all significant political action occurs at the national level need to be disabused of that perspective, particularly at early stages of RLS activity. Many of the most salient and explosive domestic political issues are fully recognisable as struggles between residents and local public authorities or interests. Furthermore, the question of how powerless persons can gain power in local affairs is of the greatest importance to a real understanding of democratic politics. The fundamental task of the RLS neighbourhood organiser is to find RLS incentives that will induce self-interested local residents to support and become active on behalf of an RLS nursery, RLS day-care centre, RLS housing-cluster, RLS co-operative market, RLS employment centre, RLS recreational centre, RLS homework/tutoring group, RLS work-transportation service, legal aid service, credit union, etc. Incentives are crucial in understanding the difficulties which RLS spokesmen and ideologists face in their efforts to attract and organise Xmen on behalf of RLS. The success of interest-group organisation – and that is what RLS efforts are – depends on much more than ideological appeals and all such appeals must be heavily intermingled with concrete inducements.

As modern Gesellschaft forces continue to expand, the incentives of RLS-sponsored neighbourhood care, companionship and assistance in managing one's work, health and family problems become ever more meaningful, particularly in poorer neighbourhoods. An RLS stress on human relationships in modern life, on local accountability, on neighbourhood collective responsibility for all who live there, on self-help activities focused upon priority concerns of the local residents, becomes ever more meaningful if both parents are in the workforce, if public education deteriorates, and if individual family means cannot provide for the old, the sick, the newborn or the young with no place to play or study. Voluntary organisations serving such needs are not merely wishy-washy expressions of piety and good-intentions, but vital experimenters and innovators on the way to social and cultural reform. They help people to find identity and purpose, self-realisation and fulfilment, the very things that RLS must stand for both ideologically and practically. Particularly in the current climate of conservative politics and budget cutting, more people-oriented help and self-help becomes both a particularly important and a particularly effective context for introducing and fostering RLS.

RLS neighbourhood building efforts must obviously relate local spiritual beliefs, family values, informal neighbouring and self-help notions to Xish and to the ideal of 'Xmen via Xish'. In response to Durkheim's dictum that 'it is impossible to artificially resuscitate a particularistic spirit which no longer has any function', RLS must stress the functionality of Xish in terms of satisfying the deeply cherished values and needs of all ordinary, rank-and-file Xmen. But, obviously, neighbourhoodism has a strong political component and potential and the energy and effectiveness of the networks generated by RLS neighbourhoodism will be tied to the fact that they satisfy needs, make demands, have goals, address purposes. RLS neighbourhoods must be battling neighbourhoods, struggling for social, cultural, economic, political and personal dignity. Action needs an image of community that local residents can identify with and that fosters commitment as a type of functional equivalence to kinship among non-kin. Among ordinary folk, Xish cannot be pursued in and of itself, for its own sake. It must be part of the warp and woof of social life and make a meaningful difference in the neighbourhood Gemeinschaft-life and in the Gemeinschaft-strivings of ordinary people. All the social movements try, in their own ways, to fulful needs and strivings. RLS efforts must be able to do so even better than others, because kinlike affect and mutual support are part of the basic promise of the ethnicity message and of the authenticity message and, therefore, are part of the distinctiveness of RLS efforts. Neighbourhoods built on such distinctiveness and affect can go on to build Xish schools (at stages 5, 4a and even neighbourhood controlled public schools of type 4b) and Xish worksites, and move towards other selected goals on the 'strong side'.[13]

Sometimes the above advice, and the entire approach on which it is based, strikes RLS activists as contra-intuitive and as self-limiting. It is obviously harder to build Xish families, neighbourhoods and communities than to broadcast for a few hours a week (or even a day) in Xish. However, the former immediately provides a base for intergenerational continuity and a point of departure for stages that can come after it and can be supported by it, whereas the latter do not because they have no daily, intimate, socialisation foundation underlying them. At best, they can contribute to the 'spirit' necessary for such a foundation to be laid, but they do not lay it themselves. Thus, the approach being advanced here does nor counsel ignoring the higher order domains, but, rather, counsels the necessity of a prior, firm child-socialisation base to which they can contribute and from which they themselves, in turn, can derive the political support which they require, given that they will always be outweighed by their Yish counterparts.

## Problems of Focusing on RLS via 'Lower Order' Family Processes

The affective and affiliative emphases that derive from the kinship-ethnicity dimension of RLS-efforts not only directly imply the neighbour-hood community, as the fundamental link to the intergenerational transmission of Xish, but they also and equally directly imply the family, as the very building-block of such transmission. It is in the family that social support and transactions with the community have traditionally been initiated and nurtured. It is also in the family that social commitments have traditionally been nurtured. Above all, it is in the family that a peculiar bond with language and language activities (conversation, games, stories, songs, proverbs and felicitous expressions, verbalised emotion, verbal ritual and verbal play) is fostered, shared and fashioned into personal and social identity. Unfortunately, the 'traditional' family has become harder and harder to find and to maintain. It has been eroded by the very same universalising macro-forces that erode small languages and caring neighbourhoods.

Good RLS neighbourhood organisation, therefore, must include pro-grammes designed to provide social support for families (particularly young families) through: the provision of home visits by RLS-oriented social workers; the organisation of parent groups for a variety of pur-poses, but for RLS-parenting as well; the organisation of drop-in centres for assistance with any and all family problems but for assistance with RLS as well. Such initially 'formal support systems' should aim at gener-ating informal or internal support systems within the families they serve so that the latter will have less and less need for the formal supports. RLS family support efforts cannot be oblivious to the fact that all competent parenting (not to mention RLS-oriented parenting) must be grounded in the norms, values and behaviours of a particular culture. Nowadays, parents must often be taught not only parenting but also their own culture, and this inevitably becomes part of the task of RLS.

Of course, all of this assumes that it is possible to break out of the impersonality and uniformity of Gesellschaft and to ameliorate the loss of Gemeinschaft without thereby creating more bureaucratic problems than one solves. RLS-inspired neighbourhood and family services must constantly be founded on consultation and co-operation, on self-liquidation of formal structures as genuine participation increases, and, above all, on the realisation that it is unrealistic to expect reversals within a few years of the myriad of neighbourhood and family problems that have evolved over the past century or more. Naturally, all planning entails some unexpected negative side-effects as well. Nevertheless, these can be minimised if RLS-efforts are conducted in an experimental, consultative, self-correcting and self-liquidating mood.

The Yish mainstream itself has failed at correcting the very neighbourhood and family problems that RLS faces if it is to succeed. Certainly RLS should distance itself from the Orwellian vision of a war-ravaged world in which the functions of the family have been taken over by stultifying and impersonal child-rearing institutions. Quite the contrary! RLS should be at the forefront of returning neighbourhoods, schools and families to the values, norms and behaviours that have preferential and historical validity for them. Many of the problems of Yish society itself are due to the very fact that most larger societal systems will not work without important input from the family. Although it is far from clear that RLS-efforts will be more successful than others that have attempted to influence family patterns, its inevitably smaller scale and its greater focus on the young, the old, the sick, the poor and the neglected are its greatest safeguards and its basic strengths. The small successes that it can attain (small in the light of the enormity of the problems that it must tackle) will be beacons of promise for others who are willing to be involved in an ennobling struggle even though it is a struggle that they cannot fully win.[14]

The basic dilemma of RLS efforts everywhere is that their success requires overcoming the very problems of modern life that the strongest societies and cultures have not been able to overcome. The basic strength of RLS efforts is that they can afford to take a less ponderous, more grassroots approach to these problems and, thereby, seek to come to the attention of and become identified with those whose lives they aim to change.

## The School: The Bridge Between the 'Weak Side' and the 'Strong Side' Approaches to RLS

For RLS success the school must be an integral part of the family–neighbourhood axis of child socialisation and identity-commitment formation. Schools cannot succeed, whether their goal be RLS or merely history or mathematics instruction, if the relationship between teachers, parents and students is such that they are estranged from each other and from the curriculum. 'Schools are the children of the community', it has been wisely said, but this adage is little more than novel verbiage, 'educationese', because the state of affairs that it describes has become an impossible dream, purely 'pie in the sky' as far as most education is concerned. On the one hand, mainstream parents and communities have little to say about what goes on in the schools that their children attend. On the other hand, mainstream schools themselves do not seem to comprehend the extent to which the school has been challenged, every bit as much as has the family, as the major force in providing children with the skills, attitudes and behaviours upon which success in modern life increasingly depends.

Precisely because such a high proportion of families are either of the 'single parent' variety or of the 'both parents working' variety (only some 7% of American families currently consist of two parents, one of whom stays at home during the years in which the children are at school), student participation in neighbourhood and community activities has become much more crucial for later success than ever before. Childcare/playgroup arrangements that involve contact with adult specialists in tutoring, computers, dance, drama, writing, library research, athletics, scouting and after-school jobs contribute to an amazing widening of perspective and learning experiences, as well as to a diversification of interests and interactive competence, that have great significance not only for academic success but for success in the larger society thereafter.

The above out-of-school agencies and activities have substantially usurped the traditional role of the family as the major partner of the school, and, in addition, they are all neighbourhood/community related arenas of crucial language use, language views and language competencies. The type 5 school can attempt to be the institutional resource that corresponds to Xish in this connection. So can type 4a schools to some extent, although they probably require an auxilliary agency, such as the type 5 school, in order to divide up the day and the onerous responsibilities of constantly relating Xish to childlife, to local needs and resources, to changing demands of the worksphere, to the entertainment sphere and the knowledge sphere. The RLS school must no longer be concerned only with ethnically encumbered attitudes, knowledge, skills and beliefs, but also with relating Xish to the rapidly changing world in which the language must constantly scramble in order to find a place for itself, most particularly so if diglossic arrangements with the world at large are ideologically unacceptable.[15]

## Additional Concerns and Perspectives

The foregoing remarks are not intended to make it seem that RLS is impossible or doomed to failure. They are intended to make it clear why it is so hard to succeed at it. Successful RLS implies remaking social reality and that is very hard for minorities to do. The social meaning of being a minority is that one is forced to spend almost all of one's resources on damage control, i.e. on merely staying alive within a reality that is not of one's own making and not even under one's own substantial ability to influence. If we add to these widely generalisable difficulties those of also engaging in and achieving acceptance of a modicum of corpus planning, at least in order to stay abreast of 'popular modernity', those of traditional second languages which cannot count on the usual home and neighbourhood process for their intergenerational transmissibility, those of purported national and official languages which cannot come close to fully controlling the 'high side' even within their own territorial borders, also the particular problems of 'expected shortgevity' that beset urban, immigrant minorities, then one may well conclude that the task is not only a formidable one but a hopeless one as well. Such a conclusion is belied by the success cases we have glanced at, Hebrew in Ottoman and Pre-Mandate Palestine, Catalan in Spain and French in Quebec. None of these successes was pre-ordained or occurred without struggle and reverses and all of them qualified as 'successes', whether or not their leaders admitted it to the rank and file, well before cultural autonomy was attained. In addition, the status of Basque seems salvageable and that of Irish has stabilised, something which appeared quite impossible only some two generations ago, albeit at a much lower level of utilisation than can be considered optimal.

Rebuilding society is very hard, even for those who are its masters. The eight stage model, with its stress on the foundational nature (not the exclusive nature) of stage 6, must not be 'fluffed off' by the conundrum that 'all stages are more fully interdependent than the model maintains'. Such a view provides no insight into intergenerational mother tongue transmission and how it differs from social influence processes more generally. Such a view disregards the very limited successes of countless RLS efforts (Frisian, Irish, Maori and American/Australian immigrational being foremost among them), that have been guided by it. Such an analysis provides no guide to action because it has no approach as to priorities and no evaluative prespective as to the differences between long-range and short-range 'success'. Such a comment merely promotes busywork in all directions, thereby foreclosing all prospects of success in connection with solving what is a most difficult problem at any rate. It is similarly not advisable to point to the myriad of 'additional factors' that can be appended to or derived from the eight stage RLS model. Untold learning, interactional, communicational, attitudinal and other psychosocial, intercultural and inter-linguistic dimensions can be proliferated *ad infinitum*. But to do so is to ultimately obfuscate the intergenerational transmission issue rather than to clarify it, by endlessly delaying the realisation that RLS efforts must attempt to do a few crucial things well and early, rather than be delayed until academics can shed light on all possible interpersonal, intergroup and interlinguistic issues related to it.

RLS entails sociocultural reforms on behalf of an ethnic ideal that are already so fargoing, even if they remain on the 'weak side', as to be extremely dubious of attainment. Nevertheless, such efforts go on and on, paying homage to human persistence in building the kind of life that is more consistent with deeply held societal values. Indeed, RLS is a peculiarly and admirably human endeavour, after all is said and done, an endeavour to rebuild life, to attain an ideal of cultural democracy and justice, to meet felt responsibilities *vis-à-vis* one's identity, to behaviourally implement the traditions to which one subscribes, to safeguard and activate perceived cultural imperatives and sanctities or, at least, to make supreme efforts on their behalf and to 'go down trying', if necessary. The methods and priorities utilised in this quest can often be improved upon, they can be rendered more rational with respect to priorities, more knowledgeable with respect to precedents the world over, more informed *vis-à-vis* the social science theories and findings that might bear upon them. This is what I have tried to provide in my treatment in this paper. The sanctity of the task, however, cannot be improved upon. Like all sanctities, it is an absolute for those who see it and hear it and savour it with inner commitment and faith.

## Notes

1. Prepared for the Fourth International Conference on Minority Languages, Ljouwert (Netherlands), 20–24 June 1989, and constituting Chapter 10 of my *Reversing Language Shift* (Multilingual Matters, 1991).
2. For some of the earliest but still timely Western objections to the legitimacy claims of minority indigenous ethnic groups see Lord Acton (1862) [1907] and Engels (1866). The more general and enduring roadblocks to an appreciation of ethnicity in human behaviour are discussed in my *Language, Ethnicity and Racism* (1977) (reprinted: 1989).
3. On the rationality/irrationality and modernity/non-modernity of revitalisation efforts, in comparison to current cultural planning of our own day and age, see Barber (1941), Champagne (1983), Kehoe (1989), Linton (1943), Wallace (1956), Thornton (1986) and Traugott (1978).
4. On the dilemmas of forgotten values and those who pursue them, see Institute of Cultural Conservatism (1987) and Klein (1976).
5. The major work on cultural persistence is still that of Spicer (1980) and his pupils, e.g. Castile (1981) and Moore (1981). Although pioneering and stimulating to this day, this work requires updating and, above all, a more systematic approach to the theory and practice of cultural persistence.
6. For useful introductions to eighteenth and nineteenth century British and French theories of social change and, therefore, to social theory more generally, see Berman (1970), Janos (1986) and Ryan (1969).
7. Sperber (1976) and Borowski (1984) provide thoughtful reviews of the communes and other alternative life-styles of the 1960s and 1970s and of the various factors which led to the variance in their success and durability.

8. Ample evidence of recent Marxist and non-Marxist rethinking of ethnicity can be gleaned from Baumgarten (1982), Fishman (1983[1985]), Hall (1983), Hechter and Appelbaum (1982), Lipset (1985), McCarthy and Zahn (1973), Nielsen (1980), Olzak (1983), Ragin (1979) and Wax (1974). A rather full review of the literature and a critique of its minor innovations and major inadequacies can be found in Fishman op. cit., Olzak op. cit. and Yinger (1985).

9. See Bonacich *et al.* (1972), De Marchi and Boileau (1982), Lieberson (1963), Said (1977), Suhrke and Noble (1973) and Yinger (1985) for indications of the ubiquitous, relatively permanent and non-theatening nature of ethnicity in many modern contexts.

10. The importance of the initial and ongoing clarification of goals and beliefs for effective social action is discussed by Aidala (1984), Tilly (1978) and Wuthnow (1976).

11. High implicationality has proven to be attainable only in relatively few social behavioural domains (including a few sociolinguistic areas among them, see Rickford, 1987, 1991). Even there scalability may be more attractive because of its apparent conceptual elegance than because of any enhanced predictive or explanatory validity that it attains or provides.

12. Geertz clearly sketches the role of economic factors in fostering more pervasive cultural change (see, e.g. his 1963 volume), but he is particularly stimulating for our own concerns in connection with his stress on gradualism and transitionalism with respect to most traditional/Gemeinschaft and modern/Gesellschaft characterisation and the large variety of combinations between modernist and tradition even when economic modernisation is ongoing. Corners and nooks of worksphere RLS may well present themselves even under conditions of ongoing worksphere modernisation under Yish impetus.

13. For examples of research and theory on the ability of minorities to influence and wrest concessions from majorities see Hirsch and Gutierrez (1972) and Moscovici *et al.* (1985). Collective action and social action are reviewed by Tilly (1978) and Crowell (1968). The huge amount of literature on neighbourhood organisation can be sampled via works such as Arzac (1982), Burton (1986), Hallman (1977), O'Brien (1975) and Scott (1981). Burton's book constitutes a review and critique of the fruitful pioneering work in this area by Philip Abrams. For a compendium of the most recent work on organisation theory more generally, see Morgan (1989).

14. Methods, difficulties and doubts re planned efforts to strengthen modern family dynamics are provocatively reviewed in Burton (1986), Curran (1983), McCubbin *et al.* (1985), Moynihan (1986) and Ziegler and Weiss (1985).

15. For a fine discussion of the school's changed relationship to family and school see Heath and McLaughlin (1987).

## References

Aidala, Angela A. (1984) Worldviews, ideologies and social experimentation: Clarification and replication of 'The Consciousness Reformation'. *Journal for the Scientific Study of Religion* 23, 44–59.

Albrecht, Johann and Gill-Chin, Lim (1986) A search of alternative planning theory: Use of critical theory. *Journal of Architectural and Planning Research* 3, 117–131.

Arzac, Adriana A. (1982) The development of community competence through a neighborhood organization. PhD dissertation, University of Texas, Houston, School of Public Health.

Barber, Bernard (1941) Acculturation and Messianic movements. *American Sociological Review* 6, 663–669.

Baumgarten, Murray (1982) *City Scriptures.* Cambridge: Harvard University Press.

Berman, M. (1970) *The Politics of Authenticity: Radical Individualism and the Emergence of Modern Society.* New York, Atheneum.

Bonacich, E. *et al.* (1972) A theory of ethnic antagonism: The split labor market. *American Sociological Review* 37, 547–549.

Borowski, Karol (1984) *Attempting an Alternative Society.* Norwood: Norwood Editions.

Burton, Martin (1986) *Neighbors: The Work of Philip Abrams.* Cambridge: Cambridge University Press.

Burke, Kenneth (1954) *Permanence and Change* (revised edition). Los Altos: Hermes.

Castile, George P. (1981) Issues in the analysis of enduring cultural systems. In G.P. Castile and Gilbert Kusher (eds) *Persistent Peoples: Cultural Enclaves in Perspective* (pp. xv–xxii). Tucson: University of Arizona Press.

Champagne, Duane (1983) Social structure, revitalization movements and state building: Social change in four native American societies. *American Sociological Review* 48, 754–763.

Crowell, George (1968) *Society Against Itself.* Philadelphia: Westminster Press.

Curran, D. (1983) *Traits of Healthy Family.* Minneapolis: Winston.

De Marchi, Bruna and Boileau, Anna Maria (eds) (1982) *Boundaries and Minorities in Westen Europe.* Milan: Franco Angeli.

Dolitsky, A. and Kuzmina, L. (1986) Cultural change vs. persistence: A case from Old Believer settlements. *Arctic* 39, 223–231.

Fishman, Joshua A. (1983) Epilogue: The rise and fall of the ethnic revival in the United States. *Journal of Intercultural Studies* 4 (3), 5–46. Reprinted in Fishman J.A. *et al.* (1985) *Rise and Fall of the Ethnic Revival.* Berlin: Mouton de Gruyter.

Geertz, Clifford (1963) *Peddlers and Princes: Social Change and Economic Modernization in Two Indonesian Towns.* Chicago: University of Chicago Press.

Hall, Thomas, D. (1983) Peripheries, regions of refuge and non-state societies: Toward a theory of reactive social change. *Social Quarterly* 64, 582–597.

Hallman, Howard W. (1977) *The Organization and Operation of Neighborhood Councils: A Practical Guide.* New York: Praeger.

Heath, Shirley B. and McLaughlin, Milbrey Wallin (1987) A child resource policy: Moving beyond dependence on school and family. *Phi Delta Kappan* 68, 576–580.

Hechter, Michael and Appelbaum, Malka (1982) A theory of ethnic collective action. *International Migration Review* 16, 412–434.

Hirsch, Herbert and Gutierrez, Armando (1972) *Learning to be Militant: Ethnic Identify and the Development of Political Militance in a Chicano Community.* San Francisco: R. & E. Research Associates.

Institute for Cultural Conservatism (1987) *Cultural Conservatism: Towards a New Agenda.* Lanham: University Press of America.

Janos, Andrew C. (1986) *Politics and Paradigms: Changing Theories of Change in Social Science.* Stanford: Stanford University Press.

Jenkins, J. Craig (1983) Resource mobilization theory and the study of social movements. *Annual Review of Sociology* 9, 527–553.

Juliani, R.N. (1982) Ethnicity: Myth, social reality and ideology. *Contemporary Sociology* 11, 368–370.

Kehoe, Alice Beck (1989) *Ghost Dance Religion: Ethnohistory and Revitalization.* Fort Worth: Holt, Rinehart & Winston.

Kent, Susan (1983) The differential acceptance of cultural change: An archaeological test-case. *Historical Archaeology* 17, 56–63.

Klein, Donald (1976) Dynamics of resistance to change: The defenders. In Bennis, Warren *et al.* (eds) *The Planning of Change* (3rd edn) (pp. 117–126). New York: Holt, Rinehart & Winston.

Lieberson, Stanley (1963) *Ethnic Patterns in American Cities*. New York: Free Press.

Linton, Ralph (1943) Nativistic movements. *American Anthropologist* 45, 231–240.

Lipset, Seymour M. (1985) *Consensus and Conflict: Essays in Political Sociology*. New Brunswick: Transaction Books.

McCarthy, J. and Zahn, M.N. (1973) *The Trend of Social Movements*. Morristown: General Learning.

McCubbin, Hamilton I. *et al.* (1985) Family dynamics: Strengthening families through action-research. In Robert N. Rapoport (ed.) *Children, Youth and Families: The Action Research Relationship* (pp. 126–165). Cambridge: Cambridge University Press.

Mindick, Burton (1986) *Social Engineering in Family Matters*. New York: Praeger.

Moore, Janet R. (1981) Persistence with change: A property of sociocultural dynamics. In G.P. Castile and Gilbert Kusher (eds) *Persistent Peoples: Cultural Enclaves in Perspective* (pp. 228–242). Tucson: University of Arizona Press.

Morgan, Gareth (1986) *Images of Organization*. Newbury Park: Sage.

——. (1989) *Creative Organization Theory*. Newbury Park: Sage.

Moscovici, Serge, *et al.* (eds) (1985) *Perspectives on Minority Influence*. Cambridge: Cambridge University Press.

Moynihan, Daniel P. (1986) *Family and Nation*. New York: Harcourt Brace, Jovanovich.

Nielsen, F. (1980) The Flemish movement in Belgium after World War II. *American Sociological Review* 45, 76–94.

O'Brien, David J. (1975) *Neighborhood Organization and Interest-Group Processes*. Princeton: Princeton University Press.

Olzark, Susan (1983) Contemporary ethnicity mobilization. *Annual Review of Sociology* 9, 355–374.

Ragin, C.C. (1979) Ethnic political mobilization. *American Sociological Review* 44, 619–634.

Rao, M.S. Changing moral values in the context of social-cultural movements. In Adrian C. Maywe (ed.) *Culture and Morality: Essays in Honor of Christopher von Furer-Haimendorf* (pp. 191–208). Delhi: Oxford University Press.

Rickford, John R. (1987) The haves and have nots: Sociolinguistic surveys and the assessment of speaker competence. *Language in Society* 16, 149–178.

——. (1991). Implicational scaling and critical age limits in models of linguistic variation, acquisition and change. In C.A. Ferguson and T. Huebner (eds) *Second Language Acquisition and Linguistic Theory*. Amsterdam: John Benjamins.

Ryan, Bryce (1969) *Social and Cultural Change*. New York: Ronald.

Said, A.A. (ed.) (1977) *Ethnicity and United States Foreign Policy*. New York: Praeger.

Sathyamurthy, T.V. (1983) *Nationalism in the Contemporary World*. London: Pinter.

Scott, David (1981) *"Don't Mourn for Me, Organize..." The Social and Political Uses of Voluntary Organization*. Sydney: Allen and Unwin.

Smith, Elsie and Clement, B.G. (1981) A union of school, community and family. *Urban Education* 16, 247–260.

Sperber, Mae T. (1976) *Search for Utopia*. Middleboro: Country Press.

Spicer, Edward H. (1980) *The Yaquis: A Cultural History*. Tucson: Arizona University Press.

Suhrke, R.P. and Noble, L.G. (eds) (1973) *Ethnic Conflict in International Relations*. New York: Praeger.

Thornton, Russell (1986) *We Shall Live Again; The 1870 and 1890 Ghost Dance Movements as Demographic Revitalization.* Cambridge: Cambridge University Press.

Tilly, Charles (1978) *From Mobilization to Revolution.* Reading: Addison-Wesley.

Traugott, Mark (1978) Reconsidering social movements. *Social Problems* 26, 38–49.

Wallace, Anthony (1956) Revitalization movements. *American Anthropologist* 58, 264–281.

Wax, Murray, L. (1974) Cultural pluralism, political power and ethnic studies. In Wilton S. Dillon (ed.) *The Cultural Drama: Modern Identities and Social Ferment* (pp. 107–120). Washington, D.C.: Smithsonian Institution.

Wolf, Eric R. (1982) *Europe and the People Without History.* Berkeley: University of California Press.

Wuthnow, Robert (1976) *The Conscious Reformation.* Berkeley: University of California Press.

Yinger, J. Milton (1985) Ethnicity. *Annual Review of Sociology* 11, 151–180.

Ziegler, Edward and Weiss, Heather (1985) Family support systems: An ecological approach to child development. In Robert N. Rapoport (ed.) *Children, Youth and Families: The Action Research Relationship* (pp. 166–205). Cambridge: Cambridge University Press.

# Chapter 6
# Reversing Language Shift: Successes, Failures, Doubts and Dilemmas

Before the advent of sociologically-informed sociolinguistic theory it was not uncommon to attempt to explain the waning of language via recourse to such intuitively popular factors as 'proximity to more powerful language' (often referred to cryptically as 'geography'); 'conviction that the language be retained' (often referred to as 'positive language attitudes' or 'wishes') and absolute number of speakers (often referred to as 'community size'). The problem with such theoretically innocent explanatory attempts is that they do not spell out or relate to societal processes, whether of intra-group interaction or inter-group interaction, that is, they are basically neither sociological (and, therefore, not sociolinguistic) nor are they related to any body of disciplined inquiry or application. It is my conviction that 'geography', 'wishes' and 'size' are all folk-concepts that need to be sociologically reinterpreted and operationalized into their manipulable societal counterparts. Reversing language shift efforts are particularly in need of both conceptually integrated social theory and a structured set of priorities for application that derives from such theory. What follows is an effort along such lines.

## What is 'Reversing Language Shift (RLS)'?

RLS constitutes that corner of the total field of status planning that is devoted to improving the sociolinguistic circumstances of languages that suffer from a negative balance of users and uses. It is not necessarily entirely an applied field of endeavor, since any hope for successful application – here as well as elsewhere – depends on the prior development of conceptually integrated diagnostic and corrective theory. When I initially laid out the field of 'language maintenance and language shift' (Fishman, 1964), it was my intention that the referents on both sides of the conjunction receive equal attention. Unfortunately, that has not proven to be the case and the negative process has received far more attention than has the positive one. Perhaps that is the result of a general bias, common both to modern humanistic and social science scholarship and to various ideologies of the left, center and right alike, to assume (and even to

prefer) the uniformation and massification of culture, based upon the massification and unification of the market and of modern technology across
cultural boundaries, i.e. to prefer social class to ethnic stratification.

As a result, 'the other side (or the plus side) of the ledger' has tended to be
neglected, if not philosophically stigmatized. The study of RLS represents an
attempt to redress the perspectival balance and to direct attention to the fact
that not only are millions upon millions of speakers of small languages on all
continents convinced of the creative and continuative contributions of their
languages (usually their mother tongues but sometimes their historically
associated religious languages) to their personal and collective lives, but
that many millions are also engaged in individual and collective efforts to
assist their threatened mother tongues to reverse the language shift processes that threaten or that have engulfed them.

Language shift can impinge on various societal communicative functions and, accordingly, the study of RLS must be concerned with the
entire sociofunctional profile of language use in any particular community under study. However, sociofunctional features of language use are
neither universals nor fixed and they must, in all honesty, be established
anew empirically whenever a hitherto unstudied (or not recently studied)
ethnolinguistic collectivity is examined. Nevertheless, due to the worldwide encroachment of western-derived modernization, it is possible
to make heuristic use of a parsimonious subset of functions that tend to
be rather generally encountered. In our discussion, below, these socio-
functions will be discussed from the point of view of RLS-efforts for the
purpose of attaining and augmenting *intergenerational mother-tongue
transmission*. The intergenerational transmission of regional languages
(lingua francas), of languages of wider econotechnical communication,
or of religious classicals (in general, the intergenerational transmission
of additional languages for special purposes) has been discussed elsewhere (Fishman, 1991: Chapter 12), although it should be stressed that
the theoretical underpinnings of that discussion are the same as that
which follows here.

## A Conceptually Parsimonious Approach to Describing and Prescribing: The Graded Intergenerational Dislocation Scale (GIDS)

It would be conceptually parsimonious to adopt an approach to analyzing RLS situations such that it would simultaneously (a) lend itself
to comparative (that is, to between-language) description or analysis;
and also (b) indicate the nature (location) and intensity (seriousness) of
the sociofunctional disarray impacting any particular cases under discussion. Simply put, RLS is in need of an approach to sociofunctional analysis

which will both *describe* the situation and *prescribe* the necessary ameliorative steps, at one and the same time, in so far as the needs of threatened languages are concerned. Table 6.1 represents an effort along those very lines and constitutes a minor modification of a prior version that has recently appeared in print elsewhere (Fishman, 1990).

Table 6.1 must be read from the bottom up to appreciate the fact that the RLS-circumstances and efforts toward the bottom of the table represent more fundamental stages of sociofunctional dislocation. Stage 8 indicates the greatest dislocation of all (from the point of view of achieving intergenerational mother tongue continuity), namely, a language which has lapsed into general disuse sufficiently long ago that it is now in need of reconstruction from shreds of evidence that can be provided by its last speakers and other incomplete and even vestigial sources. In order to shorten the number of steps in the table (the number can be greatly increased if finer functional distinctions are desired), stage 8 also includes those languages for which ample written evidence is available but which have lost their native speakers to such a degree that these languages must first be learned as second languages before further sociofunctional

**Table 6.1** Toward a theory of Reversing Language Shift

| *Stages of Reversing Language Shift*: Severity of intergenerational dislocation (read from the bottom up) |
| --- |
| 1. Education, worksphere, mass media and governmental operations at higher and nationwide levels |
| 2. Local/regional mass-media and governmental services |
| 3. The local/regional (i.e. non-neighborhood) worksphere, both among Xmen and among Ymen |
| 4b. Public schools for Xish children, offering some instruction via Xish, but substantially under Yish curricular and staffing control |
| 4a. Schools in lieu of compulsory education and substantially under Xish curricular and staffing control |
| II. *RLS to transcend diglossia, subsequent to its attainment* |
| (5. Schools for literacy acquisition, for the old and for the young, and not in lieu of compulsory education) |
| 6. The intergenerational and demographically concentrated home–family–neighborhood: the basis of mother tongue transmission |
| 7. Cultural interaction in Xish primarily involving the community-based older generation |
| 8. Reconstructing Xish and adult acquisition of XSL |
| I. *RLS to attain diglossia (assuming prior ideological clarification)* |

repertoire expansion can be envisioned for them. All in all, stage 8 represents maximal dislocation precisely because it constitutes language use outside of natural society, that is, outside of daily societal interaction among individuals actually implementing Xish ('ex-ish', our abbreviation for any particular language undergoing shift) in their normal, ongoing, community-based ethnocultural lives.

Note, however, that even the attainment (or implementation) of such cultural interaction on a community basis is insufficient for *inter*generational mother tongue continuity if the community of speakers consists of individuals who are primarily past childbearing age (stage 7). Indeed, it is precisely the fashioning (attainment or retention) of Xish-implementing *inter*generational and demographically concentrated home–family–community life, and the diglossic sheltering of such life from the inroads upon Xish intimacy that can stem from Yish ('why-ish', our abbreviation for the competitively stronger language surrounding Xish), that is the *sine qua non* of mother tongue transmission (stage 6). *All efforts that come later may help shelter stage 6 but cannot substitute for it*, nor, as we will see, can they directly help in its creation or attainment. Other characteristics of Table 6.1, and the underlying theory that it represents, will become clear from the ensuing discussion of ambivalences that often enfeeble RLS-efforts on behalf of intergenerational mother tongue continuity.

In general terms, stage 6 may be viewed as the dynamic fulcrum of a field of forces. If stage 6 is not attained, the less contributory to the intergenerational continuity of Xish will be the RLS efforts concentrated at other stages. Efforts closer to stage 6 are more nearly under Xish community control and, therefore, do not depend crucially on Yish support, cooperation or permission. Although the approach sketched here assumes that *something can always be done on behalf of threatened languages* (even for those at stage 8), it clearly implies that not everything that is done will contribute with equal directness to intergenerational mother tongue continuity. This conclusion (often a contra-intuitive one for RLS-workers) will be spelled out in the three sections that follow.

## Ambivalence 1: The Premature Attraction and Distraction of Pursuing High Status/Power Functions

The striving toward Xish implementation in and control of econotechnical modernity, a striving which is so typical of the modern situation which we have assumed generally to be part of the total language shift process impinging upon Xish, leads to an overly early concentration on stages 4 through 1 among those working on behalf of RLS. Such premature efforts to cross the continental divide between *attaining diglossic protection* for Xish and *dismantling diglossic L status* for Xish in favor of diglossic H status (or even monolingual Xish self-sufficiency) is evidenced by rushing into efforts on behalf of Xish schooling-in-lieu-of-compulsory-education and even by a stress on Xish use in the non-neighborhood worksphere, media and governmental operations. RLS efforts which pursue such goals prematurely are inevitably faced by several problems. On the one hand, these goals engender intergroup conflict precisely with respect to function in which Xmen are weakest relative to Ymen and where they will most often initially require Yish support and cooperation, even if only a nominal Xish presence is to be approved and funded.

Unfortunately, any nominal Xish presence in upper status and power functions will more often than not be completely overshadowed (if not totally eclipsed) by the vastly more frequent and often far superior Yish presence in those very same functions. The unequal struggle for 'recognition' in these high status and power functions frequently renders RLS efforts completely hopeless, disillusioned and innocent of concrete results. What is worse, the overly-early concentration on high status and power goals not only does not feed back directly to stage 6 but often postpones the tackling of stage 6 until it is too late from the point of view of capitalizing on still available Xish demographic concentrations and on Xish speakers who are still of childbearing age.

While the attainment of type 4a schools (primarily Xish staffed and regulated) or even 4b schools (primarily Yish staffed and regulated but intended for Xish children) certainly constituted a worthwhile RLS goal, nevertheless, many Yish-dominated years must pass before the graduates of such schools can found new Xish speaking families of their own. Of course, such schools can serve to further motivate and protect stage 6, but stage 6 must be alive and well for such motivation and protection to transpire. Finally, and specifically in relation to schools, various post-modernization processes have served to render the school–home relationship more tenuous than ever before (Fishman, 1991: Chapter 13), even for Yish, thereby rendering schools above type 5 quite questionable investments of time and effort for RLS movements that are still weak and without stage 6 foundations securely under their control.

The Irish RLS case was long a prime example of the inadvisability of disproportionate concentration on stage 4 relative to stage 6, and of the resulting institutionalization of Irish as an *occasional second language* among the school-focused middle class (each successive generation of which has nevertheless started, and generally still starts out [even after three generations of governmentally sponsored RLS-efforts], totally without Irish when it arrives in school), rather than as a mother tongue and informal medium among members of Irish society more generally. The current case of battle-fatigue among Irish RLSers, and the substantial peripheralization of their struggle *vis-à-vis* the interests of society more generally, can be attributed to their precipitous over-concentration on GIDS stages that do not substantially feed-back to intergenerational mother tongue continuity.

## Ambivalence 2: First Attaining and then Overcoming Diglossia, and Doing Each at an Appropriate Time

If the headlong rush into highly improbable (if not totally impossible) competition with Yish represents a distinct danger for the success of RLS efforts on behalf of intergenerational mother tongue continuity, then the insufficient pursuit of substantially self-regulated modern status and power functions, even when such can be erected upon a strong stage 6 base, constitutes an equally great (although far less common) danger to such efforts. A disproportional stress on traditionalism, revivalism or other expressions of 'anthropological revitalization' exposes RLS efforts to the risk of being rejected by Xmen who seek a path marked by both modernity and Xishness. In the absence of sufficient RLS interest in ration-ally defining the priorities to be followed in forging such a path, RLS may come to be viewed as anachronistic or backward looking and more sym-biotic alternatives to it (combining Xishness and Yish in *some* fashion) may come into being (e.g. movements on behalf of 'Xmen-via-Yish' as rivals and competitors with the RLS movement *per se* among Xmen). Some of the Ultra-Orthodox Yiddish speaking communities in New York are exposed to this very dilemma today as young people protest against the communities' overly slow progression from stage 4 to stage 3. The insuffi-cient availability of stage 3 functions under Ultra-Orthodox sponsorship is leading more and more young people into the Yish controlled work-sphere (and into social mobility via that worksphere), with evident effect on their own intragroup use of Yiddish.

Given that both the premature abandonment of the diglossic protection of stage 6 and the overly prolonged inability to transcend the encapsula-tion of stage 6 are clearly problematic *vis-à-vis* RLS success, it is, never-theless, clear that the attainment of diglossic protection for Xish by weak RLS movements lacking in stage 6 is infinitely more common and difficult (and less glamorous) than is its subsequent gradual transcen-dence by an RLS movement with a secure basis in everyday inter-generational life. RLS movements are ethnicity linked and they must build upon the putative kinship claim of all ethnicity movements in order to counteract the blandishments of greater (and often even purport-edly unlimited) individual social mobility via Yish and through Yish insti-tutions, blandishments which render Xmen less philosophically disposed toward the behavioral and motivational prerequisites of RLS-movements on behalf of the 'Xmen-via-Xish' model. The Irish and Frisian movements are good examples of the difficulties encountered in this very diglossia-attaining connection. Stage 6 never having been reconstituted on a sufficiently ample base, there is no widely available safe-harbor in daily life against the influences of the upper Yish-controlled stages.

On the other hand, the transcendence of diglossic bilingualism into virtually monolingual Xish *de facto* control of everyday public and intergroup life, is often considered to be difficult to attain without civil strife. However, the actual incidence of civil strife is more genuinely related to the removal of authoritarian control after periods of both long term and short term deprivation (Fishman–Solano, 1990) than to RLS processes or other language related processes themselves. The Franco-Canadian and the Catalan RLS cases are both examples of relatively successful negotiations of this difficult passage, the latter being almost entirely without serious intergroup recriminations between indigenous Catalans and immigrant Castilian speakers thus far. Note, however, that without successfully attaining and maintaining stage 6, no transcendence of that stage is possible. There is a dilemma here of no mean proportions.

## Ambivalence 3: The Difficulty of Planning Spontaneity and Intimacy

The basic problem of weak RLS movements is whether the attainment and maintenance of stage 6 is at all susceptible to planning. Given that intergenerational mother tongue transmission is a function of the childhood intimacy and spontaneity that characterizes home–family–neighborhood life, this problem boils down to whether this complex of culturally infused interpersonal processes can only be informally cultivated '*in vivo*', so to speak, or whether it can be fostered by rational planning. The evidence supporting the latter alternative is, quite frankly, sparse indeed. The major RLS success cases of the 20th century generally entered the fray while their stage 6 processes were still (or already) rather intact at least in some language islands. Attempts to build stage 6 directly (e.g. the community and housing schemes of Irish RLS efforts in the mid to late 1980s) have demonstrated how elusive the informal interaction processes really are and how difficult it is to really plan them or to do so without destroying them. Yet the revernacularization of Hebrew in Palestine on the part of secular (indeed, anti-clerical) Zionists was accomplished precisely along the lines of giving priority to self-regulatory home–family–community building for the attainment of intergenerational mother tongue transmission and reached its goal during the immediate pre- and post-World War I decades, much before any power and status functions (beyond the settlements and their community nursery and elementary schools) were seriously entertained on a broader societal base.

Obviously there is considerable room for ideological clarification (more about this below) and for neighborhood organization expertise and organization-theory expertise in general within the total RLS enterprise. Nevertheless, the dilemma which underlies this third area of ambivalence must be recognized as such. Intergenerational mother tongue transmission depends on processes which have too long remained overlooked by RLS movements but, to make matters worse, even when squarely acknowledged, these processes are difficult to plan because they require the establishment and fostering of interactional contexts and relationships which are difficult to plan and to cultivate as long as Xish-imbeddedness in Yish-dominated everyday sociocultural processes remains uninterrupted. It was the very ability of the new Zionist settlements to break away from their dependence on all other Jewish and non-Jewish norms and associations, both in the diaspora and in Palestine itself, that made it possible for them to create home–family–neighborhood (= settlement) contexts in which their preferred Xish was protected and could finally attain intergenerational roots. It was only thereafter that efforts to hebraize others and higher sociocultural processes were focused upon. On the other hand, Eliezer ben Yehuda, who had focused upon such higher order processes from the very outset (c. 1890) was distinctly unsuccessful in vernacularizing Hebrew, regardless of his subsequent symbolic status in that very connection.

## A Glance at A Few Selected Cases

Table 6.2 presents data on the standing of a baker's dozen of RLS cases with respect to their present GIDS status. These cases are drawn from three continents (North America, Europe and Asia/Pacific) and include both indigenous and immigrant groups. Both the right and the left margins of Part A of the table consist primarily of the GIDS stages that were presented in Table 6.1, above, and that have provided the basis of most of the foregoing discussion. The only addition to the table proper is the notation *IC* (ideological clarification) which has been scored on a three point scale (+, +−, −) reflecting the availability of positive consensuality within the 13 studied RLS circles today. The total GIDS score (referred to as *Ts*) for each case consists of the grand total of all of the numbers representing stages at which major RLS efforts are concentrated today on behalf of that case. Higher total scores indicate efforts that are still focused on societally more dislocated stages. The highest (most dislocated) scores are obtained for Maori, Irish, Yiddish in secularist circles in New York City and selected Australian Aboriginal 'outstation' cases. The lowest (least dislocated) scores are obtained for

**Table 6.2** Graded Intergenerational Dislocation Stages (GIDS) in 13 monitored RLS settings

| Part A | AA | AIR | B | C | FQ | F | H | I | M | NR | S | YO | YS | |
|---|---|---|---|---|---|---|---|---|---|---|---|---|---|---|
| 1 | | | × | × | × | | × | | | | | | | 1 |
| 2 | | × | × | × | | × | | × | | | | × | | 2 |
| 3 | | | × | × | | | | | | | | × | | 3 |
| 4b | | | | | | × | | | × | | × | | | 4b |
| 4a | × | × | × | | | | | × | | × | | × | | 4a |
| 5 | | | | | | | | | × | | | | × | 5 |
| 6* | + − | − | − | + | + | − | + | − | − | + − | + − | + | − | 6* |
| 7 | × | × | | | | × | | × | × | × | × | | × | 7 |
| 8 | × | | × | | | | | × | × | | | | × | 8 |
| IC* | + − | + | + | + | + | + | + − | + − | + − | + − | + − | + − | + − | IC* |

*Continued*

**Table 6.2**  (*Continued*)

**Part A**

| | AA | AIR | B | C | FQ | F | H | I | M | NR | S | YO | YS | |
|---|---|---|---|---|---|---|---|---|---|---|---|---|---|---|
| Ts** | 19 | 13 | 18 | 6 | 1 | 13 | 1 | 21 | 24 | 11 | 11 | 7 | 20 | Ts** |
| | AA | AIR | B | C | FQ | F | H | I | M | NR | S | YO | YS | |
| Mean | 6.3 | 5.3 | 5.6 | 2 | 1 | 5.3 | 1 | 5.2 | 6 | 5.4 | 5.2 | 3.5 | 6.7 | Mean |

**Part B**

*Average Ts for − or + − at stage 6: 15.75; at IC: 14.13
Average Ts for + at stage 6: 3.75; at IC: 10.20

**Languages ranked by the *sum* of their GIDS scores (Ts):

| | +on 6 | +on IC |
|---|---|---|
| 1 = FQ, II | × | × × |
| 6 = C | × | × × |
| 7 = YO (NYC) | × | |
| 10 = S(NYCPR) | | |
| 11 = NR | | × × |
| 13 = AIR, F | | × × |
| 18 = B | | |
| 20 = YS (NYC) | | |
| 21 = I | | |
| 24 = M | | |

Hebrew in Israel, French in Quebec, Catalan in the Autonomous Catalan Community and Yiddish in Ultra-Orthodox circles in New York. Another way of estimating the current relative positions of these 13 communities is by examining their mean GIDS scores. The correlation between the Total GIDS score and the Mean GIDS score is 0.79, implying that the Ts is not merely an artifact of the number and variety of efforts involved.

It is quite clear from Part A of Table 6.2 that there are some cases significantly involved in efforts above the 'continental divide' that are, nevertheless, still in a poor state of health with respect to their overall RLS status (e.g. Irish and Basque). There are also even more obviously a few cases where there is little if any ideological focus (IC) on RLS which are doing relatively well with respect to their overall RLS standing (e.g. Navaho [selected reservation] and Ultra-Orthodox Yiddish in New York). Part B of Table 6.2 reveals that the consideration that really seems to distinguish between cases doing well and cases doing less well or poorly, as far as RLS is concerned, is whether stage 6 (home–neighborhood–community) is substantially under self-regulatory RLS auspices.

The average total GIDS score for the four cases in which this is so is 3.75, whereas the average total GIDS score for the nine cases in which it is not so is 15.75. The difference in total GIDS scores between cases with and without positive ideological consensuality is less impressive (10.20 vs. 14.13), although it too is clearly in the right direction (detailed information concerning all 13 cases can be found in Fishman, 1991). Current ambivalence regarding the importance of Hebrew in Israel (particularly in comparison with the unanimity as to the importance of the 'Xmen-via-Xish' position among Francophones in Quebec and among Catalans in the Autonomous Catalan Community) is attributable to philosophical pluralism on this issue, a pluralism which can be attributed to the post-struggle phase which Xish has now achieved there. The IC analysis clearly implies that even an RLS-engineered ideo-logical consensus (by no means the same as spontaneous 'positive attitudes' or 'positive wishes' relative to Xish) is of clearly lesser RLS importance than establishing Xish supremacy *vis-à-vis* the societal pro-cesses of everyday home-family-community life.

Obviously, Table 6.2 does not try to show the historical development that has occurred with respect to the RLS statuses of the speech com-munities involved. Clearly, it deals only with the reasonably current situations in each case. A series of such tables, decade by decade from the beginning of this century, would unambiguously reveal which cases have advanced, which have regressed and which have remained stationary with respect to their respective RLS status. I have attempted to present the relevant information precisely for such an analysis and to do so in a less compressed non-tabular (that is, in narrative) form in Fishman (1991).

## Some Concluding and Summary Observations

Our discussion has helped clarify why 'geographic' considerations, 'absolute size' considerations and attitudinal/motivational ('wishes') considerations cannot be considered either conceptually fruitful or, indeed, manipulably rewarding considerations in connection with understanding RLS differentials. Letzeburgisch, the vernacular of Luxembourg, is 'next door' (indeed, surrounded by) two world languages, French and German, both of which are even part of the very Xish identity-and-behavior pattern that Letzeburgisch itself serves to clinch. Furthermore, Letzeburgisch mother tongue speakers constitute a rather small speech community and one which gives its mother tongue rather little explicit ideological attention. Rather than fixating on the former non-manipulable intra-group considerations we have tended to emphasize intergroup processes and a search for manipulable 'planning' considerations. Nevertheless, a number of ambiguities and dilemmas must be recognized as plaguing or rendering extremely difficult the pursuit of RLS. Even things that are well understood, however, are not necessarily reparable.

Intergenerational linguistic continuity may safely focus on the school, on the church or on the workplace if specific non-mother tongue functions are being aimed at. However, if intergenerational mother-tongue transmission is being aimed at, there is no parsimonious substitute for focusing on the home–neighborhood–community processes which bind together adults and children (most frequently, but not only, grandparents and grandchildren and parents and children) in early bonds of intergenerational and spontaneous affect, intimacy, identity and loyalty. This is not to say that this arena is itself sufficient to guarantee that mother tongue focused RLS will succeed, but it is to say that RLS control of this arena is necessary, a *sine qua non*. Subsequent stages provide it with additional latitude and instrumental reinforcement. Much before diglossic arrangements are fully transcended there are types of schooling (particularly type 5 and 4a) that can support this arena materially and with only meager dependence on Yish regulation, approval or support. Thereafter, Xish with a firm, demographically concentrated community base can increasingly pursue economic and even political co-regulatory power. The increasing attainment of such power leads to cultural autonomy arrangements and to realistic possibilities of further political arrangements as well.

## References

Fishman, Joshua A. (1964) Language maintenance and language shift as a field of inquiry. *Linguistics* 9, 32–70.

——. (1990) What is reversing language shift (RLS) and how can it succeed? *Journal of Multilingual and Multicultural Development* 11, 5–36.

——. (1991) *Reversing Language Shift*. Clevedon: Multilingual Matters. (See Chapter 12: 'The intergenerational transmission of "additional" languages for special purposes' for an analysis of the intergenerational transmission of non-mother tongues; Chapter 13: 'Limitations on school-effectiveness in connection with mother tongue transmission' for a discussion of the societal prerequisites of school effectiveness.)

—— and Frank R. Solano (1990) Civil strife and linguistic heterogeneity/homogeneity: An empirical examination. *Canadian Review of Studies in Nationalism* 17, 131–146.

## Abbreviations

AA = Australian Aborigines (selected cases)
AIR = Australian Immigrant (post-World War II)
B = Basque
C = Catalan
FQ = Francophone Quebec
F = Frisian
H = Hebrew
I = Irish
M = Maori
NR = Navaho (selected reservation community 1)
S = Spanish: New York City Puerto Ricans
YO = Yiddish Ultra-Orthodox (NYC)
YS = Yiddish Secular (NYC)
IC = Ideological clarification
Numbers = GIDS stages (X = stage[s] currently receiving most attention in RLS efforts)
Ts = Total dislocation score
+ = present or positive
− = absent or negative
+− = ambivalent or uncertain

# Chapter 7
# *Language Revitalization*

In 1963–1964, when I was rewriting what was ultimately to become my *Language Loyalty in the United States* (1966), I coined the expression 'language maintenance and language shift' to designate the ebb and flow continuum with respect to the number of users and uses of languages. It was not an elegant phrase, particularly if there was a need to repeat it frequently in any one article, but it managed to convey my interest in the manifold possibilities facing small languages and small language communities the world over. I had begun by studying the non-English languages of the United States and had wound up defining a field of inquiry that had both international and historical dimensions.

Although the polar extremes of the continuum were both of equal interest to me and seemed to be equally stressed in the designation, the ensuing years saw a marked concentration of interest at the negative pole, i.e. at the shift side of the dynamics of sociocultural change. Subsequently, such terms as language loss, language attrition, language replacement, language displacement, language endangerment and various others, began to be used and, on occasion, distinguished one from the other in conjunction with a large variety of language debilitating possibilities that came to be recognized. Since most sociolinguistic research is conducted under majoritarian auspices and since the self-declared purposes (or at least the egos) of majoritarian sponsors are gratified by the weakening of smaller languages and minority language communities, language debilitation phenomena of various degrees and tempos came to be widely and frequently studied. Meanwhile, the plus side of the ledger remained oddly unexamined, particularly so when small languages and small language communities were under review. There seemed to be an unspoken assumption that they were not long for this world and that nothing much of any generalizable significance could either be said about or done for them.

The 'ethnic revival' of the mid-sixties to the mid- and late-seventies gradually forced many perceptive investigators in the Developed World to revise their views about such matters (Fishman, 1985). Small languages and small language communities, even when these pertained to immigrant groups, often displayed not only a reluctance to fade away but an amazing capacity to stand their ground, to attract and hold the devotion of individuals sufficiently trained to help them plan their futures, to try to maximize their chances of intergenerational ethnocultural continuity and, in general, to attempt to utilize the methods of modernity against being swallowed up whole by mainstream modernity itself. Accordingly, a new, more refined 'lexicon of the positive pole' has come to be needed. What follows is an attempt to suggest such a lexicon in the hope that more standardized usage in this connection will facilitate understanding of the phenomena and processes under consideration. Although I will suggest that the term 'language maintenance' continue to be used, I will advocate that it be restricted to only one of four different varieties of *language reinforcement processes* which, together, constitute the complete 'positive pole' of the users and uses continuum Again, although my initial concern stems from a consideration of contextually disadvantaged languages, the entire range of reinforcing phenomena should be of interest to students of all languages whatsoever. The great and mighty languages of the world are also encountered in contexts in which they and those who use them are in need of assistance.

*Language reinforcement: processes and efforts.* Four different varieties of language reinforcement will be differentiated from each other. In each case, a few bibliographic items will be mentioned, although the major purpose of this essay is the *reorganization* of knowledge rather than its detailed *review and enumeration*.

## Language Revival or Revitalization

Since I use the term 'language reinforcement' for the 'positive pole' as a whole, I would, therefore, like to suggest that the term that the editors of this volume have assigned for this article ('Revitalization') be reserved only for a small section of the total topic under discussion. I would also suggest that no hair-line distinctions be drawn at this time between 'revival', 'revitalization', 'revivication' and other terms which draw upon the image of 'imparting life', particularly since many languages do not have a variety of etymologically related synonyms in this semantic area. The phenomenon for which I would like to reserve the term 'revival' is the rather unusual one of the *revernacularization* of a language no longer being spoken on a societal basis. I do not propose that we actually use the term 'revernacularization' for this entire process, because that term might actually be better reserved for languages that are no longer being natively spoken anywhere. As rare as revivals are, revernacularizations are even rarer as societal phenomena. The major instance of successful revernacularization is the case of modern Hebrew (Fellman, 1973; Bar-Adon, 1975). However, more common revivals have occurred in connection with languages which remain(ed) spoken only in the countryside whereas city-folk, at best, learn(ed) to read them or to 'appreciate' their past classical, literary or folkloristic manifestations. Attempts to create Latin speaking, Sanscrit speaking or Geez speaking communities would be instances of attempts at revernavularization revivals. (If there have been any such attempts – and I think there have, just on the basis of passing references to them – I am not aware of any detailed literature about them.)

However, when the Czech intelligentsia set aside German and turned back to Czech (Namier, 1944; Paneth, 1939; Wikemann, 1967), when the late 19th and early 20th century Jewish intelligentsia of Eastern Europe (let us say that of Vilne [Vilnius], e.g.) set aside Russian, Polish and German and switched to Yiddish (Birnbaum, 1905[1991]), when Irish nationalists turned from Irish-admiration to the Irish speech found by then only in various isolated Gaeltachts (Advisory Planning Committee 1989), those were all instances of revivals 'pure and simple', no revernacularizations as such being required. Accordingly, there are revival movements even for English, French and German in various pockets scattered around the globe today, where the totally relinguified offspring of individuals who once spoke those vernaculars are now trying to return societally to the linguistic patrimony of their real or putative ancestors. Since it is precisely the societal phenomenon that interests us, then it is the societal status of the language rather than its linguistic status that the term 'revival' should denote. Revivals should be recognized in small scale societal terms as well as in connection with more massive phenomena, just as we do when we speak of religious revivals, economic revivals, literary revivals and even literacy revivals, regardless of the scale of the societal units involved. Revivals constitute stages 8 and 7 of my 'Graded Intergenerational Dislocation Scale-GIDS' (Fishman, 1992) with respect to attaining intergenerational mother-tongue continuity. Not only are revivals typically engineered by adults, but frequently by adults who are themselves past childbearing age. Accordingly, revivals do not yet speak to, let alone guarantee, the types of reinforcement that only intergenerational continuity can address.

## Reversing Language Shift

Obviously, the attainment of adult 'native like' fluency is only the beginning of the reinforcement saga. Revivers may be poor or very mediocre guarantors of the intergenerational future, precisely because they are so often focused on much more elementary gratifications, namely those of current face-to-face community interaction. However, such gratifications do not necessarily attain intergenerational momentum, primarily because they commonly do not apply to sufficient numbers or to a sufficient range of sociocultural functions to maintain such momentum even if it is initially attained. Accordingly, reinforcement efforts typically take additional steps, aim at higher goals, than the 'mere' revival of adult-level fluency. The crucial (and often overlooked or insufficiently valued) basis of all further reinforcement progress is based upon the involvement of the younger generation in the reinforcement process and, together with and through it, the attainment of neighborhood and community life in the language that is to be reinforced. The development of community organizations for economic assistance and job training, political participation and involvement, child care and education, religious observance, physical and mental health care, recreational activity, all of which constitute the modern neighborhood and community and are the modern supports of home and family life, on the one hand, and the building blocks of societal efforts to relinguify (or at least co-relinguify) the major institutions of modern life: the school, the church, the workplace, the media and the government, at least in their local or regional manifestations.

To the extent that the functions implied by the above institutions were once discharged, at least in part and for intra-communal purposes, via the language to be reinforced, the efforts to bolster intergenerational ethnolinguistic continuity by returning the language to these functions are rightly referred to as 'reversing language shift' efforts. The language is being returned, if initially only to a modest extent, to functions that were associated (or co-associated) with it and to functions which any community that is in touch with the surrounding modern world must wish to influence and regulate (or, at least, co-regulate) on its own behalf, if its own intergenerational ethnolinguistic viability is to have at least a chance of succeeding. The initial attainment, daily implementation and protection of such functions is currently on the agenda for Frisian (Gorter *et al.*, 1988), Maori (Benton, 1984), for Romansch (Biligmeier, 1983), for certain Amerindian languages (particularly in Canada, but also for various Navajo reservation sites in the USA; see, e.g. Rosier & Holm, 1980), for most parts of the Basque country (other than Guipuzcoa, see, e.g. Garmendia, 1992), etc. The crucial consideration, here, is to attain and safeguard the linguistic normalization of home–family–neighborhood–community functioning, rather than rushing headlong into repertoire expansion for more symbolic or econotechnically powerful purposes that are, therefore, removed from the social interactions of most people during most parts of their day. These efforts pertain primarily to stages 6, 5 and 4 on the 'GIDS Scale' (Fishman, 1992).

## Language Maintenance

Reversing language shift is a never-ending struggle for most small languages and small language communities. However, often the stage is reached when it is not the attainment of new functions which is either the status planning or corpus planning issue, but, rather, the constant effort, an attention that is required to avoid and counteract slippage. This is truly termed 'language maintenance', because its agenda consists of efforts to maintain in practice and throughout the speech community the repertoire expansion already negotiated by the most committed or in certain localities. Typically, and as was also the case earlier, the reinforcement effort's reach must exceed its grasp, if only in order to safeguard and generalize the grasp that has already been attained. Thus, language maintenance efforts often make recourse to the higher level coordination of efforts and to the formalization and augmentation of governmental authority on behalf of the language. This is clearly the case for much Catalan exertion today (Weber & Strubell i Trueta, 1991), for Afrikaans (Juta, 1961) and even for French in Quebec (Handler, 1988). However, even the defenders and guardians of such relatively 'safe' and ideologically unthreatened languages as Israeli Hebrew still seem to recognize, at times, the need to call the faithful to rise to the defense of the ethnonational tongue, particularly when the intrusions of English seem to become excessively common in governmental and in everyday affairs. Language maintenance corresponds to stages 3, 2 and 1 of the GIDS scale (Fishman, 1991).

## Language Spread

The reinforcement of a few erstwhile threatened languages has, in part, reached the stage where they are also being advocated for and among ethnolinguistic 'outsiders' and, indeed, when they spread among speakers of other mother tongues as a means of interethnic communication with the 'insiders'. This is true for Catalan and Basque, *vis-à-vis* the large numbers of Spanish speakers who have been attracted to their industrially more advanced midsts. This is also true of Afrikaans among various Black Africans (for some of whom, it should be noted, Afrikaans has become not only a lingua franca but also a mother tongue [Alexander, 1990]). The phenomenon of language spread applies to Israeli Hebrew among Palestinian Arabs and, of course, to French in Quebec among Anglo-Canadians. In some of the above mentioned examples, language spread has been fostered via the legal system, requirements having been instituted making the formerly threatened language obligatory (or co-obligatory) in certain functions (public education, worksphere, mass media, signage, government, etc.). The ability to adopt and enforce such measures is itself an indication of the momentum and power that can be attained by language reinforcement efforts.

## Cautions

A brief presentation such as this cannot analyze all of the subtleties of language reinforcement, particularly with respect to its practical aspects and dilemmas (see, however, Fishman, 1993b). Thus, the two cautions that *will* be presented here are mere attempts to focus on some major concerns. First of all, the above listed stages and types of language reinforcement are not to be taken to be discrete or linear in nature. Actually, they are overlapping and interacting. Basque in Gipuzcoa is further along on the road to language spread than it is, generally speaking, in Bilbao, but in Vitoria-Gasteiz a language maintenance struggle is needed and elsewhere in Alava even revival efforts are still 'iffy'. Although the average of all of the foregoing realities is squarely in the reversing language shift arena, that average masks the more advanced situation in certain important speech networks and the very tenuous nature of Basque usage and even Basque attitudes in very many others throughout the Autonomous Basque Community. Accordingly, language reinforcement efforts must be investigated and pursued on a local, almost network by network basis, rather than in whole language terms. The boundary between reversing language shift and language maintenance may not be a hard and fast one but rather, more a subtle change of emphases in particular situations. Similarly, stages may also be largely or even entirely bypassed. Thus, immigrant languages often aspire to post-revival language maintenance and skip over all or most of the reversing language shift stage (thereby endangering their own success due to self-restriction of functions).

Furthermore, language reinforcement is not an isolatable undertaking, to be engaged in independently from political and economic change efforts more widely, including language planning, neighborhood organization and political action. The most successful language reinforcement movements of this century (that on behalf of Hebrew in Ottoman and British controlled Palestine, that on behalf of French in Quebec and that on behalf of Catalan in Spain) have all been all-encompassing movements, reaching far beyond language alone. Without such a reach they could not have succeeded, as they did, as language reinforcement efforts. Language reinforcement is, essentially, a well-nigh revolutionary reconstitution of society and, indeed, without such a reconstitution it cannot suceed. For language reinforcement to 'take', previous power positions in society must be transferred to or strongly impacted by segments of minority society and their previous incumbents must either be replaced or relinguified. Relinguification often means reethnification. It is a difficult and sensitive issue and must be expected to meet up with opposition.

Finally, it should not be denied that language reinforcement is a self-interest related activity. As the self-interests of some are advanced the self-interests of others retreat or are adversely effected. When oppositely oriented interest-related activities involve different ethnolinguistic groups, the result may well be intergroup conflict. It is probably true that adherents of small languages and language communities, operating on behalf of their own greater sociocultural self-regulation, cannot conceivably inflict on the majorities in whose midsts they live the kinds of punishment that majorities take for granted when inflicted on minorities. Nevertheless, language reinforcement efforts are not all sweetness and light. They are not innocent of self-interest and cannot be expected to be. Unless they are to lead to an infinite crescendo of grievances and counter-grievances, they must include compromises far short of the questionable goal of every language being legally recognized and supported for every conceivable function under the sun (Fishman, 1993a). The pursuit of ethnolinguistic democracy must have reasonable and feasible goals, both for its own sake and for the sake of humanity at large.

### Bibliography (selected)

Advisory Planning Committee (1989) *The Irish Language in a Changing Society: Shaping the Future*. Dublin.
Alexander, Neville (1990) Die Onderrig van Afrikaans in 'n Demokratiese Suid-Afrika. *Language Projects' Review* 5, 13–14.
Bar-Adon, Aaron (1975) *The Rise and Decline of a Dialect*. The Hague.
Benton, Richard (1984) *Te rito o the korari: Maori Language and New Zealand's National Identity*. Wellington.
Billigmeier, R.H. (1983) *Land und Volk der Rätoromanen, eine Kultur- und Sprachgeschichte*. Frauenfeld.
Birnbaum, Natan (1905, 1991) Ostjüdische Aufgaben. In: *Bukowinaer Post* (Tshernovits). Seperatdruck. Translated into Yiddish as 'Di uvdes fun mizrekh-eyropeyishe yidn' by Joshua A. Fishman. In: *Yivo-bleter* 1 (n.s.), 109–128.
Fellman, Jack (1973) *The Revival of a Classical Tongue*. The Hague.
Fishman, Joshua A. (1991) *Reversing Language Shift*. Clevedon.
_____. (1993a) Ethnolinguistic democracy: varieties, degrees and limits. *Language International* 5, 11–17.
_____. (1993b) Reversing language shift: successes, failures, doubts and dilemmas. In: Hakon Jahr, Ernst (ed.) *Language Conflict and Language Planning*, (pp. 69–82). Berlin.
_____ et al. (1985) *Rise and Fall of the Ethnic Revival*. Berlin.
Garmendia, M. Carmen (1992) *Appearance of M. Carmen Garmendia, Secretary General for Language Policy of the Basque Government, before the Institutions and Home Affairs, Commission of the Basque Parliament*. Vitoria-Gasteiz.
Gorter, Durk *et al.* (1984) *Taal yn Fryslan*. Ljouwert.
Handler, Richard (1988) *Nationalism and the Poltics of Culture in Quebec*. Madison.
Juta, Conrad J. (1961) *Aspects of Afrikaner Nationalism, 1900–1964*. Pietermaritzburg.
Namier, L.B. (1944) *1848: The Revolution of the Intellectuals*. London.
Paneth, Philip (1939) *Czechs Against Germans*. London.
Rosier, Paul and Holm, Wayne (1980) *The Rock Point Experience: A Longitudinal Study of a Navajo School Program*. Washington.
Webber, Jude and Strubell i Trueta, Miquel (1991) *The Catalan Language: Progress Towards Normalization*. Sheffield.
Wikemann, Elizabeth (1967) *Czechs and Germans*. London.
Woolard, Kathryn A (1989) *Double Talk Bilingualism and the Politics of Ethnicity in Catalonia*. Stanford.

*Chapter 8*

# Good Conferences in a Wicked World: On Some Worrisome Problems in the Study of Language Maintenance and Language Shift

On the completion of yet another very good conference on language maintenance and language shift, it may be appropriate to pause to consider the twin questions of (a) *what* makes for a good conference and (b) *when* good conferences may just not be enough, relative to the responsibilities that rest upon us.

## What Is a Good Conference?

Conference going – conference listening, conference speaking and conference learning – is a distinctly modern mode of interaction, both within science and within society more generally. The language sciences and language-focused social action have both benefited tremendously from the conference mode (Fishman, 1993) during the past century. Like all of you, indeed like all of my colleagues the world over, I have been going to conferences all of my professional life. I vividly remember how I was carefully socialized into the conference attending circuit as a graduate student, by my own professorial mentors. These same mentors then also helped make sure that my first conference presentation was at a suitably high (or even recondite) level (Fishman, 1954).

Forty years have passed since then and literally hundreds of conferences have flown by. Nevertheless, when I ask myself which ones I still remember, the number shrinks appreciably, to barely a dozen. Finally, if I ask myself, which of these conferences really made a contribution to my own thinking or to my own post-conference research or social action, I am left with only two or three! These two or three tend to have very similar characteristics. They were all small, involving roughly

15–20 people in each instance. They were all topically focused rather than simply disciplinary or interdisciplinary. And they all aimed at post-conference follow through in very concrete ways, e.g. a follow-up meeting within a year's time, a proclamation for world-wide dissemination and a joint international study by the participants. Some of the aforementioned characteristics of conferences 'that really made a difference' are, at first blush, quite contraintuitive. Conference planners and sponsors often try to have as large a conference as possible. A large number of attendees yields correspondingly lower hotel charges and various 'perks' for the organizers themselves. An omnibus agenda permits more people to attend, to present (and, therefore, to get their way paid by their employers), and to find something on the program that is related to one's own research or teaching. Nevertheless, precisely because such conferences are a mile wide and an inch deep, they are also predictably 'forgettable'. They do less to advance the field than one would optimally hope.

As one who, after 35 years of involvement, still spends most waking hours immersed in the study of language maintenance and language shift, I have often thought about what could be done to improve conferences in this field. I am obviously gratified by this field's growth in numbers and its development in topical complexity and methodological sophistication, a growth, complexity and sophistication which its conferences obviously also mirror. I am also tremendously pleased by the growing efforts to attract participants from outside of the industrialized West, difficult though that is (given the serious lack of funding that characterizes the current phase of academic enterprises). Our field is still sufficiently young, it seems to me, and the amount of disagreement within it sufficiently great, that it may still not be contra-indicated to bring together somewhat larger groups and to foster exchanges of opinion and experience within the field as a whole. Nevertheless, the time for smaller, more focused and more criterially evaluated 'working conferences' is rapidly approaching, even for us, and I would like to make a few suggestions in that direction. This field of inquiry began as a 'Gemeinschaft' and its relatively rapid success (in terms of number of courses, conferences, journals, books, organizations, etc.) has quickly converted it into a 'Gesellschaft'. This level of social functioning inevitably leads to anomie, mechanization and routinization. Perhaps the time has come to put more 'Gemeinschaft' back into our functioning and into our thinking.

## The Wicked World

But there are other good reasons why more attention to small groups, each meeting around a topical focus, would be highly advisable. It would enable our field to come to grips with the reality of language maintenance and language shift 'as it is lived', felt, experienced, struggled with and (on occasion) coped with. Without a good injection of such 'reality linkages', language maintenance and language shift may become what medical research would become if it were all biochemistry and neurophysiology oriented and never attended to patients, their families and their communities, or what educational research would become if it were all social and behavioral science oriented and never attended to pupils, teachers, parents and communities, namely, too abstract, too removed from health and health care, on the one hand, and from learning and instruction, on the other hand, to be of maximal value to those who have to deal with either real illness or real education. This would not only be a pity and a great loss to all those who need the help of medical and educational research, but it would quickly impoverish such research *per se*. 'Abstracting' from the 'real live' setting does not lead to clarification, to the control of supposedly irrelevant factors, but, rather, to the impoverishment of research hypotheses and findings.

There are several 'real life' circumstances, pertaining to language maintenance and language shift settings the world over, that currently deserve particular attention by small groups of researchers, coming together to pursue both intellectual and practical goals.

(1) The 'ethnic cleansing' context: The fact that several newly state-building ethnolinguistic aggregates have immediately visited death and destruction upon their neighbors (and traditional rivals) has obviously colored the public reaction to language maintenance. It is necessary to point out to governments and to the public at large that a false connection has been implied here in the popular press. There is ample research evidence to demonstrate that the combination of long term deprivation and the sudden removal of superordinate coercive power leads to increased civil strife (Fishman, 1991). The terrible ethnocidal occurrences that now plague Serbs, Croatians and Bosnians, as well as the Eastern and Southern European refugees who have fled to Germany, and Georgians, Armenians and Azeris, among others, are in no way by-products of language maintenance or even of self-determination strivings among ethnolinguistic aggregates. They are primarily the residues of longstanding national rivalries and ambitions, rivalries and ambitions that have now been given free reign once the former superordinate threat of Stalinism or Titoism have been removed. The former superordinate powers themselves aggravated these rivalries and ambitions, played them against each other and, for generations, essentially stifled any opportunity to reconcile them. These policies were genocidal along the traditional lines of the Western great power (note, e.g.

the history of French policies toward Bretons and Occitans, or the history of British behavior toward the Irish, Welsh and Scots).

While this does not excuse the inexcusable mayhem perpetrated by newly appearing small powers it also should not leave the great powers off the hook for the genocide that they have long practiced and continue to practice to this very day against indigenous and immigrant minorities within their own national borders. Language maintenance, voluntaristically pursued and democratically supported, is a moral and legal right that Western democracies ignore at their own peril, to the detriment of innocent minorities and to the detriment of their own democratic ethos, which no amount of finger-pointing at Serbs, Croatians, Armenians and Georgians can disguise. A small group of language maintenance specialists meeting to review ongoing genocides in the democratic West and to highlight overlooked interethnic power sharing in the new states (e.g. in Slovenia, in the Ukraine, in Kazakhstan, etc.) would be able to set the record straight by exploring *minority language maintenance policies on vastly different sociopolitical and socioeconomic orders*. We would all benefit from such a review and it could subsequently be expanded to include additional areas of the world than the ones mentioned above, as well.

(2) We have been strangely – and for me, very painfully – silent about the fact that roughly a third of the world's languages are now threatened with extinction within their own traditionally indigenous areas. Others have issued calls protesting this dismal development and Unesco has even proclaimed an 'Indigenous Peoples Year'. But the actual state of the indigenous languages of the world – merely in terms of their capacity for intergenerational transmission – remains essentially underdocumented if not entirely undocumented. What is even less understood and appreciated is 'what it is that is lost when a language dies'. Since language death is both a result of and an indicator of severe sociocultural dislocation, it is closely associated with definite costs in terms of social disorganization: heightened levels of mental and physical illness, increased crime, lowered per capita productivity, lowered educational attainment and the destruction of communal functioning and communal authenticity. These costs have never been carefully estimated and it would be a distinct and feasible contribution to do so, were a workgroup on *the economics of language and language loss* to be formed. Although there are a number of 'economic linguists' in our own ranks (Jernudd, Coulmas and Grin immediately come to mind, but I know from a forthcoming issue of the *International Journal of the Sociology of Language* that there are at least half a dozen others as well), a topic such as this would require working together with

additional economists as well as sociologists specializing in the various types of social disorganization. Concentration on this issue would reveal the extent to which our area of specialization can seriously contribute to an appreciation of *the sociocultural and socio-economic costs of language attrition, language shift and language loss.*

(3)   As researchers in an area of specialization that is essentially outside of and broader than education, we tend to be surprisingly mesmerized by schools and by schooling. Perhaps this is a matter of practical convenience (schools provide 'captive subjects' for our data collection forays), perhaps it is a matter of funding (ministries and boards of education provide research grants for ourselves and our students), or perhaps it is merely a sign of our innocence (we are products of far more than the usual number of years of schooling and, as bookish folk are wont to do, we tend to think of education as the dominant factor in our society and culture). All of this would be understandable and harmless enough, were it not for the fact that we tend to make societal extrapolations on this basis – favoring education as the cure-all for sociolinguistic ills – as well. I have noticed this repeatedly. When I was studying reversing language shift, most sociolinguists with whom I discussed my work were convinced that 'the schools could turn any language around', oblivious of the fact that exactly this has proven to be impossible in almost every well documented case. Now that I am at work on 1940–1950 status change experienced by English in former British and American colonies, I once again encounter this exaggerated attention to the schools, among colleagues who are trying to explain why English did or did not experience substantial status-change in their respective countries.

What disturbs me about this approach, is not only that it is so completely an 'average man-in-the-street' analysis of social processes and social problem solution (after all, my next door neighbor also 'knows' that the schools can fix anything if they were only seriously inclined to do so), but that it is so devoid of either theory or data *vis-à-vis* the intergenerational transmission of language in society and culture. To put this yet another way, given that almost any reversing language shift effort should involve the schools too (I say 'almost any', because there are cultures in which school involvement in such a process is specifically ruled out, either because the schools are 'enemy instruments' and, therefore, they cannot be trusted or because the vernacular is not considered 'schoolworthy' and schools are focused on a different language entirely), one must still ask 'what kind of school' and 'what kind of schooling', particularly in the light of the manifold past failures along these lines. Convening a small group of specialists to discuss, analyze, plan research on and review research findings pertaining to *this* question, formulated in *this* way, that would really be worthwhile! Why do Basque and Maori schools succeed where Irish and Frisian schools fail? Why do Old Order Amish and Jewish Ultra-Orthodox schools succeed while nearly all other minority schools in the USA fail? A comparative sociology of education in the service of reversing language shift is long overdue and a focused invitational conference on this topic would be a real contribution.

(4)   And while we are on 'reversing language shift' (Fishman, 1991), let me add that it would be highly desirable to pay more attention to the various other facets of the total language maintenance phenomenon as well. One particularly overlooked aspect of that complex societal endeavor is the 'Language Movement'. All over the world one can encounter organized groups who devote their time, money, effort, fervor and devotion to fostering a threatened language-in-culture that is particularly dear to its members. These groups differ from each other in every conceivable way (size, resources, absence or presence (and if the latter, type) of political affiliation, absence or presence of religious affiliation, absence or presence of territorial goals, degree of more general communal involvement beyond language *per se*, acceptance or rejection of bilingualism, technical linguistic sophistication and concern, types of language focused activities engaged in (education, publications, political efforts, research, literary competitions, literacy campaigns, camping, youth groups, choruses, theatrical groups, child care), etc.). All of these topics would benefit from comparative synchronic study across language lines, of course, but they should also be studied diachronically relative to some criterion or other of reversing language shift. Such studies would be particularly useful outside of Europe – e.g. in conjunction with Ainu, Berber, Yiddish, Romani, Maori, Koori, etc. – although many smaller and minoritized languages in Europe also remain relatively unexplored (e.g. Rusyn, Alsatian, Sorbian, Saami, etc.). A conference to initiate and foster research on such movements would not only be intellectually rewarding but could be highly useful to the futures of many of the languages as well.

## Beyond Academic Exercises

What do all of the above suggestions have in common? They all reflect my concern that the study of language maintenance and language shift may, unconsciously, have been coopted by the very same establishments that are ultimately responsible for or involved in and contributors to most of the sociolinguistic dislocation that has now reached epidemic proportions in the world round about us. They subsidize our conferences, they subscribe to our journals, they maintain the universities that provide most of us with our livelihoods. We depend on them to promote us, to send us students and to award us prizes. The routinization, over-intellectualization, under-involvement and general lack of topical bite or conclusiveness that marks our conferences (and makes us satisfied with going on from one conference to another *ad infinitum*), leaves us painfully unaware of or self-protectedly sheltered from the suffering and pain, the tears and travail, hopes and aspirations of the peoples, societies and cultures we are studying. Of course, it is partly our duty to be objective intellectualizers, rather than manning the barricades and staffing the emergency wards. But just as law-school professors must spend some time in courts, jails and law-offices in order to remain in touch with law and justice as real-life processes, rather than just as abstractions, so we must periodically draw closer to the realities of the world that we are studying. Topically focused conferences might help us realize how detached from our actual subject matter we have become. Ultimately, however, good conferences are not enough, no matter how focused they may be, to help us understand the wicked world. We constantly need to search for ways to be immersed in that world in a helping capacity and to emerge from it with new empirical and theoretical insights, sensitivities, intuitions and . . . yes, also responsi-bilities. In a world that is as deeply splattered with social and cultural tragedy as ours is, good conferences – even better conferences – are not enough, and they are not only not enough for the amelioration of eth-nolinguistic dislocation, they are not even enough for the more powerful intellectualization that our field of endeavor requires and deserves.

## Bibliography

Fishman, J.A. (1954) The role of the culture-group affiliation of the 'judge' in Thurstone attitude-scale construction (Abstract, with Irving Lorge). *American Psychologist* 9, 368–369.

_____. (1991) Interpolity perspective on the relationships between linguistic het-erogeneity, civil strife and per capita gross national product. *Applied Linguistics* 1, 5–18.

_____. (1991) *Reversing Language Shift*. Clevedon, Multilingual Matters.

_____. (1993) *The Earliest Stage of Language Planning: The 'First Congress' Phenom-enon*. Berlin, Mouton.

## Chapter 9

# Prospects for Reversing Language Shift (RLS) in Australia: Evidence from its Aboriginal and Immigrant Languages

The amazingly variegated country and continent of Australia is often overlooked in RLS discussions but, actually, some of the most interesting and contrasted processes and policies are to be encountered there. The Aborigines ('Austraindians' might be the American term for that continent's pre-European natives), on the one hand, and the post-World War II immigrants and their children, on the other hand, represent two very different sociolinguistic constellations and, also, two very different sets of experiences and expectations *vis-à-vis* the Australian anglo and anglified mainstream. Although the 'bottom line' may be a similarly disappointing (or even shocking) one in both cases, there is nevertheless a great deal that has been accomplished against great odds, certainly in terms of idealism and ennoblement through struggle, if not yet in terms of RLS *per se*. However, the story is not over yet and the future is by no means preordained.

## Immigrational Diversity and Adversity: Cultivation and Resistance

Since the end of World War II, 'White' (i.e. non-Aboriginal) Australia has undergone a massive immigrational transfusion and transformation. A society that had preferred to remain under-populated during the pre-war years, rather than risk the cultural diversity that would be introduced by Orientals, other Asians (e.g. from India or Indonesia), 'Kanaka' (Pacific Islanders) and even by non-anglo Europeans, decided that its political and economic future had much more to lose than to gain from such exclusiveness. Although Europeans remained the immigrants of choice, various West Asian, South Asian, East Asian, South East Asian and Pacific Island immigrants were also admitted. Some two million non-angloceltic newcomers arrived in a country of roughly seven to eight million inhabitants all in all, and, at least initially, were received with relatively little racism and were acknowledged to be upright, family and mobility oriented citizens and worthy contributors to Australia's commercial and economic development.

With the coming to power of the Labour Party in 1972 (at a time that coincided with the 'ethnic revival', i.e. with an upsurge of self-conscious identity explorations among minority ethnics in Australia and, toward the tail-end of that process, in much of the Western world more generally), new immigrants found a particularly receptive environment also on the cultural front, with a degree of governmental assistance and acceptance that might well have been unprecedented in English mother tongue countries anywhere previously, including Australia itself. Although the 'peak of positiveness' attained in the early 80s has now been passed and voices of opposition and criticism are heard more often, the fact still remains that one out of every 12 Australians now speaks a language other than English at home (CLOTEs is the acronym by which the 'Community Languages Other Than English' are sometimes referred to, the more widespread designation simply being 'community language') and the amounts and kinds of support and recognition that these immigration-based languages receive is still noteworthy, even if their futures are far from assured.

## The Aboriginal Scene: Plus ça Change ...?

The Aboriginal scene has also undergone considerable change since the end of World War II and its re-evaluation in historical perspective has become more common, particularly given that 1988 represented the 200th anniversary of British settlement in Australia. Almost all are agreed that the first 125–150 years of this period constitute a shameful (and, in many cases, even a genocidally catastrophic) story of the destruction of traditional Aboriginal peoples via the expropriation of their traditional lands, the despoiling of their sacred sites, and their inhuman treatment in various ways, not stopping short of mass expulsions, forced re-settlement in inhospitable regions, mass poisonings, shootings and the separation of families (particularly the forced – and often Church-sponsored – separation of children from their parents).

The results were an initially huge increase in Aboriginal mortality (due to both maltreatment by Europeans and contagion from European diseases against which Aborigines had, as yet, developed no resistance) resulting in the total population dropping from more than a quarter million to roughly 80,000 in little over a century and a half. Although a demographic recovery has subsequently occurred, Aboriginal life is still marked by some of the highest rates of alcoholism, illness, discriminatory arrest and detention, unemployment, suicide and other indices of personal and social dislocation to be found anywhere in the world. For those who imagine that nothing could be worse than North and South American policies *vis-à-vis* the Amerindians it should be pointed out (without in any way seeking to apologize for those policies) that hundreds of treaties were signed (and broken) with Amerindians by the various American authorities, whereas Australia's Aborigines were long not really considered to be humans at all and, therefore, little in the way of treaties or negotiations of any kind were undertaken with them to begin with, and what little there was, whether oral or written, was subsequently simply ignored. They were merely 'expendable objects' and particularly so for the cattlemen, sheep raisers and mineral (or other natural resources) investors.

A change for the better was heralded in a 1967 referendum which gave the Federal ('Commonwealth') government authority in Aboriginal affairs, which, in turn, enabled a more enlightened approach to get underway when the Labour Party came to power (1972). State and Federal governments instituted provisions for recognizing and returning Aboriginal lands, for protecting Aboriginal sacred sites and for permitting Aborigines a measure of self-regulation with respect to their settlements, the education of their children and the use of their languages in the public media in their vicinity. Many of these promises have been subsequently abandoned or seriously compromised and others have led to little more than endless delays, legal wranglings, successive investigatory commissions, public recriminations (some of which have attained international notoriety, whether for their pro- or anti-Aboriginal positions), revived and vociferous racism and bitter political infighting.

The interested reader will find no difficulty in locating the extensive literatures dealing with all of these matters: the original horrors, the new promises, the continuing disappointments and the endless struggles (most recently, particularly in connection with the Aboriginal Land Rights issue).[1] Even as late as 1989, Survival International USA delivered thousands of signatures collected in 36 states and in 21 countries to the Australian embassy in Washington, supporting Aboriginal demands for land rights legislation. In the previous year, a Royal Commission on [Aboriginal] Deaths in [Police] Custody was established, with provision for Aboriginal input into its final report (due in 1990). We can only refer to all of these matters in passing – although the issues involved, particularly the issue of returning traditional lands, are basic ones for the very survival of Aboriginal languages and cultures – but we must remember to keep them in mind as we turn our focused attention to the RLS-efforts that accompany them.

### Stage 8: Reassembling the Language

None of the European or other immigrant languages are at an advanced state of disrepair and, even were that to be the case in connection with the oldest and smallest among them, the necessary 'repairs' would probably be undertaken elsewhere, in their respective home countries, rather than in Australia. In connection with the continent's Aboriginal languages, however, there are hundreds of languages and dialects (yes, hundreds) that require such repair and Australia proper is obviously the main location in which such repairs are and must be undertaken.

The exact number of Aboriginal languages and dialects that were spoken when Europeans first came to Australia is difficult to ascertain. The recently published *Language Atlas: Pacific*[2] lists over 700 languages and dialects but other specialists (e.g. Black, 1983) usually refer to a lower figure, namely, 'nearly 270 distinct languages'. If the former estimate is accepted it becomes clear that 80% of this number are either already extinct or have so few remaining speakers (less than 100) that their early demise is virtually a foregone conclusion. If the latter estimate is preferred, the results are nearly the same. Only some 50 languages remain that are relatively widely spoken (and often written) and of these only 18 have at least 500 speakers and, taken together, account for 25,000 of the approximately 30,000 remaining speakers of Aboriginal languages in Australia today.[3] Pessimistic observers conclude that only some two or three of these will retain any substantial vitality into the twenty-first century. Clearly, modern Australia has been a veritable graveyard of indigenous languages and the study of dying languages as well as the reassembly of dead and momentarily expiring ones has become a major linguistic occupation and preoccupation. Although such efforts add considerably to scholarly (and, ultimately, to the intelligent layman's) appreciation of human diversity, ingenuity and, in more recent days (since 'last living speakers' have also begun to be more intensively studied) cultural dedication as well, they provide scant comfort for the Aboriginal RLS advocate. Unfortunately, this is all the comfort that there can be in many cases.

### Stage 7: The Elderly Among Themselves: Learning, Relearning and Use Without Intergenerational Family or Integrated Community Functions

At this stage several of the older immigration-based languages (and some of the newer ones too, where the most rapid sociocultural change has occurred) enter our story. Particularly in small immigrant communities in the more rural hinterlands, outside of the major urban areas, but in some of the old ethnic neighborhoods of the latter as well, it is not an uncommon occurrence for 'old-timers' to get together with each other and to use the 'old language' when they do. There are innumerable small gatherings full of good fellowship and quiet camaraderie, programs of considerable cultural (literary, musical, educational) sophistication, at which not a single person of childbearing age or younger is or can be present. At this stage ethnic languages continue to be spoken with complete proficiency, even if code-switching to English is often quite common, but the intergenerational heirs of these languages are 'conspicuous by their scarcity'. Because of the relative recency of massive post-World War II immigration to Australia this scenario is not yet common among Italian, German, Croatian, Greek, Macedonian, Chinese, Vietnamese, Russian, Hebrew or other languages of recent arrivals (but note that there are now no direct linguistic heirs of the earlier waves of German, Italian or Chinese speakers). Various recent language policies of Australian authorities and institutions have also tended to slow down some of the processes whereby this stage assumes 'typical' proportions. Nevertheless, unless subsequent stages soon become more successful than they have been thus far, this is the stage that will become clearly predominant during the 1990s. Once this stage becomes predominant, a virtual sociocultural revolution in the lives of young people is required before it can again be superseded on an intergenerational and community-wide basis.

It is among Aborigines, particularly among those who are speakers of languages other than the top 18, that we not only most often find this stage but that we find it in its most painfully enfeebled manifestations. Thus, a brochure inviting Gooris (more usually 'Kooris', an increasingly popular indigenous self-designation applying to and uniting all Aborigines and favored by some as a collective term to replace Aborigine/Aboriginal) to participate in a series of six weekly seminars about Bundjalung,[4] a language of Southeast Australia that is now down to its last few dozen speakers, promises that the seminars will enable them to 'learn more about a language that existed in these areas, learn the sounds of Bundjalung, and ... use ... Bundjalung words and phrases in ... everyday (English) conversation'. This, indeed, is a type of Reversing Language Shift, but it is RLS of the last possible and most urgent kind. The fact that it can no longer lead to proficiency (not to mention intergenerational proficiency, which now seems to be an unobtainable goal for Bundjalung and scores of other Aboriginal languages) makes it no less important and, possibly, no less contributory to identity and self-concept.

Another Aboriginal venture at this stage has to do with the collective preparation and subsequent enjoyment of 'alphabet books' in a few language communities. These books (booklets would be the more appropriate characterization) contain one English letter (upper and lower case) on each page, as well as an English word beginning with

Notes:

| | |
|---|---|
| ☐ | Creole |
| ☐ | Aboriginal English |
| ○ | Languages with more than 500 speakers (as listed) |
| ◌ | Languages with more than 250 speakers (but less than 500) |
| — - — - — | Limit of complete communication in Aboriginal languages |

N.B.: The numbers of speakers of each language are approximations listed for guidance only.

| Language | Speakers | Language | Speakers |
|---|---|---|---|
| 1. Kriol | 15 000 | 12. Western Desert, western | 900 total |
| 2. Torres Strait creole | 15 000 | a. Manyjilyjarra | 500 |
| 3. Western Desert, eastern | 3 000 total | b. Yulharidja | 200 |
| a. Pitjantjatjara | 1 000 | c. Martu Wangka | 200 |
| b. Pintupi and Luritja | 800 | 13. Murrinh-Patha | 800 |
| c. Kgaanyatjarra | 700 | 14. Nyangumarta | 700-800 |
| d. Gugadja | 300 | 15. Miriam | 700? |
| e. Wangkatja | 200-300 | 16. Yindjibarndi | 600 |
| 4. Aranda dialects: | 3 000 total | 17. Guugu Yimidhirr | 600 |
| a. Western Aranda | 1 000 | 18. Burarra | 400-600 |
| b. Eastern Aranda | 1 000 | 19. Dhangu dialects: | |
| c. Anmatjirra | 800 | a. Gaalpu | 200 |
| 5. Warlpiri | 2 800 | b. Wangurri | 150 |
| 6. Kala Lagaw Ya | 2 800 | 20. Alyawarra | 400-500 |
| 7. Dhuwal-Dhuwala dialects | 1 600-1 700 total | 21. Nunggubuyu | 300-400 |
| | | 22. Garawa | 300-400 |
| a. Gupapyungu | 450 | 23. Wik-Munkan | 300 |
| b. Gumarj | 250 500 | 24. Kitya | 300 |
| c. Djambarrpuyngu | 250-450 | 25. Kuku-Yalanji | 300 |
| 8. Tiwi | 1 400 | 26. Ritharngu | 300 |
| 9. Walmajarn | 1 300 | 27. Gurindji | 250 |
| 10. Anindilyakwa | 1 000 | 28. Djaru | 250 |
| 11. Gunwinggu | 900 | Source: Australian Institute of Aboriginal Studies | |

**Figure 9.1.** Prominent Australian Aboriginal Languages (Source: Senate Standing Committee on Education and the Arts, 1984)

that letter, the indigenous equivalent of that word, and a folksy illus-
trated story or explanation related to the indigenous word. Local linguists and teachers have taken to preparing such alphabet books in
ways that maximize local participation in the selection of the words
whose indigenous equivalents are felt to be of greatest use or interest,
and in the joint authorship of the accompanying stories. Wherever
possible, local artists are approached to illustrate the booklets, and
the entire interactive process is tape-recorded so as to preserve other
indigenous words and phrases that often are utilized in the discussions
that surround and constitute the total enterprise. These booklets are
then allowed to circulate among the participants (and particularly
among the oldest members of their communities) in try-out versions
and are then revised before finally being published by school or
other local developmental authorities.

Although indigenous people often feel that these little alphabet books
help them 'repossess their history', these publications have sometimes
also become very popular among tourists and other non-Aborigines in
the local areas who have bought many copies of them at airports and
other local shops. Minor though these books may be in terms of more
functionally ambitious RLS proper, they have been experienced as local
triumphs in symbolic and interpersonal respects pertaining to the indigenous identities involved. Indeed, it is for this reason that these efforts
are discussed for the first time here, rather than in stage 8, above, or in
stages 6 or 4a, below. Adults who fully realize the extent of the Xish
language attrition and culture change that is going on round about
them are the prime movers, and possibly the prime benefactors, in connection with these 'little alphabet books'. They see them as symbolic of
a former, all-encompassing way of life, a pattern which youngsters can
no longer reassemble in their mind's eye, and which would vanish
without a trace were it not for the booklets produced in order to impart
a whiff of their authentic flavor.[5] Under the new National Language
Policy (see below), the National Aboriginal Language Program now provides some support for such and similar initiatives, a welcome but basically ineffectual RLS departure from the uncaring policies of the recent
past.

A basic problem for the intergenerational transmission of immigrant
languages in Australia (some would say: 'the basic problem') is the fact
that they do not have their own relatively inviolate space, their own concentrated communities in which their own language-and-culture can
dominate or at least where like-minded RLS-minded families can easily
reinforce one another by dint of daily interaction and implementation
of similar norms and values. Such relatively self-contained communities

(in rural areas) and neighborhoods (in urban areas) are not uncommon during the early first generation years and the oldest children in immigrant families frequently grew up in such settings. However, differential social mobility leads to residential mobility as well and the primary settlements are slowly eroded as the most successful immigrants leave them behind for more comfortable, more attractive and more prestigious quarters.

Secondary settlement areas are, almost without exception, urban or suburban (contributing to the early demise or enfeeblement of rural ethnic communities), of low population density and ethnically mixed or 'non-ethnic' in composition. Language maintenance becomes dependent not on natural, daily neighborhood interaction but on relatively infrequent institutional and extra-neighborhood 'visits' to co-ethnic stores, schools, clubs, churches, family and friends (some of whom have remained in the 'old neighborhoods' and are, therefore, inevitably tainted by the stigma of 'not having made it'), visits that are too scattered to provide a critical mass *vis-à-vis* either natural language use or cultural implementation for a new generation that never experienced the full-blown 'real thing'. Younger children of immigrants are largely socialized in such contexts and second generation ethnics tend to raise their own families in these contexts, again almost without exception.

These secondary settlement areas themselves are not sufficiently self-regulatory *vis-à-vis* ethnolinguistic socialization and *vis-à-vis* the implementation of daily Xish language-in-culture to foster the reliable intergenerational transmission of immigrant languages in open and mobility-affording host contexts. The 'visits to ethnic addresses and points of interest' are clearly insufficient to substitute for what is lacking in daily life. Such visits can contribute to identifying with the symbols of ethnic culture but they are not sufficient for maintaining a full and evolving ethnolinguistic repertoire, let alone the substantially self-regulatory ethnolinguistic social boundaries on which ethnolinguistic intergenerational continuity ultimately depends. As Xishness withdraws into a more selective corner of the total life space it gets along with only snatches of Xish (linguistically), 'Xish appreciation' at best, just as it is increasingly based on memories of, stories about, and judicious ('inoffensive') selections from Xish culture. The path to functioning as Xmen-via-Yish is paved with good intentions and is well underway in most post-World War II immigrant-derived communities in Australia today. The lack (indeed, the increasing lack) of intergenerational linkages and Xish community-wide functions for the immigrant languages is becoming increasingly evident, to outside scholars and policy makers and to inside Xmen alike.[6]

## Stage 6: Family–Neighborhood–Community Based Language Maintenance in Which the Link to the Younger Generation is Established and Retained

That which the immigrant languages have generally been unable to do, particularly in the larger urban centers of southeastern Australia (Melbourne and Sydney) in which most of them are so overwhelmingly concentrated, has, to a very modest degree, been accomplished by a very few Aboriginal languages in the remoter areas of central, western and northwestern Australia. Actually, there is a two-part tale to be told in this connection, one chapter of which exemplifies the negative consequences of a type of intergenerational concentration in which ethnocultural self-regulation is either minimal or out of the question entirely, and the other chapter of which exemplifies intergenerational concentration precisely for the purpose of attaining greater ethnocultural self-regulation. The first chapter, another sad chapter in the long Aboriginal tale of suffering under white rule, deals with the forced removal (under the Protection Acts) of most Aborigines in the northern and central regions of the country into 'settlements', 'missions' or 'reserves'. The Acts, ostensibly passed in order to protect Aborigines from being gunned down on their own lands, in fact gave the local authorities the right to legally force Aborigines off their land and then transfer or assign these lands to White individuals or companies.

Both by design and by ignorance, ethnoculturally diverse (and, therefore, also linguistically diverse) and, often, traditionally antagonistic Aboriginal populations were resettled together, under the administration of white managers, on impoverished soil and in climatically severe locations considered to be of no conceivable agricultural, pastoral or mineral value to Whites. Here, the very hopelessness of their situation resulted both in Aboriginal sociocultural dislocation and anomie (since it was impossible to observe traditional site-related ceremonies and practices there) and in rampant Aboriginal personal dislocation (alcoholism, violence, widespread illness and malnutrition, increased infant mortality, shortened life-spans, etc.). Many Aborigines still live under such wretched conditions today, even though their legal circumstances have changed with the granting of citizenship and political rights in the 1960s, because of a combination of inertia, discrimination and lack of the necessary skills that would make it possible for them to compete successfully for the rewards available to other minorities within mainstream society. Under these horrendous circumstances RLS is impossible, even though intergenerational communities exist. Negative self-concepts and negative views toward Aboriginal cultures abound, concepts that foster further language shift and ludicrous identification with the oppressor, rather than with one's own heritage.

Beginning in the 1960s, roughly at the same time as the first beginnings of the 'ethnic revival' in much of the rest of the world (but, probably, in no way directly linked to that still insufficiently understood more general phenomenon), there began a self-directed movement to leave the above-mentioned disruptive settings and to resettle in 'outstations' where Aborigines could more completely regulate their own lives by concentrating primarily on otherwise unpopulated or 'undesirable' traditional lands. Most of these first 'outstations' – receiving no governmental support or assistance and being actively discouraged or opposed by white authorities – failed and were subsequently abandoned. However, after a decade of continued efforts along these lines, and, finally, with encouragement from newly supportive governmental spokesmen and programs, an increasing number of outstations began to stabilize in the 1970s. By now, there are nearly 600 such settlements (not all of them being permanently occupied at any particular time due to the seasonal movements in which some groups traditionally or innovatively participate), the total universe of such settlements being very varied in many demographic, material and cultural respects.

These communities, most of them very small in terms of the number of residents living in them, now accommodate approximately 10,000 inhabitants all in all, or only between 3% and 4% of the entire Aboriginal population, most of whom live in country towns and urban centers, either unable or unwilling to move to outstations. Life in the outstations is far from easy, but it is a life in accord with one or another Aboriginal culture and, therefore, a life that is also played out in the appropriate vernacular and liturgical languages pertaining to these cultures. More and more of these outstations are also beginning to provide supportive contexts for Aboriginal customs, Aboriginal music (traditional and new) and Aboriginal foods and for such innovations as Aboriginal literacy and, more generally, for the self-regulated adoption and adaptation of modern artifacts and knowledge, on the one hand, and their combination with Aboriginal counterparts, on the other hand. A common slogan in such settlements (and one that we will encounter again in our discussion of schooling, below) is 'both ways' or 'two ways', implying that *it is not a total isolation from the modern world that is desired at all, but, rather, an ability to retain that which is selected from the tradition alongside that which is adopted from the outside,* and to do both the one and the other under community control of the decision-making, implementation and evaluation processes.

Neither the current importance nor the future stability of the outstations should be exaggerated. Most Aboriginal cultures and languages cannot possibly benefit from them because of the physical remoteness and limited economic prospects of these settlements. Nevertheless, they provide interesting and important examples of how RLS depends on 'first things first' and how stage 6 becomes the launching pad for further crucial stages, the relationship between the outstations and the Aboriginal land rights efforts being a particularly intimate and symbiotic one.[7]

Immigrant languages in Australia have yet to consciously develop and maintain intergenerationally intact communities that are similarly self-regulating in cultural respects and, therefore, that have similar RLS potential. Their conceptual, residential and occupational over-identification with and involvement in mainstream modernity submerges them entirely in processes that they can neither control nor mitigate. All of their language maintenance efforts, discussed below, are, therefore, built on shifting sands and are unlikely to result in intergenerational mother tongue transmission beyond the second generation, language shift often taking place within the very first (the immigrant) generation itself.

### Stage 5: Literacy Via Agencies or Institutions that are Entirely Under Xish Control and that do NOT Need to Meet or Satisfy Yish Standards Re Compulsory Education

Immigrant languages in Australia are served by impressively large numbers of community-supported ethnic group schools. These schools meet during after-school hours or on weekends, primarily in quarters of their own (although sometimes quarters are rented from public schools, libraries or other public agencies) and do not intend to meet compulsory education requirements (although Australian public school authorities can grant 'academic credits', upon examination, in connection with many of the languages that students acquire in these schools). The two parenthetical phrases inserted above imply that immigrant ethnic group schools are not totally outside of the public reward (and control) system in Australia, but they are still primarily self-contained and, as such, deserve to be considered here.

There are various estimates of the number of schools and pupils that are involved in stage 5 efforts pertaining to immigrant languages in Australia. A 1985 government report estimated that in 1983 there were over 65,000 students attending 1200 ethnic schools (primarily in the states of Victoria, in which Melbourne is located, and New South Wales, in which Sydney is located) and studying 51 different languages. In addition, there were more than twice as many more studying in 'insertion classes' run by ethnic community organizations, for at least one hour once a week, but held in public schools during regular school hours. The language maintenance emphases of these schools, their co-emphases on the transmission of traditional and authentic cultural values and behaviors which foster language learning, and the extreme variety of languages that the totality of these schools encompass were also governmentally recognized as making noteworthy contributions to the non-English language resources that are considered to be of value to Australia (based on the fact that an estimated 65% of the students attending these schools speak at home the language that they are studying in their ethnic school) and, therefore, as meriting a measure of financial support from both the Commonwealth and the State governments.

Greater collaboration between the ethnic community supplementary schools and the public schools is envisaged in South Australia in accord with the recent Kisoylous Report (and similar moves are underway in Victoria), in which sharing of teachers, exchange of credits and other such measures are envisaged. The sophistication and the sympathetic stance revealed by these recent governmental views and arrangements is further attested to by the recognition that such support and collaboration could entail an inevitable degree of loss of autonomy for the schools (the government wanting to set some standards re adequacy of facilities, curricular soundness and teacher certification in the schools receiving its support) and that any 'other measures which may further weaken this autonomy should be treated with some caution'.[8]

While it is difficult to estimate either the degree of language mastery actually attained in these schools or the amount of government support that they receive, let alone the language maintenance consequences of such support, it is quite clear that these schools are being encouraged, on the one hand, and increasingly influenced, on the other hand. The funding of curriculum and educational materials centers for these schools, the institution of teaching credentials and the organization of seminars for teachers already credentialed, and the recognition (via certification) of students from these schools who have reached a sufficient level of achievement, these are all encouraging signs of appreciation which maintenance and RLS activists would be happy to attain in all other modern, Westernized countries throughout the world. On the other hand, it is worrisome that there is no sign at all that the efforts of these schools, whether with or without governmental help, have generally had any demonstrably positive consequences insofar as RLS is concerned, particularly given the ongoing residential mobility and 'thinning out' of Australia's urban second generation population which makes attendance at these schools an increasingly 'time consuming' pursuit. The more recent budgetary squeeze in Australian education, particularly in education that is not directly oriented toward increased production and technological capacity, has also added a strong element of doubt as to how much longer governmental co-funding of ethnic group schools will continue. In addition, the increasing governmental stress on the major diplomatic and commercial languages of the Pacific rim (Japanese, Mandarin, Korean, Indonesian) also tends to downplay (and to eat up funds that might otherwise be available for) instruction of most ethnic community languages.

The additional fact that these schools almost completely overlook the maintenance and cultivation of literacy among their graduates (and in their parental support-constituencies as well) is yet another reason to doubt whether they ultimately can make a reliable contribution to RLS. Without any corresponding and vibrant adult literacy with which to link up, second or third generation childhood literacy in an immigrant language tends to be little more than a fleeting rite of initiation, a *rite de passage* that marks a stage which is left behind almost as soon as it is reached.[9]

In the Aboriginal sector, community-operated literacy imparting institutions, whether for children or for adults, are still few and far between and particularly so under auspices that have nothing to do with meeting the educational requirements that have been governmentally instituted. Examples of such programs on a small scale are the one-week and two-week adult courses in Alyawarre (400–500 speakers), Warumungu (? speakers), Warlmanpa (? speakers) and Warlpiri (2800 speakers) conducted in and around Tennant Creek, Northern Territory, by the Barkly Region Aboriginal Language Center. There are also a few tertiary level institutions located in areas near Aboriginal concentrations (e.g. the Institute for Aboriginal Development in Alice Springs, NT) that offer vernacular literacy courses at a non-degree adult education level, often, but not always, as preliminary to their more focused efforts to foster English reading and writing. In addition, there are also missionary groups that offer vernacular literacy courses to adult Aborigines (and to younger Aborigines as well) in conjunction with their more basic Christianizing and Bible study emphases. All in all, however, the disparity between Australian governmental assistance to ethnic community stage 5 schools for immigrants and their children and its thinly disguised lack of interest in the establishment of networks of such schools for Aborigines is quite marked, notwithstanding the support for a few Aboriginal community schools under the program providing grants for ethnic community schools more generally. The first constituency is being helped to pass into an 'Xmen-via-Yish' (English) stage by means of generously subsidized cooption into the Yish system; the other, by a surfeit of what is, at best, a variant of benign neglect.

### Stage 4a: Xish-Sponsored and Conducted Schools that are Attended In Lieu of Meeting Compulsory Education Requirements

There seems to be no complete census of the all-day schools teaching ethnic 'community languages' and sponsored primarily by the various immigrant-based ethnic groups in Australia. I would estimate that there are no more than 50 such schools, all in all, and probably fewer than that, all but a few handfuls of them being at the elementary school level, with approximately 10,000 students. The lion's share of these schools are under religious auspicies, Hebrew (and, much more rarely, Yiddish too) being taught in the Jewish ones, Greek in most of the Orthodox ones and Italian, German, Polish, Spanish, Portuguese, Vietnamese and perhaps a very few other languages too in the multi-ethnic Catholic ones. All of these schools receive direct and indirect governmental funds which cover a very sizeable proportion of their costs, the remaining costs being covered by tuition fees and community fund-raising efforts. The amount of time devoted to ethnic community language acquisition and, subsequently, to ethnic community language use in the study of other ethnic subjects varies tremendously, from no more than a few hours per week (and as an elective subject to boot) and only in certain years of study, to approximately half of the entire school day in all years of instruction. The results also vary greatly, from little more than passive language appreciation all the way through to fluent speech and creative writing.

In the infrequent cases where these schools still correspond to stable population concentrations in primary settlement ethnic neighborhoods, they, their teachers and their lay school boards undoubtedly make a contribution to intergenerational language maintenance, at least into the adolescent years, when out-of-community influences and opportunities begin to become predominant among pupils. Social mobility and its resulting residential dislocations become the ultimate arbiters of whether the ethnic day-school education provided with so much voluntary dedication and ethnic community effort has any intergenerational impact on the RLS front, or whether it remains little more than a residual memory as far as everyday language use is concerned. The latter outcome already appears to be far more typical than the former one and may be expected to become increasingly so.

In the Aboriginal ranks such schools (usually referred to as 'independent schools') are both few in number and small in size – no more than nine or ten in all, as of early 1989, the exact number being somewhat difficult to pin down due to the fact that there are a few schools of an interstitial type that reveal both type 4a and type 4b characteristics. These are government-funded but under Aboriginal curricular, personnel and administrative control (like the Navajo 'contract schools') and are all situated in areas in which a good bit of Aboriginal self-regulation in many other respects is also common. Most of the type 4a schools initially came into being thanks to the support received from church and other charitable funds. Several, located in very remote areas, were established by Aborigines contrary to the explicit advice and warnings of the State educational authorities, who were convinced that 'there is no practical possibility of the children in homeland centres receiving a complete school program [particularly insofar as English and mathematics are concerned] at a level comparable to that in [the government's] central schools'.[10] The criterion for this judgment was doubtlessly the future success of Aboriginal students in communicating with white Australians and 'getting ahead' in social contexts dominated by them. But this could no longer be an appropriate criterion of a desirable school program for parents who opted to live in settings where their own culture, rather than that of white Australia alone, would be a major component of everyday life. It should also be noted that not all independent Aboriginal schools are in 'outstations' – indeed, several of them are in towns and urban areas (e.g. in Townsville, Perth, Alice Springs, etc.) but that it was there that the notion of autonomous Aboriginal life-style and educational process first took hold.

One of the very first independent Aboriginal schools was the one established in Strelley, Western Australia, in 1976. It soon developed several campuses in neighboring communities, all of them administered entirely by local Aboriginal school boards. These schools were noteworthy for their emphases on the traditional Aboriginal religious lore and laws of the region that they served, thus providing the ultimate justification for stressing vernacular languages as well. Interestingly and appropriately enough, the school programs were preceded by extensive *adult vernacular literacy programs* (one in Nyangumarta [roughly 800 speakers] and the other in Manjiljarra [roughly 500 speakers]). In this fashion, *children were later socialized into the educated use of languages that their elders could already read and write*, literacy thereupon uniting the generations rather than separating them. English too is taught, of course, but as a foreign language.

Of the handful of other independent and vernacular-stressing schools (and, it should be noted, not all independent Aboriginal schools are vernacular-stressing, if for no other reason than the fact that most Aborigines no longer control a vernacular that they can stress and, therefore, other guiding educational rationales must be operative among a segment of Aborigines seeking greater independence from white society), the best known by far is the Yipirinya ( = 'caterpillar', a reality in local fauna and a character in local Aboriginal lore) School in Alice Springs (south-central Northern Territory). Its fame is partly based on its long struggle (1979–1984) for governmental recognition (and, therefore, financial assistance) since the Northern Territory educational authorities seemed to be set on making an example of it (due to its Aboriginal curricular content, shortened in-school-day as a result of frequent school-sponsored visits to the 'bush', and preference for and reliance upon uncertified Aboriginal – and, often, on elderly Aboriginal – teachers). After five

years of inadequate funding (supplied by church and charitable organizations, both from Australia and abroad), terribly inadequate quarters, and
inadequate ability to attain its own programmatic goals, the school was
not only 'registered' by the authorities (after a Supreme Court decision
in its favor), but vindicated by 'higher authorities'. The House of
Representatives' Select Committee on Aboriginal Education (1985) came
to the conclusion, partly on the basis of the notoriety attained by the
Yipirinya School's struggle, that 'the existence of alternatives in
Aboriginal education ... constitutes a strength in the community. Also,
as expressions of Aboriginal self-determination and ... community
control, Aboriginal independent schools should be encouraged' and
'recurrent funding ... should be made available' to them so that they
could operate without undue hardships. This, at long last, represented
the extension to Aborigines of the facilitative approach to independent
education that had long been available to Australia's immigrant ethnic
groups.

The Yipirinya School was initially set up by parents living in the Aboriginal peripheral camps outside of Alice Springs because the local public
schools consistently alienated their children both from education and
from Aboriginal life. The Yipirinya School, run by an all-Aboriginal
school council which makes all curricular, policy and administrative
decisions and is the official 'principal' of the school, aims at combining
both Aboriginal culture and 'whitefella skills'.[11] The school is still a relatively tiny one (roughly 60 students in its primary division and 25 in its
post-primary division, the latter not yet having been 'registered' by the
Northern Territory Education Department) but, nevertheless, it is necessary for it to trichotomize its vernacular efforts, Mparntwe Arrente
(approximately 1000 speakers), Western Arrente (approximately 1000
speakers) and Luritja (approximately 800 speakers together with a
variety also known as Pintupi) all being utilized with different student
groups drawn from nine different Aboriginal camps in and around
Alice Springs.

As in the Navajo and Maori schools that we have discussed in Chapters
7 and 8, the Yipirinya School makes substantial use of older members of
the local Aboriginal cultures in connection with its traditional studies,
both on and off campus (e.g. in weekly expeditions into the 'bush'
where familiarization with Aboriginal lore and its relationship to local
flora and fauna is acquired in a more natural setting directly related to
the very tales, songs, dances and religious practices being taught). On
the other hand, non-Aboriginal teachers are employed by the School
Council to teach English and other non-Aboriginal subject matter,
thereby further emphasizing the distinction between what is 'own' and
what is 'foreign'. A new intergroup consensus as to the overall success

of the school is evidenced by the fact that it has recently begun to plan additional new buildings (above and beyond those recently completed), these plans being pursued with funds from the Commonwealth educational authorities. Thus, against great odds, the long and painful struggle for another (the ninth) independent Aboriginal school, a school that is able to pick and choose its own way in the difficult quest for 'two ways' education for Aboriginal children, seems to be drawing to a successful – even if only locally significant – conclusion. Above all, finally, Yipirinya is an example of how RLS requires that language and culture be pursued together, holistically and intergenerationally, with enough, unembarrassed, voluntary self-separation from the mainstream so that distinctiveness can be attained, maintained and selectively modified and combined with the culture of the surrounding 'big brother'. In 1988, when the Yipirinya School moved from its inadequate, initial 'mobile home' structure into a larger, governmentally funded new site in Alice Springs, this was taken (and rightfully so) as a positive indication of a new stage in the recognition of its hard-won autonomy.

Some of the other independent schools have succeeded against even greater cultural odds than those faced by the Yipirinya School. At the Kulkarriya Community School children have been guided back to Walmajarri-at-school, after they and their older siblings (and, indeed, most adults under 30 years of age) had already shifted to Kriol and to English. This was done as a result of parental/grandparental insistence and careful supervision of their new community school. Local observers now expect these children to begin utilizing Walmajarri in their out-of-school and community interactions in the near future. If the language can then be societally nurtured until these youngsters have children of their own, preferably via intensifying stage 6 and 5 efforts for young and middle-aged adults too, thereby recreating a community that functions increasingly via the language, then a revival of Walmajarri can be said to have occurred.

### Stage 4b: Xish Programs in Yish Schools

The more dubious effectiveness of pursuing the RLS goal of fostering Xmen-via-Xish by being an invited guest in institutions obviously controlled by Yish authorities is evident in Australia in conjunction with both immigrant and Aboriginal languages. In the immigrant fold this approach is exemplified by the roughly 56,000 children attending 'insertion classes' which are sponsored in whole or in part by ethnic schools or organizations – although paid for by public education funds – and held *during regular school hours in the very quarters of the full-time public schools.* As in the case of the ethnic schools *per se* (see stage 5, above) a large variety of immigrant languages are instructed in this fashion (although, generally, during fewer hours per week) and a large number of part-time teachers are involved (and require State certificates in order to be retained for this purpose). However, the relative insignificance of this effort for RLS purposes is revealed by the fact that only 22% of all students in insertion classes are studying a language which is also spoken in their homes.

There are, of course, some positive outcomes of these efforts as well as of the even more mainstream-embedded efforts to introduce more and more community languages into the standard foreign language offerings of the public schools (elementary and secondary) themselves.[12] Among such positive outcomes are certainly (a) the 33% increase during recent years (1976–1986) in the number of candidates opting to be examined in foreign languages upon high school graduation (the absolute numbers rising from 20,000 to 30,000 during this period, and increasing again in 1987, despite overall declines in school enrollments and in foreign language enrollments) and (b) a similar increase in the number of tertiary level students preparing to become language teachers in general and 'ethnic community language' teachers in particular, and, therefore, a notable increase and a growing diversification in the language offerings of the tertiary institutions themselves.[13]

When all is said and done, however, these outcomes may help broaden and deepen Australian education and may even contribute somewhat to strengthening Australia's trade and political contacts with much of the rest of the world (both of these outcomes being rewarded and fostered from a variety of in-school and post-school sources of recognition and reinforcement), but their contribution to RLS is more likely to be extremely negligible, particularly so in light of the basic weaknesses in stage 6 (see above). Languages which have no assured environments and functions of their own can still be learned, but they are by and large ever so much more quickly lost, with the entire acquisition and loss experience being shrugged off as a frivolity of childhood and adolescence. RLS cannot be built out of such intergenerationally disconnected stuff, although such efforts contribute to 'interest in the language' and, thereby, may buy some time (at the most, until the native-speaking grandparents are gone; at the least, far less time than that) during which more substantive attempts can be launched.

### Stage 3: The Xish Work Spheres (Serving Xmen and/or Ymen)

There is very little to report in connection with RLS efforts in Australia at the stage 3 level. Even when the immigrant-derived population is occupationally clustered, such clustering is not of an intergenerational nature due to the social and demographic mobility of the second generations. As a result, the work sphere is not an organized RLS facilitator, not even when Xmen work together with each other nor even when other Xmen are their major employers or customers. Indeed, all of the usual immigrant stereotypes and negative associations *vis-à-vis* their own languages as disadvantages are encountered at work among both first and second generation immigrants, even though there are still many workplaces in which older immigrant workers continue informally to use their own languages among themselves. Significantly enough, such negative views are encountered, both overtly and covertly, even in such government-sponsored or co-sponsored enterprises on behalf of fostering 'multiculturism' as the ethnic schools (whether full-time or part-time), insertion classes and radio/television programming (see stage 2, below). Even in these contexts it is common to hear English spoken between those very individuals whose job responsibilities are, temporarily, those of ethnic mother tongue custodianship. Almost all of these folks, and particularly the second generation contingents among them, reveal that their work is 'just a job' and that they see no future in their language, neither individually nor socioculturally.

The situation is somewhat different among a substantial proportion of young Aborigines only in the 'outstations'. As might be expected, these are virtually always encountered speaking their own languages 'at work', particularly since the Western distinctions between 'home' and 'work' are not really applicable in such settings. Interestingly enough, the Aborigines living in these outstations have also been judged (by a white researcher commissioned by the Ministry of Aboriginal Affairs) to constitute 'the most economically independent [Aborigines] in the Northern Territory'.[14] Work and economic factors more generally are aspects of culture. RLS obtains when language and culture (including language and work) are intergenerationally integrated. When such integration between language and culture is not possible in the work sphere, all is not lost. But it becomes even more crucial to achieve that integration in the more foundational and self-regulated domains of the total interaction between language and culture.

### Stage 2: Local Mass Media and Governmental Services

As will be evident from our previous chapters, local mass media and governmental services can make positive contributions to RLS only to the extent that they are directly related to and connected to fundamental family–neighborhood–community functioning. They may well extend the vocabulary and help foster the 'modernity' images of the languages associated with them, thereby improving the attitudes toward these languages among their speakers. But the impact of this attitudinal improvement is soon lost insofar as RLS is concerned, unless that impact is explicitly and quickly fed back to the establishment, functioning and protection of the families, neighborhoods and communities in which these languages can be intergenerationally transmitted as mother tongues. Such 'feedback' contributions of the mass media and governmental services must be specifically planned and kept in mind. This is not merely because threatened languages cannot easily wait for generations until indirect effects may possibly build up sufficient 'atmosphere effect' to influence intergenerational mother tongue transmission. The need for positive feedback to stage 6 is also crucial because, if left to their own devices, local mass media and governmental services easily become negative RLS factors, because even when conducted partially in Xish they tend to tie their clienteles into larger, Yish-centered listening and viewing patterns too, indeed, into larger frames of reference than Xish or Xmen-via-Xish *per se*.

The Australian Department of Immigration and Ethnic Affairs estimated that there were about 100 immigrant-based ethnic newspapers in Australia in 1984, modally weeklies, with a combined readership (including both subscribers and pass-along readers) of approximately half a million. Even now, however, when the period of mass immigration is still relatively recent history, these periodical publications typically have a rather meager second generation readership (even when they introduce special youth sections in English or undertake to publish in both Xish and English in each of their sections). Apparently, second generation literacy in Xish is too weak and its commitments to Xish (or even to Xishness) too peripheral to require an Xish press, in whatever language, for their satisfaction. Accordingly, as is also the case in the USA, most Xish periodicals never make the transitions either to bilingual or to all-English formats. Such transitions assume an Xmen-via-Yish market and there is either no such market out there or it doesn't require a press of its own for its functioning. In either case, lacking the more fundamental supports at earlier stages, there is very little that the immigrant press is able to do that is immediately translatable into RLS payoff.[15]

Hardly any periodical press seems to exist in Aboriginal languages too (and there are also only a very few publishers who specialize in simple books and brochures in such languages), probably because of the continuing rarity of adult and adolescent literacy in these languages. During the coming decade or two, this may change at several of the larger Aboriginal settlements, some of which already publish weekly, monthly or irregular news-sheets (e.g. the Amjinginyi newsletter of the Barkly Region Aboriginal Languages Center), provided that the youngsters educated at the independent schools remain concentrated in their home communities, rather than spreading out and settling elsewhere in numbers too small and too diffused to contribute to effective family, neighborhood and community building.

The absence of any substantial second generation interest in the immigrant-based foreign language press is generally paralleled by a lack of interest on the part of that same generation in foreign language radio, on the one hand, and the much more substantial second generation interest in foreign language television and films, on the other hand. Of course, the level of interest in the latter may benefit considerably from the English subtitles with which they are both commonly accompanied. All in all, a great deal of attention and a sizeable amount of funding is currently being lavished on non-print media utilizing immigrant-based languages with very meager (if any) evidence of positive RLS consequences being derived therefrom. The positive social climate and public acceptability of ethnic community languages to which television and radio contribute is 'something', of course, but that 'something' is, in itself, not effective RLS, precisely because it is not intergenerationally linked from the point of view of mother tongue transmission.

In 1984, 40 radio stations throughout Australia broadcast in immigrant-based community languages for a total of nearly 600 hours per week (or an average of 15 hours per week per station). Four of these stations, in Adelaide, Brisbane, Melbourne and Sydney respectively, were full-time ethnic radio stations. To take the last-mentioned as an example, Radio 2EA broadcast in 53 'community languages of Australia' in 1985 (see Table 9.1), the more prominent of which (Greek, Italian, Arabic, Turkish and 'Yugoslav' – Serbian, Croatian, Slovenian and/or Macedonian) had daily or twice-daily broadcasts. These broadcasts and their counterparts elsewhere attracted a Commonwealth Government subsidy of $650,000, not counting the subsidies paid to stations to train the personnel involved in producing the programs and in presenting them. Nevertheless, it should be observed (as, indeed, it was observed by the media authorities themselves) that most of the programs were focused on entertainment (rather than on information) and that they were most successful in reaching the poorly educated with little knowledge of English (and, therefore, least successful in reaching a second generation listernership).

The situation with respect to immigrant language television and films is somewhat similar to what we have presented above for radio. Such broadcasts are much more recent in origin but they have already been expanded from Sydney and Melbourne to Canberra, all State capitals and several other cities (see Table 9.2). In 1985–1986, 29 languages were involved for an average of five and a quarter hours per day, constituting half of the total broadcast hours on the channel set aside for this purpose (Channel 0/28). These programs are considered to have informational and intercultural functions as well, due to their built-in community service announcement (three minutes out of every hour) and subtitles. It has become clear that these telecasts and films have a wide English-speaking

**Table 9.1** The non-English radio channel in Sydney, Newcastle and Wollongong (1985) broadcasts in 53 community languages every week

| Time | Monday | Tuesday | Wednesday | Thursday | Friday | Saturday | Sunday |
|---|---|---|---|---|---|---|---|
| 06:00 | Greek | Greek | Greek | Greek | Greek | Greek | Greek |
| 06:45 | Arabic | Arabic | Arabic | Arabic | Arabic | Arabic | Arabic |
| 07:30 | Croatian | Macedonian | Croatian | Serbian | Macedonian | Croatian | Slovenian |
| 08:15 | Italian | Italian | Italian | Italian | Italian | Italian | Italian |
| 09:00 | Assyrian | Polish | Polish | Armenian | Turkish | Hungarian | Dutch |
| 10:00 | German | Maltese | German | Portuguese | German | Lithuanian | Jewish[b] |
| 11:00 | Dutch | Ukrainian | Russian | Hungarian | Urdu | German | Ukrainian |
| 11:30 | Dutch | Ukrainian | Russian | Hungarian | Hindustani | German | Ukrainian |
| 12:00 | Spanish | Maltese | Spanish | Maltese | Spanish | Maltese | Maltese |
| 13:00 | Norwegian | Music | Aboriginal | Laotian | Khmer | Spanish | German |
| 13:30 | Bengali | 'Insight' | Aboriginal | Laotian | Music | Spanish | German |
| 14:00 | Tamil/Gujarati[c] | French | Vietnamese | Spanish | Jewish[b] | Music | Polish |

*(Continued)*

**Table 9.1** *Continued*

| Time | Monday | Tuesday | Wednesday | Thursday | Friday | Saturday | Sunday |
|---|---|---|---|---|---|---|---|
| 14:30 | Sinhalese/Punjabi[c] | French | Vietnamese | Spanish | Jewish[b] | Music | Polish |
| 15:00 | Arabic | Mandarin | Cantonese | Arabic | Russian | Russian | Arabic |
| 16:00 | Vietnamese | Korean | Swedish | Dutch | Tongan | Latvian | French |
| 16:30 | Vietnamese | Korean | Danish | Dutch | Fijian | Latvian | French |
| 17:00 | Turkish | Turkish | Turkish | Turkish | Turkish | Turkish | Turkish |
| 17:45 | Italian | Italian | Italian | Italian | Italian | Italian | Italian |
| 18:30 | Greek | Greek | Greek | Greek | Greek | Greek | Greek |
| 19:15 | Cantonese | Armenian | Jewish[b] | Mandarin | Assyrian | Romanian | Hindustani |
| 20:15 | Portuguese | Byelorusian | German | Slovak | Pilipino | Finnish | Czech |
| 21:15 | Hungarian | Spanish | Spanish | Ukrainin | Vietnamese | Estonian | Spanish |
| 22:15 | Serbian | Slovenian | Macedonian | Croatian | Serbian | Macedonian | Croatian |
| 23:00 | Celtic[a] | Serbian | Latvian | French | Arabic | German | Special |

[a]1st Monday in month: Gaelic-Scottish
2nd Monday in month: Welsh
3rd Monday in month: Gaelic-Irish
*Source:* Radio 2EA brochure.

[b]Presented in Hebrew, Yiddish and English
[c]Alternate weeks

**Table 9.2** English and non-English language television in Australia, 1985–1986

| Language | Number of hours | % of total program time |
|---|---|---|
| Arabic | 77.02 | 2.42 |
| Armenian | 4.30 | 0.13 |
| Bahsa Indonesian | 13.73 | 0.43 |
| Bulgarian | 12.23 | 0.38 |
| Chinese languages[a] | 82.76 | 2.60 |
| Czech | 83.74 | 2.63 |
| Danish | 35.09 | 1.10 |
| Dutch | 37.74 | 1.18 |
| English[a] | 1313.76 | 41.24 |
| Farsi | 0.85 | 0.03 |
| Finnish | 15.00 | 0.47 |
| Flemish | 3.60 | 0.11 |
| French | 154.92 | 4.86 |
| Gaelic | 1.05 | 0.03 |
| Georgian | 1.28 | 0.04 |
| German | 158.48 | 4.98 |
| Greek | 225.83 | 7.09 |
| Hebrew | 12.35 | 0.39 |
| Hungarian | 33.07 | 1.04 |
| Icelandic | 3.12 | 0.10 |
| Indian languages[a] | 26.49 | 0.83 |
| Italian | 297.65 | 9.34 |
| Japanese | 59.36 | 1.86 |
| Maltese | 7.27 | 0.23 |
| Marathi | 1.92 | 0.06 |
| More than one language | 2.26 | 0.07 |
| No dialogue | 31.06 | 0.98 |
| Norwegian | 12.01 | 0.38 |
| Pidgin English | 3.78 | 0.12 |
| Polish | 86.49 | 2.72 |
| Portuguese | 19.83 | 0.62 |
| Russian | 24.09 | 0.76 |

*(Continued)*

**Table 9.2**    *Continued*

| Language | Number of hours | % of total program time |
|----------|-----------------|-------------------------|
| Spanish | 117.11 | 3.68 |
| Swedish | 30.60 | 0.96 |
| Tagalog | 1.48 | 0.05 |
| Thai | 4.04 | 0.13 |
| Turkish | 30.66 | 0.96 |
| Ukrainian | 4.59 | 0.14 |
| Welsh | 1.27 | 0.04 |
| Yiddish | 1.48 | 0.05 |
| Yugoslav languages[a] | 151.90 | 4.77 |
| | 3185.26 | 100.00 |
| [a]Breakdown as follows: | | |
| *Chinese languages* | | |
| Cantonese | 34.29 | 1.08 |
| Mandarin | 48.47 | 1.52 |
| *English* | | |
| English | 620.64 | 19.48 |
| English (SBS TV Productions) | 693.12 | 21.76 |
| *Indian languages* | | |
| Bengali | 9.82 | 0.31 |
| Hindi | 16.67 | 0.52 |
| *Yugoslav languages* | | |
| Croatian | 6.79 | 0.21 |
| Macedonian | 13.26 | 0.42 |
| Serbian | 40.21 | 1.26 |
| Serbo-Croatian | 66.46 | 2.09 |
| Slovenia | 25.18 | 0.79 |

*Source*: Lo Bianco (1987)

following as well (particularly for their classic foreign films and for their in-depth news coverage); what is totally unclear (or even distinctly dubious) is whether they have any genuine RLS value. To have such, they would need to be much more conscientiously focused on home, family, child and youth material which could be copied and distributed for VCR cassette use in homes, community centers and schools. The social psychological impact of the mass media, strong though it may be either momentarily or cumulatively, is, in itself, not a safe bet for RLS. Families simply do not pass on threatened languages to their children because of a few hours per week of mass media programming, nor do children become mother tongue speakers of Xish on that basis.

Broadcasting in Aboriginal languages, so important because of the relative lack of literacy even in the most retentive Aboriginal communities, took a major leap ahead in 1980 – notwithstanding the small and scattered audiences involved – when an Aboriginal group in Alice Springs formed CAAMA (Central Australian Aboriginal Media Association). The Association now has a $100,000 budget provided by the Commonwealth Government (very little really and constantly at risk of being discontinued) and broadcasts for part of its 16-hour radio day in English and part (more than half) in Pitjantjatjara, Warlpiri and Arandic (Arrente). There are also a few other radio stations broadcasting regularly in Aboriginal languages, all of them very short of funds for this purpose although some of them have produced very worthwhile (indeed, even prizewinning) programs.

There are also, at present, only roughly a dozen stations in all of Australia that even present programs for Aboriginal listeners in English. Audio-tapes of *Aboriginal News*, the newsletter of the Queensland Department of Employment, Education and Training, are produced in various Aboriginal languages by the Townsville Aboriginal and Islander Media Association in order to get around the problem of Aboriginal illiteracy. All in all, however, the Aboriginal market is too small, and too scattered, for many successful media programs in Aboriginal languages and it would require heavy governmental subsidization for this number to grow significantly in the future. Once again, the contrast between policy with respect to the immigrant-based languages and policy with respect to the Aboriginal languages is a painful one indeed.

In 1987 CAAMA's television offshoot, IMPARJA (from the Arrente word for 'track' or 'footprint'), was founded and began broadcasting in Aboriginal languages for three-quarters of an hour/week [!], that being all of the time that could be spared due to competitive financial pressures. Somewhat prematurely, a local Aboriginal RLS activist has concluded that 'now [that] we have our own TV and video we can put our own things on ... We can fight fire with fire'. Unfortunately, that is neither a wise policy (presenting 'Dallas' dubbed in Warlpiri is a total waste of time and money) nor a feasible one in practical terms. Unless carefully watched and counterbalanced, the overall growth in English media availability in the remoter areas (due to the rapid growth of satellite-directed broadcasting and rebroadcasting) and the further acceptance of English as an Aboriginal language merely because it is the only feasible Aboriginal lingua franca, is likely to be many, many times greater than the growth of its Aboriginal counterparts. Playing with fire is a dangerous thing to do for those who have very little that they can fall back upon should they get burned. The Aborigines' languages do need modern print and non-print media in their struggles for RLS, but these must be non-competitive with the English media and, instead, must concentrate on fostering the type of Aboriginal life and reinforcing those sociocultural contexts which Aborigines can control and on which RLS depends.[16] Encouraging efforts along these very lines are now underway at taping centers of CAAMA and IMPARJA and at the Video Center of the Barkly Region Aboriginal Languages Center (Northern Territory).

### Stage 1: Higher Education, Regional or Central Governmental Activity, National Media and Higher/Specialized Work Sphere

It is evident from our examination of the prior stages that there is very little of RLS significance to report at this most advanced stage, the stage that is most fully controlled by and for the Yish establishment (unless explicit provisions exist for local cultural autonomy). There are, of course, several ethnic studies/ethnic languages programs and research centers (and even a few Aboriginal studies/languages programs and research centers) at various major and minor Australian universities, some of which (e.g. Batchelor, Northern Territory) are explicitly teaching about RLS and its needs, processes and priorities. There is also a degree of top-flight media involvement in the large investment that has been made in community language broadcasting and in the more meager support that has been allotted to Aboriginal language broadcasting. More noticeable and more noteworthy than any of the foregoing is the effort to engage in language policy planning at the Commonwealth level and in several of the individual states. Many ethnics and some Aborigines have even been invited to participate in more than a token sense in this planning. Very few Yish establishments throughout the world have done either the one or the other and Australia deserves recognition in both connections,[17] as well as in connection with appropriating or allocating over $90 million for the period 1987–1991 for the purposes of implementing the National Language Policy finally adopted in 1987.

However, when all is said and done, the RLS outlook in Australia is far bleaker than the sheer amount of RLS activity currently ongoing might seem to imply. Aboriginal languages are dying at the rate of one or more a year and language shift continues unabated in the immigrant-based 'community languages' fold. This is a tremendous attrition for a country that recognizes, as few others do, its own dire need for languages other than English and that has shown as much admiration, recognition and support as Australia has for the languages still spoken within its borders. Unfortunately, as we have noted so many times before, good intentions are not enough and the steps taken or about to be taken are either largely unrelated, non-productive or even counter-productive as far as intergenerational RLS-payoff is concerned.

Something (although not much) can still be saved, but it will probably be up to the language communities themselves, more than up to the Government, to point to the required family–home–neighborhood–community foundations of such possible salvation. When the right way is finally recognized, the Aboriginal willingness to withdraw to 'outstations' will be understood in all of its metaphorical power. Self-help and self-regulation in everyday intergenerational mother tongue transmission contexts, safeguarded by boundary setting and boundary preservation, are the *sine qua non* of RLS. Money and planning along such lines by national authorities are unlikely, given the ethos of shared participationism that dominates both democratic and authoritarian regimes today. Small-scale self-regulation and self-help at the local level is the inevitable only way out for the saving remnant that really takes RLS seriously. For the others, 'language appreciation' and Xmen-via-Yish may be the rewards and the consolations of widest currency.[18]

Australian policies and processes constitute a positive but ineffective approach to RLS on behalf of recent immigrant languages and a negative but potentially effective approach to RLS on behalf of Aboriginal languages. Because of its relative proximity to and ultimate commercial connectedness with South and Southeast Asia Australia may well be the first anglo-establishment country to break out of the prison of English monolingualism. However, few of its immigrant language communities and none of its Aboriginal language communities will benefit directly from this self-liberation. Indeed, over the long run (during the next fifty years or so), a few Aboriginal languages associated with 'outstations' and genuine community schools may be far more successful on the RLS scene than any of the recently proliferated immigrant languages currently marked by social mobility and urban demographic dispersion, on the one hand, and by a luxuriant growth of language courses, radio programs and television broadcasts, on the other hand. This will come about because a very few, fortunate (i.e. governmentally benignly neglected) Aboriginal languages are genuinely linked to the intergenerational mother tongue transmission process rooted as it is in home–family–neighborhood and community, whereas no such linkage generally exists in connection with the highly publicized efforts on behalf of immigrant languages. Ultimately, therefore, and with the exception of a few obvious South and Southeast Asian languages plus a few major European tongues that are really needed for Australia's own commercial

Table 9.3 Recommendations from the 'National Policy on Languages' Report

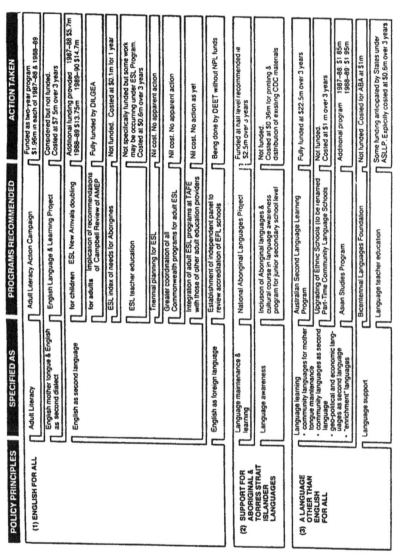

| POLICY PRINCIPLES | SPECIFIED AS | PROGRAMS RECOMMENDED | ACTION TAKEN |
|---|---|---|---|
| (1) ENGLISH FOR ALL | Adult Literacy | Adult Literacy Action Campaign | Funded as two-year program $1.95m in each of 1987–88 & 1988–89 |
| | English mother tongue & English as second dialect | English Language & Learning Project | Considered but not funded. Costed at $7.5m over 3 years |
| | English as second language | for children    ESL New Arrivals doubling | Additional funding provided    1987–88 $5.7m 1988–89 $13.75m    1989–90 $14.7m |
| | | for adults    Implication of recommendations of Campbell Review of AMEP | Fully funded by DILGEA |
| | | ESL index of needs for Aborigines | Not funded.   Costed at $0.1m for 1 year |
| | | ESL teacher education | Not specifically funded but some work may be occurring under ESL Program. Costed at $0.6m over 3 years |
| | | Triennial planning for ESL | Nil cost. No apparent action |
| | | Greater coordination of all Commonwealth programs for adult ESL | Nil cost. No apparent action |
| | | Integration of adult ESL programs at TAFE with those of other adult education providers | Nil cost. No action as yet |
| | English as foreign language | Establishment of independent panel to review accreditation of EFL schools | Being done by DEET without NPL funds |
| (2) SUPPORT FOR ABORIGINAL & TORRES STRAIT ISLANDER LANGUAGES | Language maintenance & learning | National Aboriginal Languages Project | Funded at half level recommended ie $2.5m over 3 years |
| | Language awareness | Inclusion of Aboriginal languages & cultural course in language awareness program for junior secondary school level | Not funded. Costed at $0.36m for printing & distribution of existing CDC materials |
| (3) A LANGUAGE OTHER THAN ENGLISH FOR ALL | Language learning<br>• community languages for mother tongue maintenance<br>• community languages as second language<br>• geo-political and economic languages as second language<br>• "enrichment" languages | Australian Second Language Learning Program | Fully funded at $22.5m over 3 years |
| | | Upgrading of Ethnic Schools (to be renamed Part-Time Community Language Schools | Not funded. Costed at $1m over 3 years |
| | | Asian Studies Program | Additional program    1987–88, $1.85m 1988–89 $1.95m |
| | Language support | Bicentennial Languages Foundation | Not funded Costed for ABA at $1m |
| | | Language teacher education | Some funding anticipated by States under ASLLP. Explicitly costed at $0.5m over 3 years |

*(Continued)*

Table 9.3 *Continued*

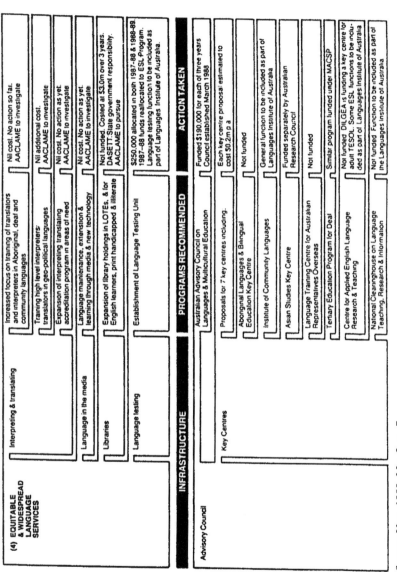

| | | PROGRAMS RECOMMENDED | ACTION TAKEN |
|---|---|---|---|
| **(4) EQUITABLE & WIDESPREAD LANGUAGE SERVICES** | Interpreting & translating | Increased focus on training of translators and interpreters in Aboriginal, deaf and community languages | Nil cost. No action so far. AACLAME to investigate |
| | | Training high level interpreters; translators in geo-political languages | Nil additional cost. AACLAME to investigate |
| | | Expansion of interpreting translating accreditation program in areas of need | Nil cost. No action as yet. AACLAME to investigate |
| | Language in the media | Language maintenance, extension & learning through media & new technology | Nil cost. No action as yet. AACLAME to investigate |
| | Libraries | Expansion of library holdings in LOTEs, & for English learners, print handicapped & illiterate | Not funded. Costed at $3.0m over 3 years. DASETT. State government responsibility. AACLAME to pursue |
| | Language testing | Establishment of Language Testing Unit | $250,000 allocated in both 1987-88 & 1988-89. 1987-88 funds reallocated to ESL Program. Language testing function to be included as part of Languages Institute of Australia. |
| **INFRASTRUCTURE** | | | |
| Advisory Council | | Australian Advisory Council on Languages & Multicultural Education | Funded $190,000 for each of three years Council established March 1988 |
| | Key Centres | Proposals for 7 key centres including: | Each key centre proposal estimated to cost $0.2m p.a |
| | | Aboriginal Languages & Bilingual Education Key Centre | Not funded |
| | | Institute of Community Languages | General function to be included as part of Languages Institute of Australia |
| | | Asian Studies Key Centre | Funded separately by Australian Research Council |
| | | Language Training Centre for Australian Representatives Overseas | Not funded |
| | | Tertiary Education Program for Deaf | Similar program funded under MACSP |
| | | Centre for Applied English Language Research & Teaching | Not funded DILGEA is funding a key centre for adult TESOL. Some ESL functions to be included as part of Languages Institute of Australia |
| | | National Clearinghouse on Language Teaching, Research & Information | Not funded Function to be included as part of the Languages Institute of Australia |

*Source:* Vox, 1989, No. 2, p. 5

advancement, Australia will yet be the graveyard of dozens upon dozens of its immigrant languages, through the self-destruction of their community bases, even as it is already the graveyard of an even larger number of its decimated Aboriginal languages.

Efforts that are not sequentially planned from an informed RLS perspective rarely result in RLS, regardless of how colorful and expensive they may be, just as any organized sociopolitical actions that vastly outgrow their demographic foundations must come a cropper. Without the possibility of a solution based upon the territorial principle, such as that which assists various Aboriginal cultures and outstations in their struggles for survival, and without the spirit of *primum mobile* which also applies to Aborigines and to a few isolated immigrant settlements alone, most immigrant speech communities must fall back on their own internal family and community dynamics to generate RLS and even to prime the less-than-RLS efforts of governmental agencies. These speech communities are currently far from being aware of how distant they really are from assuring intergenerational mother tongue transmission of those very languages whose superficial institutional flourishes the government is currently supporting for an increasingly aging first generation.[19]

## Notes

1. A good starting place for sampling both Aboriginal and Anglo-Australian perspectives during the past century and a half is a volume by Mattingley and Hampton (1988). The issues of *Survival International, Cultural Survival Quarterly* and *pogrom: Zeitschrift der Gesellschaft für bedrohte Völker* are excellent sources of current information (see, e.g. Altman & Dillon, 1986; Duelke, 1984; and Ludwig, 1985). A recent excellent addition to the periodical literature in this area is *Land Rights News* (P.O. Box 3321, Alice Springs, NT 5750, Australia), which is published for the Northern Territory Land Councils but provides a review of news and opinions pertaining to Aborigines and their concerns as well as their accomplishments throughout the country. Thus, its September 1988 issue (Vol. 2, No. 10) includes reports on: the outspoken racism of spokesmen of the Returned Service League, urgent questions raised by the Royal Commission into Aboriginal Deaths in Custody (108 Aboriginal deaths while in custody since 1980), a report by the chairperson of the UN's Working Group on Indigenous Populations urging greater Aboriginal self-management and self-determination in Australia, the protest by Aboriginal spokesmen against the International Labor Organization's minimalist position with respect to the rights of indigenous populations, an extensive listing of tertiary education offerings and opportunities for Aborigines, an update on the bilingual/bicultural Yipirinya School (to be discussed below), and dozens of brief articles about various ongoing efforts to provide (and to deny) land rights in various parts of Australia.

2. Stephen Wurm's and Shiro Hattori's (1981) *Language Atlas: Pacific* contains four separate maps covering the various parts of Australia, dividing it into Southeastern, Eastern, Northern and Western regions. This atlas gives estimated numbers of speakers as well as bibliographic references in each case and is an invaluable tool for all those interested in the number, diversity and spatial distribution of the Aboriginal languages.

3. We will follow Black's (1983) lead by not including creole languages in our discussion of Aboriginal languages. The two major creoles (Kriol and Torres Strait Creole, both of them English-related), each with some 15,000 speakers (including second language speakers), are of considerable importance in their respective areas and represent cases of language genesis and of newly established language-and-ethnicity linkages which should not be lost sight of in considering the manifold cultural dislocations that initially lead to language shift and language death. Creoles are a reminder that authenticity 'comes to be' rather than springs full-formed from the head of Jove. Nevertheless, RLS adherents are attached to their preferred and already legitimated authenticity and are not consoled by the possibility of future authenticities to come. Creole partisans, of course, frequently engage in RLS-efforts of their own, when threatened by contextually more powerful language and culture constellations.

4. Wurm and Hattori refer to this language as Banjalang (with six dialects) and estimate that it may have had 30 speakers in the late 1970s and early 1980s. Eve Fesl (Director, Aboriginal Languages Center, Monash University), formerly an instructor at the Seminar, estimates 30 speakers today, although she points out that there might be a somewhat larger number if it were possible to count those who hide their language skills in order to avoid the hardships (both for themselves and for their children) visited on former generations of speakers of Aboriginal languages or in order to keep the language from changing as a result of its use by inexperienced 'semi-speakers' (personal communication). The invitation to the series referred to mentions that 'through our language program we hope to reaffirm our cultural relationships ... We hope to compile the history and stories that were part of our daily lives and traditions. People with language knowledge are invited to share it with us.' The availability and spread of an indigenous aggregative term for all Aborigines (Gooris/Kooris) is suggestive of a growing intergroup identity among them, over and above former and current ethnolinguistic demarcations. The term Goori/Kuri itself stems from the Southeastern coastal area, some 300 miles north of Sydney. Wurm and Hattori list '7?' speakers for Kuri and '9??' for the Yuin-Kuric grouping (10 dialects, all but three of which are extinct).

5. I am indebted to Tamsin Donaldson, Australian Institute of Aboriginal Studies, for my information about the 'little alphabet books' in general and specifically for details of their construction in several different Aboriginal language settings. Donaldson's paper 'From speaking Ngiyaampaa to speaking English' (1985) is an excellent account of the rapidity of shift in many Aboriginal settings and is a great help in appreciating the special attitude-building role of the 'little alphabet books' at a time when English is already the common vehicle of communication among all but the oldest members of a particular group.

6. For the scholarly documentation of the above processes, see: Clyne (1982, 1985, 1988); McAllister (1986); and Pauwels (1988) (the latter being an excellent collection of recent papers on 'the future of ethnic languages in Australia').

While the number of claimants of community languages other than English is still rising for languages most of whose speakers are either recent arrivals or whose immigration is still ongoing (e.g. Arabic, Spanish, Vietnamese, Chinese, etc.), intergenerational maintenance is usually very poor beyond the second generation and is even often poor beyond the first, if not within the first generation itself.

7. The material variety of the outstations is nicely described and summarized in 'Desert Homeland Centres – Their Physical Development', Department of Aboriginal Affairs Occasional Reports, 1977 (August), No. 4. I am not entirely sure of how widespread the designation 'Homeland' has become but it seems to me to have a distinctly more positive designation than 'outstation'. *Land Rights News* is a good source of information about publication houses (such as Magabala Books) and a variety of musical groups that have come into being to serve the outstations in general and RLS-efforts in particular. Most of my information on the 'outstations' is derived from material placed at my disposition by Eve Fesl.

8. The governmental report referred to here is that of the Senate Standing Committee on Education and the Arts, 1984. Another very useful source for this discussion (but even more so, in connection with our discussion of radio and television, stage 2) is that of Foster and Stockley (1984). I am grateful to Joseph Lo Bianco, Michael Clyne and Manfred Klarberg for providing me with various published and unpublished governmental, organizational and private reports pertaining to ethnic community schools and other related immigrant-RLS issues in Australia.

9. The attainment of adult literacy in community languages is the goal of the government-sponsored, multi-ethnic Victorian School of Languages, which teaches 30 languages in over a dozen centers in the metropolitan Melbourne and Geelong (Victoria's second largest city) areas. This school is not under ethnic auspices (although some of its branches are mono-ethnic and are even conducted on mono-ethnic institutional premises), however, and, although its students attend of their own volition, it feeds back relatively little to the strengthening of community ethnolinguistic stability because most of its students are pursuing very focused, instrumental language goals. Many of its students are of high school age or older and utilize its courses in order to qualify for high school certification in the community language which they initially acquired in childhood but subsequently largely ceased to speak. Also not included in our discussion are the many non-ethnic proprietary schools now teaching Japanese in order to meet the needs of Australia's rapidly expanding commercial ties with Japan. I am indebted to Annette Schmidt (Australian Institute for Aboriginal Studies, Canberra) for providing me with much valuable information regarding the adult literacy efforts (and other adult education efforts) in various Aboriginal languages.

10. This quotation is from the 'Report of the House of Representatives Select Committee on Aboriginal Education 1985', p. 116. The bulk of my information on Aboriginal type 4a schools is derived from Eve Fesl's dissertation (1989), *Land Rights News*, 1988, 2, No. 10 ('Yipirinya: Making two-way education a reality'), Lo Bianco (1987), Senate Standing Committee on Education and the Arts report *A National Language Policy* (1984), von Tesmar (1988) and very informative and lengthy correspondence with Annette Schmidt, Stephen Harris (Batchelor College, Batchelor, Northern Territory) and Eirlys Richards (Summer Institute of Linguistics, Berrimah, Northern Territory).

11. The contrastive juxtaposition and combination of own *culture* vs. foreign (Western) *skills* constantly reoccurs in late European (i.e. in Eastern and Southern European) and in Afro-Asian nationalisms, the former being viewed as humanistically and philosophically superior and nourishing to the soul, while the latter are 'merely' technically advanced but philosophically empty. The complementary nature of these two, own ethnocultural lore and traditions, on the other, and foreign technical 'know-how', on the one hand, implies that there need be no deep-seated ideological conflict between the two and, therefore, that they can be combined under proper indigenous auspices and supervision. Like the ethnonationalisms that came before it, Aboriginal self-determination is not a wholesale rejection of the modern Western world, but rather, a defense of thought-and-value systems of their own and a willingness to strengthen that defense by the utilization of modern means, as necessary. For further elaboration of the symbiotic nature of modernizing ethnonationalisms, see my *Language and Nationalism* (1972; republished in its entirety in my *Language and Ethnicity*, 1989).

12. The variety of immigrant languages offered in the foreign language programs of the public schools and the proportion of students studying such languages is probably greater in Australia (particularly in the southeastern states of Victoria, New South Wales and South Australia in which most immigrants have settled) than anywhere else in the Western world. In the state of South Australia, e.g. just to cite evidence outside of the major ethnic enclaves of Melbourne (Victoria) and Sydney (New South Wales), nearly 20% of the elementary school students and 40% of the secondary school students were studying languages, the major enrollments being in German and French but with Italian, Indonesian, Greek, Mandarin and Japanese also being well represented and a considerable contingent being found for Serbocroatian as well. It should also be pointed out that a number of Aboriginal languages are offered in public primary schools in most of the larger Aboriginal settlements in South Australia, enrollment being particularly high (over 600) for Pitjantjatjara (1200–1300 speakers in South Australia and Northern Territory).

13. My familiarity with respect to stage 4b developments within the immigrant languages fold derives from my personal fieldwork during a prolonged visit to Australia in 1985 and from extensive discussions and correspondence with Joseph Lo Bianco and Manfred Klarberg. Klarberg's article (1987) on 1976–1986 trends with respect to the High School Certificate examinations in the foreign language field should be of considerable interest to language education authorities elsewhere. The more meager type 4b efforts in conjunction with Aboriginal languages are reviewed in the Senate Standing Committee on Education and the Arts' 1984 report which enumerates 25 'bilingual programs' in government schools for Aborigines. Needless to say, all of the foregoing are of a transitional nature. Lo Bianco's 1987 report also lists a few short-term offerings (fewer than a dozen all in all and of only 1–3 years duration) of Aboriginal languages as 'foreign languages' in public and in Catholic schools. From correspondence with Annette Schmidt I have learned of two type 4b programs involving Aboriginal languages that were recently (1989) discontinued due to the lack of qualified staff and administrative uninterest and/or resistance. I am also very grateful to Dorothy Tunbridge, Adnyamathanha Language and Culture Program, for once more reminding me that type 4b programs that have no real RLS consequences of

an overt language use sort may, nevertheless, still have a significant positive impact on reawakening and fostering ethnic identity. Nevertheless, with respect to RLS, such programs ultimately contribute more to Xmen-via-Yish than to Xmen-via-Xish life-patterns.

14. Altman, Jon, *Aboriginal Employment and Education News*, 1988, No. 17, p. 18.
15. The major sources of information concerning the immigrant-based foreign language press in Australia are Gilson and Zubrzycki (1967), Clyne (1982) and Terezakis (1982). The Senate Standing Committee on Education and the Arts' 1985 report mentions two forthcoming studies (commissioned by the Department of Immigration and Ethnic Affairs) of the contents of Greek and Arabic newspapers in Sydney and of Turkish and Yugoslav newspapers in Melbourne. Neither of these studies seem to have been released as of early 1989, when the bulk of this chapter was written.
16. Useful information concerning immigrant language and Aboriginal language non-print media is provided in Anon. (1988a, 1988b), Australian Institute of Multicultural Affairs (1982), Clyne (1982), Ethnic Television Review Panel (1980), Jernudd (1969), Language Maintenance Newsletter (School of Australian Linguistics, P.O. Batchelor, NT 5791), *Land Rights News*, 1988, 2, No. 10, and The Senate Standing Committee on Education and the Arts (1984). During my 1985 fieldwork visit I also gathered much information from stations/channels and broadcasters in the Melbourne and Sydney areas. Still unreported in any systematic fashion are the more limited RLS-efforts via ethnic theater and ethnic choral groups, both of which function among immigrant groups as well as Aboriginal groups.
17. Several major publications have resulted from these planning efforts, among them Commonwealth Department of Education (1982), Applied Linguistics Association of Australia and Australian Linguistic Society (PLANLangPol Committee) (1983), Senate Standing Committee on Education and the Arts (1984), National Advisory and Coordinating Committee on Multicultural Education (1987) and Lo Bianco (1987). The latter is a report that has potentially major implications for RLS, although, as yet, it addresses this issue indirectly and without the explicit attention that it requires if RLS is to be successfully attained. Language maintenance is on the report's agenda, however: see Table 9.3. The National Language Institute, established in 1989, has a center focusing on 'Language in Society', located at Monash University (Clayton, Victoria). This center could help redirect attention to the fact that RLS is not yet really on the Australian agenda.
18. From the huge literature on Australian Aboriginal and immigrant groups and their languages, I would like to mention just a few, not referred to above, that were of substantial additional help to me in my RLS inquiries in connection with that part of the world. In the immigrant languages sector: Lo Bianco (1989) (also contains information on Aboriginal languages and on sign language [for the deaf] in Victoria) and the successive issues of *Vox* (the journal of the Australian Advisory Council on Languages and Multicultural Education, which began publishing in 1988). In the Aboriginal sector: the successive issues of *Land Rights News* (a publication of the Northern Territory Land Councils, which began publishing in 1987), the successive issues of *Language Maintenance Newsletter* (beginning in 1986), *Aboriginal Australians* (=*Report No. 35* [revised edition, 1988] of the Minority Rights Group, London), Loveday (1982), Prior and Wunungmurra (1987) and Reyburn (1988). Other materials that I found useful or stimulating in the preparation of this chapter, although I have not cited them directly, are Baldauf and Luke (1990), Bavin and Shopen (1988), Collman (1988), Cronin (1988), Foster

and Stockey (1988), Johnson (1987), Kalantzis, Cope and Slade (1989), Spurr (1988) and Thieberger (1988).

19. My sincere thanks to Michael Clyne, who enabled me to spend five weeks in Australia in 1985, and to him, Joseph Lo Bianco, Steven Harris, Fred Klarberg and Eve Fesl for their manifold assistance, criticism and encouragement in connection with the preparation of this formulation of the RLS situation in immigrant and Aboriginal Australia. Needless to say, any errors of fact or interpretation are my own.

## References

Altman, Jon and Dillon, Michael (1986) [1985], Aboriginal land rights in Australia. *Cultural Survival Quarterly* 10, 2, 53–54 (adaptation of their article 'Watching brief on Land Rights', *Australian Society*, June 1985).

Anon. (1988a) Maningride media gets a new home. *Land Rights News* 2 (10), 2.

——. (1988b) FM tests for 'a foot in the door' for TAIM. *Land Rights News* 2 (10), 15.

Applied Linguistics Association of Australia and Australian Linguistic Society (PLANLangPol Committee) (1983) *A National Language Policy for Australia*. Kensington: ALAA/ALS (PC).

Australian Institute of Multicultural Affairs (1982) *Evaluation of Post-Arrival Education Programs and Services*. Melbourne: AIMA.

Baldauf, Richard Jr and Luke, Allan (eds) (1990) *Language Planning and Education in Australasia and the South Pacific*. Clevedon: Multilingual Matters.

Bavin, Edith L. and Shopen, Timothy (1988) Walpiri in the 80s: An overview of research into language variation and child language. In B. Rigsby and S. Romaine (eds) *The Language[s?] of Australia*. Sydney: Cambridge University Press.

Black, Paul (1983) *Aboriginal Languages of the Northern Territory*. Darwin: School of Australian Linguistics/Darwin Community College.

Clyne, Michael (1982) *Multilingual Australia: Resources–Needs*. Melbourne: River Seine.

——. (1985) Language maintenance and language shift: some data from Australia. In Nessa Wolfson and Joan Manes (eds) *Language of Inequality*. Berlin: Mouton, 195–206.

——. (1988) Community languages in the home: a first progress report. *Vox* 1, 22–27.

Collman, Jeff (1988) *Fringe-Dwellers and Welfare: An Aboriginal Response to Bureaucracy*. St Lucia: University of Queensland Press.

Commonwealth Department of Education (1982) *Towards a National Language Policy*. Canberra: Australian Government Publishing Service.

Cronin, Darryl (1988) Land rights; is that all we really want? *Land Rights News* 2 (10), 34–35.

Donaldson, Tamsin (1985) From speaking Ngiyaampaa to speaking English. *Aboriginal History* 9, 126–147.

Duelke, Britta (1984) Aborigines in Northern Territory. *pogrom: Zeitschrift für bedrohte Völker* 15 (108), 50–55.

Ethnic Television Review Panel (1980) *Programming for the Multicultural/Multilingual Television Service: Objectives and Policies* (Third Report). Canberra: ETRP.

Fesl, Eve (1989) Language Policy Formulation and Implementation: An Historical Perspective on Australian Languages. PhD dissertation, Monash University.

Fishman, Joshua A. (1972) [1989], *Language and Nationalism: Two Integrative Essays*. Rowley, MA: Newbury House. Reprinted in its entirety as part of *Language and Ethnicity in Minority Sociolinguistic Perspective*. Clevedon: Multilingual Matters, 97–175 and 269–367.

Foster, Lois and Stockley, David (1984) *Multiculturism: The Changing Australian Paradigm.* Clevedon: Multilingual Matters.

——. (1988) *Australian Multiculturism: A Documentary History and Critique.* Clevedon: Multilingual Matters.

Gilson, M. and Zubrzycki, J. (1967) *The Foreign Language Press in Australia, 1948–1969.* Canberra: Australian National University.

Jernudd, Björn H. (1969) Foreign language broadcasting in Victoria. *Babel* 5 (2), 24–25.

Johnson, Steve (1987) The philosophy and politics of Aboriginal language maintenance. *Australian Aboriginal Studies* (2), 54–58.

Kalantzis, Mary, Cope, Bill and Slade, Diana (1989) *Minority Languages and Dominant Culture.* London: Falmer.

Klarberg, Fred (1987) The gift of tongues is becoming an appreciating asset. *The Age* June 15, 3.

Lo Bianco, Joseph (1987) *National Policy on Languages.* Canberra: Australian Government Publishing Service.

——. (1989) *Victoria: Language Action Plan.* Melbourne: Ministry of Education.

Loveday, P. (ed.) (1982) *Service Delivery to Outstations.* Darwin: Australian National University/North Australia Research Unit.

Ludwig, Klemens (1985) *Bedrohte Völker: Ein Lexikon nationaler und religiöser Minderheiten.* Munich: Beck.

McAllister, Ian (1986) Speaking the language: language maintenance and English proficiency among immigrant youth in Australia. *Ethnic and Racial Studies* 9, 24–42.

Mattingley, Christobel and Hampton, Kenneth (eds) (1988) *Survival in Our Own Land: Aboriginal Experiences in South Australia Since 1836: Told by Nungas and Others.* Cowandilla: Wakefield.

National Advisory and Coordinating Committee on Multicultural Education (1987) *Education in and for a Multicultural Society: Issues and Strategies for Policy Making.* Canberra: NACCME.

Pauwels, Anne (ed.) (1988) The future of ethnic languages in Australia. *International Journal of the Sociology of Language,* 72 (entire issue).

Prior, John and Wunungmurra, Wali (1987) *Aboriginal Employment in Homelands and Outstations.* Casuarina: Northern Territory Open College/Department of Education.

Reyburn, Bruce (1988) The forgotten struggle of Australia's Aboriginal people. *Cultural Survival Quarterly* 12 (3), 7–10.

Senate Standing Committee on Education and the Arts (1984) *A National Language Policy.* Canberra: Parliament of the Commonwealth of Australia/Australian Government Publishing Service.

Spurr, Russell (1988) Australia goes Asian. *New York Times Magazine,* December 4, 46–49, 52 and 56.

Terezakis, Maria D. (1982) *The Content of Three Sydney Based Ethnic Newspapers.* Sydney: Macquarie University and Department of Immigration and Ethnic Affairs.

Thieberger, Nicholas (1988) *Aboriginal Language Maintenance: Some Issues and Strategies.* Masters thesis, La Trobe University.

Von Tesmar, Johannes (1988) Die Schule der kleinen Raupen; Die 'Yiprinya School' der Aborigines hat sich durchgesetzt. *Pogrom: Zeitschrift für bedrohte Völker.* 19 (141), 40–41.

Wurm, Stephen and Hattori, Shiro (1981) *Language Atlas: Pacific.* Canberra: Australian Academy of the Humanities, and Tokyo: Japanese Academy.

# Part 3

# Globalization, Power and the Status of Threatened Languages

## Chapter 10

# 'English Only': Its Ghosts, Myths and Dangers[1]

With the adoption of the English Language Amendment proposition in California in November, 1986, and with the margin in favor of that adoption being nearly three-to-one (73.2% vs. 26.8%), it is doubtlessly true that, for the first time in American history, a language-policy issue has come to the fore as a prominent internal issue in the USA. It was not by any means the first, nor, probably, the last triumph for the 'English Official/English Only' nativism of the 1980s, but it was a triumph in one of our most populous, economically developed, and modernistically oriented states. This was a triumph that signaled that gone were the days when I and other language-status specialists would have trouble explaining to American academic and lay audiences why there were those among the Irish and the Welsh, the Jews and the Poles, the Flemings and the Frisians, the Catalans and the Basques, and among various and sundry other 'emotional nationalities that get so upset about and make such an issue over' their language, whereas Americans are too solid, secure, rational and realistic to get involved in anything like that. To most Americans, 'before California', language always seemed to be such a trivial issue relative to seemingly 'real issues', issues pertaining to the economy and to foreign policy, to sports and to the weather next weekend. The prevailing stereotype in this connection, one almost equally prevalent among academicians and the lay public, was forcefully brought to my attention in 1968, when I coedited a volume entitled *Language Problems of Developing Nations*. A colleague who chanced to see a copy of this book on my shelf chided me for the redundancy in the title. 'It's like giving a book the title *The Smallness of Midgets*; only midgets are small and only undeveloped nations have language problems. You're indulging in a tautology with a title like that!' he said. How noteworthy, then, that the USA has joined the ranks of the 'developing nations', or, alternatively, that there is greater realization that no tautology is involved at all. There are many developing nations without language problems (such as El Salvador and Rwanda), as well as many developed ones with language problems (such as Belgium and Spain). Clearly, something has happened of late in the

179

USA to bring the status of English into controversial prominence, and I would like to ask what that is, why now, and why in the USA. However, first of all, I would like to start at the end and ask, 'What difference would it make?', that is, what would really change in the daily operation of government and in the daily rounds of everyday life in our country if English Official legislation continues to be adopted and is even enacted at the national level?

## What Difference Would it Really Make?

In a recent issue of the *International Journal of the Sociology of Language*, David Marshall (1986) attempts to pursue this topic in detail by examining the impact of a federal English Official amendment on the operation of six states: California, Hawaii, Texas, New Mexico, Maine and Illinois. Since there is still no definitive wording of any such amendment, he takes H.J.R. 96 and S.J.R. 167 of the 99th Congress as his basic texts. He cannot be sure just how these texts would be implemented or interpreted, were they ever to be adopted, but he generally concludes that, if taken seriously, they would require 'a great deal of [prior] law to be rewritten', whereas if left as a pious gesture, as such laws currently are in most of the states that have adopted them, they would have no impact at all on governmental services. In Illinois, for example, the passage of a law making English the 'official' language of the state in 1969 (a revision of a 1923 law that had made 'American' the official language of Illinois, a remarkable 'denomination' but one that hails back to Noah Webster's recommendation of 1790 and an 'American official' bill introduced in Congress in 1923 in order to get around the Supreme Court's ruling that had invalidated the Nebraska state law that very year!) has not hindered the Illinois [State] Educational Development ment Board from requiring that

> Agencies having direct contact with substantial numbers of non-English speaking or otherwise culturally distinct citizens shall establish occupational titles for persons having sufficient linguistic ability or cultural knowledge to be able to render effective services to such citizens [Ill. Ann. Stat. ch. 127 Par 63b109(6)].

Accordingly, Illinois continues to provide services to the public, examinations for applicants for state civil-service positions, and courses for its current employees in languages other than English. In this particular instance, Marshall concludes, 'one wonders whether it means anything for Illinois to have an official language' (Marshall, 1986: 57). This conclusion is bolstered by the fact that the law in Illinois has been on the books since 1923 (or since 1969 at the latest), permitting sufficient time to elapse for observers to judge how it is being enforced and what it is taken to mean. In all other states with 'English Official' laws (as of April, 1987: Hawaii, Tennessee, Indiana, Kentucky, Nevada, Virginia, Georgia, California, Arkansas, Mississippi and North Dakota), no such time perspective is available and only two, Nebraska and California, have included such laws as amendments to their state constitutions, that is, adopted them in a way that makes these laws relatively difficult to scrap or change. Note, however, that Nebraska has done just that, effectively repealing its 1920 'English Official' act in 1987, and that in Hawaii, a state in which the official status of English is usually ignored by 'English Only' advocates, Hawaiian too is official and, indeed, is also designated the state's 'native' language (Hawaii Rev. Stat. Sec. 5–6.5 [1983]). Just to round out the picture, before looking into the 'English Official/English Only' effort *per se*, it should be pointed out that it suffered significant defeats in 13 states in 1987, namely in Arizona, Colorado, Maryland, Montana, Nebraska, New Hampshire, Louisiana, New Mexico, Oklahoma, South Dakota, Texas, Washington, West Virginia and Wyoming. 'English Official/English Only' legislation is still pending in 17 other states, leaving only Maine, Oklahoma and Oregon untouched, one way or the other, at this time.

Frankly, it is not really possible to say what difference 'English Official' laws would make at either the state or the national governmental levels. The various bills and laws that have been formulated thus far differ in their intent and in their wording. Even where these are similar, they still differ in their implementation. In no case has their implementation been subject to a court ruling, although court cases are now being planned in California and, perhaps, also in other jurisdictions. All in all, given the decentralized nature of the American legal process with respect to law making, law enforcing and law interpreting, we can expect a great deal of variation, including patterned law avoidance, even where such laws are enacted or adopted. The same is also true internationally. Of the many countries with monolingual 'official language' legislation (Turi, 1977), many are extremely liberal in so far as using additional languages in order to adequately serve populations which require languages other than the official one. 'Official' language is often interpreted as 'language of official record', and although most countries with designated and single official languages cannot be *required* to use other than those languages they, nevertheless, frequently do so, as a matter of tradition, from a sense of decency, or as a dictate of pragmatism.

All in all, therefore, my remarks thus far add up to the propositions that (a) we don't really know yet how 'English Official' laws will be formulated, interpreted and implemented (even if the courts ultimately find them to be legal) and, therefore, (b) there is no reason yet to consider such laws to be calamities, 'worst-scene scenarios', or the beginning of 'a new order' and the end of the outgoing and accepting America that we know and love. As in Illinois, most states may consider their 'official language' laws as merely being as decorative and as innocuous as the 'official flower' and the 'official bird' laws that most states have adopted.

Of course, the law in itself is not all that counts. *Leges sine moribus vanae*, the Romans realized, just as much as *leges mori serviunt*. Laws require a certain tradition, a certain inborn sense of right and wrong, in order to be either adoptable or enforceable. It is hard to tell how the current English Official movement would turn out in these respects. On the one hand, when referendums are being debated and appeals to justice and pragmatism are highlighted, various advocates of the English Official position claim to exclude (transitional) bilingual education and emergency health, police, and fire protection services from the purview of their bills, propositions, laws and/or amendments. On the other hand, at various times and in various places, even such innocuous and governmentally unencumbered matters as Spanish language advertising by McDonalds and Burger King and bilingual customer services by Pacific Bell are attacked, by some of them, as practices that 'tend to separate our citizens and our people by language' and 'lead to dangerous divisiveness' (*Louisville* [KY] *Times*, 12. 3. 1985). Although Gerda Bikales, formerly the Executive Director of U.S. English, claims that her organization 'is not targeting advertisers', 'Nevertheless', she adds, 'the national group is not discouraging individual members from doing so.' The lack of any such discouragement leads me to suspect that the Burger King and Pacific Bell protests do not merely represent the views of a few loony extremists, but that what they are saying openly expresses the underlying unstated (hidden?) goal of the movement: to move from 'English Official' to 'English Only', that is, from English-only in government to English-only in society.

Since bilingual education is the largest and the most omnipresent non-English-language effort of the federal and of various state governments, its adherents have every right to feel nervous about its future, even when it is explicitly excluded from any particular 'English Official' agenda. Just as 'English Official' legislation, even when adopted, can remain unimplemented, so there can be a 'handwriting on the wall' ripple effect, leading to budget cuts, foot-dragging, obstructionism and negative attitudes toward non-English-language services that are clearly outside the purview of any particular legislation. The more exacerbated the debate becomes, the more likely it is to move public sentiment in the latter direction. There is cause for worry, if not for alarm, whenever the *Zeitgeist* leans in the direction of seeing diversity as an *ipso facto* threat to unity. Obviously, the current American *Zeitgeist* itself needs to be examined, that is, the cultural milieu as a whole, because more than the letter of the law is involved (and necessarily so) in bringing law into being, in interpreting law and in enforcing law. Law itself is a by-product, a dependent variable, even more than it is primum mobile or an independent variable. So, if I have stressed before that 'English Language Amendments' need not be calamities, that they need not be as bad in practice as they may seem to be in theory, then it is also possible to suspect, on the other hand, that the initial legislation is merely an entering wedge, that it really masks much worse developments and much more negative and restrictive goals *vis à-vis* the future. It will take a while for us to know which of these two alternatives will more generally carry the field. In either case, it behooves us to ask our next question: why has a concern for 'English Only/English Official' surfaced in the USA and why at this particular time in our national history? Let us consider these questions one at a time.

## Why in the USA and Why Now?

In what has been referred to as the 'century of English' (Fishman *et al.*, 1977), at a time when English is the world's most prestigious, most effective and most sought-after vehicle of communication the world over (Kachru, 1982), when political careers in non-English-mother-tongue countries are made or ruined partially on the basis of whether candidates for national office there can handle English effectively (in order to negotiate with Schultz or with Reagan or appear before the American Congress – few of whom can handle any language other than English – when they visit Washington, D.C.), when English is still spreading and gaining uses and users in the entire non-English-mother-tongue world, why should a concern for its functional protection arouse so much interest in the wealthiest, most prestigious and most powerful core-English-mother-tongue country of the world, a country in which fully 85% of the population is of English mother tongue and where anywhere between 94% and 96% of the population is English speaking (Fishman *et al.*, 1985)? It does not really seem to me that the very ubiquity of English, whether worldwide or in the USA *per se*, can be appealed to as an explanatory vehicle in answering this question. It cannot merely be that the American defenders of English, flushed by the victories of their dearly beloved tongue on a world scale, have become enraged at the 'slights' to the hegemony of English in its own, American, back-yard. No similar legislative effort to redress the internal insults to English, real or imaginary, have surfaced in other core countries of English such as England, Australia or New Zealand, all of which have substantial non-English-mother-tongue populations of their own. The general view toward non-English languages in governmental use in each of these countries is quite benevolent (re England, see Garcia & Otheguy, 1986; Linguistic Minorities Project,

1983; re Australia, Australia: Commonwealth Department of Education, 1982; Clyne, 1985; Pauwels, 1988) and even supportive in ways undreamed of in the USA. At government expense, some Australian radio and television channels are devoted exclusively to non-English broadcasting, ethnic community schools are provided with significant government subsidies and the teachers for these schools are trained at state universities, government offices and services are provided in literally dozens of languages, etc. In all of these countries there is at least as much concern for the future of English in the world, for its continuation as the *de facto* official language of record within these countries, and for a good standard of English mastery in the schools and proper English usage thereafter as in the USA, with actual school achievement in English being at least as high as and probably higher there than in the USA. Even Anglo-Canada, with all of its wounded pride at the hands of a recalcitrant (and, at times, triumphalist) francophone Quebec, is more accommodating to its language minorities, francophone and nonfrancophone alike, than would be considered either seemly or likely in the USA (Churchill & Smith, 1986; McRae & L'Allier, 1986). No, any purported American or 'English Only' self-image as the true keeper of the English flame cannot really hope to account for the phenomenon we are trying to explain. It is not English-centeredness itself (love of the language, mastery of nuances of the language, fascination with the beauty of the language *per se*) that seems to be the crucial variable. I have yet to hear of 'English Only' advocates mustering votes to increase anemic budgets so as to expand the currently small number of TESOL programs that cannot begin to accommodate the non-English and limited-English students (at the child, adolescent and adult levels) that are clamoring for admission. I have also never seen an Anglo-American parent cry at the beauty of his/her child's English, or of Shakespeare's either for that matter, although I have seen francophone and hispanophone and other parents do so, both in the USA and abroad, *vis-à-vis* their respective mother tongues and the verbal virtuosity and virtuosi to be encountered in those languages. What does seem to be crucial are certain characteristics of the recent (post-Vietnam) American experience more globally, more centrally than any preoccupation with language *per se*.

When 'English Only/English Official' advocates tell us that our linguistic minorities 'are getting the wrong message' when the US government addresses or serves them in languages other than English, presumably a message that it is not necessary to learn English in order to live and prosper in the USA, I sense a wounded *amour propre*. Otherwise, why the utterly ridiculous paranoia about the possible inability of one part of the country being able to communicate with the other?; why the nightmares of bloodshed or social conflict because of language differences? Is there any internal evidence at all to confirm such fears? Aren't the comparisons to Sri Lanka or India not only far-fetched and erroneous but completely removed from the reality of the USA as well as from the reality of these countries? And, to top things off, aren't the problems even of these countries fundamentally unrelated to linguistic heterogeneity (Fishman & Solano, 1988a, 1988b)?

No, there is a seriously wounded self-concept involved insofar as mainstream America yearns for 'English Official/English Only' to salvage its sense of propriety and law and order. Otherwise, why the imperviousness to the data on language maintenance and language shift with respect to our non-English-mother-tongue population? Why are facts so useless in the discussion? Why is it so irrelevant to 'English Official/English Only' advocates that with the exception of isolated and self-isolated groups, such as certain Amerindians, the German-speaking Old Order Amish and Hutterites, the Russian-speaking Old Believers and the Yiddish-speaking Khasidim (none of whom would be in the least bit affected by 'English Official/English Only' legislation), all other *ethnolinguistic minorities in the USA lose their ethnic mother tongue fairly completely by their second or third generations of encounter with American urban life*. Not only do they become 'English usually' speakers: they usually become 'English only' speakers by then (Veltman, 1983; Fishman *et al.*, 1985).

Hispanics are no exception to this 'iron law' as far as learning English is concerned. Their only exceptionality pertains to their slightly longer retention of Spanish as well (a one-generational difference at most), due to the continued influx of monolingual Spanish speakers into their urban barrios. As a result of this influx the concentration of Spanish speakers remains high and the economic value of Spanish remains substantial for the denizens of the barrios (Heath, 1985) for one generation beyond the general immigrant norm. Accordingly, many second- and third-generation Hispanics who haven't learned any Spanish at home, from parents and siblings who stopped speaking it themselves or who could have spoken it to them but didn't, learn it from life in the immigrant-impacted neighborhood, an impactedness that the new immigration policy of 1986 may be on the way to counteracting.

Instead of rigidly perseverating on recent arrivals who need governmental services in Spanish if their health, education, welfare and political rights are to be safeguarded, 'English Only/English Official' advocates should be asking themselves, 'why are those second- and third-generation Hispanics – who usually or only speak English by now – still living in those barrios where previously their parents and grandparents lived and where now the new immigrants concentrate?' But to ask this question would lead to yet another unknown, undesired and/or rejected data set, namely one that shows that mastery of English is almost as inoperative with respect to Hispanic social mobility as it is with respect to Black social mobility. A racist society experiencing little sustained economic growth during the past few decades has no way of massively rewarding anglophone Hispanics. Of Hispanics today, 25% live at or below the poverty level, a rate that is easily two or even three times as high as the proportion of Hispanics that are not English-speaking. Among the older immigrants English was acquired, their immigrant cultures were destroyed, and their social mobility was their payoff or reward for the dislocation experienced. Among Hispanics, Asians, and Pacific Island immigrants of the last two decades only the first two steps in this equation have been realized (due more to the dynamics of urban dislocation and mobility aspirations than to any governmental program whatsoever).

What signs of 'getting the wrong message' are there and what would the wrong message be? Are there any signs of 'separatism', of 'ethnic political parties', of 'ethnic militancy', of 'anti-Americanism', of 'ethnic terrorism'? The Black political party that surfaces during presidential primaries is certainly of no direct relevance to 'English Official' advocates since it is supported by the most uniformally anglified population in all of American society, the Black Americans (35% of whom live at or below the poverty level and 70% of whose males are predicted to be either in jail, on drugs, or in the throes of alcoholism by the year 2000 if current trends continue unabated). Why does the anglo-oriented middle bourgeoisie feel as much or more abused by government services in languages other than English than the ethnic poor and immigrants themselves feel by the rapidly diminishing scale of such services? A higher proportion of middle-class, anglo-oriented Americans have been turned off by multilingual ballots than there are non-English-mother-tongue voters who have used such ballots. More anglo-oriented Americans have been turned off by the very notion of bilingual education than there are Limited English Proficient children who have received bilingual education. The 'why should we pay for them?' syndrome, the 'why didn't my grandparents get such benefits?' syndrome, the '*we* know what's good for them' syndrome, the '*we* only want to liberate them from their ethnic self-imprisonment (because when we follow our leaders that is free choice but when they follow their leaders that is capitulating to demagoguery)' syndrome, these all boil down to the 'who's in control here anyway; we who deserve to be or those riff-raff and upstarts.?' These attitudes are all sublimations of the sense of being abused, of being taken advantage of, of being denied one's own rightful place in the sun and in the scheme of things that seems to plague so much of anglo-oriented America today. The 'English only/English Official' movement may largely represent the displacement of middle-class anglo fears and anxieties from the difficult if not intractable *real* causes of their fears and anxieties to mythical and simplistic and stereotyped scapegoats. If those with these fears are successful in passing 'English Official' amendments, this would represent another 'liberation of Grenada' rather than any mature grappling with the really monumental economic, social and political causes of conflict, unrest and contention in either America or the world at large today.

'English Official/English Only' advocates continues to stress the problems 'out there', due to and among non-English-speaking Americans. They refuse to admit to any problems 'in here', that is, among themselves and among middle-class anglified Americans more generally. There can be no doubt that such problems exist, given that it has proved to be so relatively easy for the holders of power to launch a witch-hunt in the 1980s, a patriotic 'purification' campaign against 'foreign elements', akin today to the anti-Catholic, anti-immigrant, anti-Black and anti-hyphenated-American campaigns of past eras American history. Indeed, the campaign against 'foreign contaminants' has attracted an odd mix of adherents, among them conservation/natural resources proponents, those who fear that Hispanics are plotting to force Anglos to learn Spanish as the nation's first language (a case of the pot calling the kettle black, if there ever was one), and supporters of a large variety of traditional conservative causes (such as 'right to life' [= antiabortion] and anti-gun control). Finally, having discovered that it is an issue that excites the baser instincts, it has been exploited as a fund-raising and voter-mobilization ploy for conservative candidates, causes and referenda reaching far beyond the English issue *per se*. In political parlance, it is a 'stampeder', an issue whose importance far transcends its own limits. The insecurity of the relatively secure and those who wishfully identify with them shouts out from above and around this odd assembly of defenders of middle-class good-and-welfare. It is this insecurity that needs to be examined, more than anything else, in order to understand the 'English Only/English Official' appeal on the current American political scene.

And why is anglo-oriented, middle-class America particularly insecure and upset by 'these foreigners' in its midst who are getting government services in languages other than English? Perhaps because it is America that has lost more relative leverage on the world scene than any other major power during the past two score years; perhaps because it is the American economy that has performed less glamorously than its own mythology and built-in aspirations and expectations had led its prior beneficiaries to expect; perhaps because the ethnic revival led to multicultural mutterings that finally frightened more of the mutterers and their listeners than it satisfied, gratified or influenced in any way (Fishman *et al.*, 1985); perhaps because this is the first anglo-American generation that has had to face the possibility that it and its children would not rise socially to a station in life higher than that of their parents, etc. The new insecurities of anglo-mainstream-oriented American middle-class life, combined with the widespread disappointment in the liberal ameliorative promise of the Roosevelt-to-Johnson era, have led to the 'English Only/ English Official' 'solution', a 'cheap thrill' if there ever was one. It solves none of the problems leading to the above-mentioned insecurities (indeed, it does not even recognize any of those problems) and, therefore, still leaves the way open for various other vindictive displacements or 'unloadings' or insecurity in the future. It is the classical wrong solution to the wrong problem. Indeed, even were English in America being threatened by other languages, the 'English Only/English Official' forces have failed to recognize that such a language conflict, like all other language conflicts wherever they arise, merely represents the tip of the iceberg of interethnolinguistic conflict based upon economic, political and cultural grievances. These grievances represent the real problems and not their linguistic concomitants. If interethnolinguistic divisiveness is a real threat to America, which I firmly believe it is not (that charge being no more than a currently fashionable form of nativistic witch-hunting), then 'English Only/English Official' efforts are wasting our time, leading us away from real solutions to the causes of this threat and orienting us to the pursuit of mere symptoms and byproducts of the threat. Thus, even in terms of its own definition of what ails America, 'English Only/English Official' is an abysmal failure in getting down to basic causes and, therefore, at suggesting effective solutions. By manufacturing the myth of 'giving our new arrivals the wrong message' (which, like all myths, is shrouded in vague and unspoken mysteries and allusions), it must wind up with an unreal solution. Myths, as Barthes (1972) and Woolard (in press) remind us, do not simply hide the truth, they distort it. The truth is that 'English Only/English Official' efforts cannot hide the fact that the power class (and those Anglos and non-Anglos who aspire to join its ranks) feels insecure about its own leadership role and its power prerogatives in American society; the distortion arises when others (those who are presumably 'getting the wrong message' by thinking that they too deserve some power in American life) are blamed for these insecurities and for the power class's difficulties in finding genuine solutions to them.

The profile of 'English Only' supporters revealed by the June 1986 nation-wide poll of the New York Times/Columbia Broadcasting System reveals an age, education and income progression. The older the age, the higher the income, and the higher the education, the greater the support for 'English Only', with relatively little support coming from Blacks, Hispanics or other minorities (Asians, Amerindians). This is an alarming alignment of power vs. its absence, except for an equally alarming minor reversal of this trend at the lowest end of the (white) income distribution (family income below $12,000/year), where 'English Only' sentiment out-polls that among those whose family income is at the very top of the scale (above $50,000/year). It is this latter identification of whites desperate for the taste of power – and for disassociation from non-white immigrant minorities – with those who already 'have made it' that carries with it a potentially dangerous explosive charge. Note should also be taken of the atypicality of those relatively few Hispanics who are active in mainstream politics in the USA, when interpreting the tendency of the Hispanic middle class (from whose ranks the new Director of the Office of Bilingual Education and Minority Language Affairs, Alicia Coro, and the new Direc-tor of U.S. English, Linda Chavez, are drawn) to vote for 'English Only'. The Hispanic middle class is obviously faced with a 'no-win' situation. Either they must reject the charge of anti-Americanism or they must confirm it, and the only way they can reject the charge in today's climate of opinion is to vote for 'English Only' far more frequently than do other Hispanics (29%). Hispanics pay their own price, a doubly heavy price, for their membership, or membership aspirations, in the American establishment.

## Of Times and Tides in American History

Although we have tried to grapple with the question of 'why now?', our answer, above, should not hide the fact, already alluded to, that this is not the first time in American history when immigrants and their languages have been considered suspect by significant segments of the establishment. In the early years of the Republic, Benjamin Franklin railed against the Pennsylvania Germans because of his inability to influ-ence them during election campaigns because they understood no English and he, no German. Anti-Catholicism and anti-immigration biases were prominent in the 1880s and, appropriately enough, were referred to (by adherents and detractors alike) as constituting the 'Know Nothing' party (a designation that would be quite appropriate for the ELA ideol-ogists today). During and after the First World War, we witnessed a spate of antihyphenation, antiforeigner, antiforeign language agitation and legislation (the legislation all being found unconstitutional by the end of that decade). And here we are again, in a period of retreat from affirmative action, anti-immigration legislation, budget cutting with respect to health, education and welfare programs, and serious threats to Social Security and Medicare. As before, the threat to cultural democ-racy and to continually renewed and self-maintaining ethnolinguistic diversity comes from the right of the American political spectrum, such as it is. However, as Arthur Schlesinger, Jr, has recently pointed out, 'both conservatism and reform degenerate into excess'. Just as liberal reformism produced problems by *its* solutions, so our current conservative binge is producing problems, fiscal, moral and military, by its policies and priorities. Accordingly, as the debits of conservatism begin to clearly outweigh its assets, there should come, 'shortly before or after the year 1990 ... a sharp change in the national mood and direction ... , [when power should pass to] the young men and women who came of political age in the Kennedy years' (Schlesinger, 1986). Unfortunately, it is not absolutely clear that Schlesinger is a good prophet in this particular connection, recent polls having indicated a growing conservatism (rather than a growing liberal inclination) among America's younger population. Nevertheless, their Kennedy/Vietnam/youth revolt experiences of the 1960s and 1970s may still leave them more accepting of minorities and ethnic differences and contributions than their parents were or are to this very day.

Schlesinger takes comfort from this cyclical nature of American politics, because he believes that 'the two jostling strains in American thought ... [are] indissoluble partners in the great adventure of democracy'. I agree and find consolation in the idea that no political establishment is likely to become so established as to permanently foreclose philosophical opposition and pragmatic cost-effectiveness accounting in the electorate. But another comment by Schlesinger also strikes me as basically correct and gives me greater concern in my sociolinguistic capacity. Schlesinger reminds us that 'in the American republic, conservatism and reform ... agree more than they disagree'. This is nowhere truer than in the realm of language.

## The Two-Front War: Fostering Ethnolinguistic Diversity as a National Good

My basic opposition to the 'English Only/English Official' efforts is that I would like my government to actively foster and value ethnolinguistic diversity. If Australia can declare that every child that has one should be encouraged and assisted to maintain an ancestral language other than English, and every child who does not have (or no longer has) one should be encouraged and assisted to acquire and maintain a community language other than English, then I am strengthened in my conviction that the American mind and the American heart and soul are sufficiently accepting and encouraging to make a similar statement. In pursuit of such a goal of government activity on behalf of fostering ethnolinguistic diversity as a national desideratum, I find myself stymied by the residual lack of language consciousness (certainly lack of positive language consciousness) that we have acquired from our British intellectual and legal heritage, on the one hand, and by the uniformity that is similarly shared by conservatism and liberalism, on the other hand. There is as much opposition to ethnolinguistic diversity in Marx, Engels, Roosevelt and Hart as in Lord Acton, Ronald Reagan, Jacques Barzun and Senator Hayakawa. The left (or the so-called 'liberal center') fantasizes an ethnically uniformed America as much as does the right, even if it does not act out its fantasies quite so openly and so fully. The one conceives of ethnolinguistic diversity as bourgeois nationalism that sunders the unified proletariat, and the other conceives of it as subversive extremism that destroys the established order. Both associate it with pure emotionality or even irrationality, since both see in it values and priorities that are unrelated to the maximization of productivity in the economic sphere. The mild (practically inaudible) language maintenance stance of the National Association for Bilingual Education, of the Smithsonian's annual festivals of American folklife (even that of the 1987 Festival, with its emphasis on 'America's many voices' [=languages]), of the National Council of Teachers of English, of the National Council for Black Studies, of the Linguistic Society of America, of the Conference on College Composition and Communication, of the Center for Applied Linguistics, of the National Council of the Churches of Christ in the USA, and of the American Jewish Committee's Institute of Human Relations does not begin to redress the imbalance, for most of them are merely being tolerant, rather than vibrant, with respect to fostering the non-English language resources in the USA, and others of them are engaging in special pleading, which is equally, if not more, ineffective (Smitherman-Donaldson, 1987). Nor is the constant academic call for 'more research' (note the study on 'English Language Concerns in American Life: Historical and Contemporary Dimensions', headed by Prof. Guadelupe San Miguel, of Education and Chicano Studies, University of California, Santa Barbara, with very modest Ford Foundation support) anything like a goal or an effective lever. We are a long, long way from a positive language policy, such as the one the Australians have just adopted calling for an active second language (either English or a Community Language Other Than English) for every Australian; indeed, so far away that it would be not only premature but dangerously self-defeating to engage, at any now-foreseeable date, in the requisite discussion out of which such a policy might ultimately flow. The disentanglement of linguistic pluralism from civil strife and from debits in connection with per-capita gross national product has only just begun even in academia (Fishman & Solano, 1988a, 1988b), and it will be a long time before the implications of that disentanglement trickle down to the lay public and its leaders.

As an unabashed linguistic pluralist, I have not only the 'English Only/ English Official' forces to contend with but also all those forces, whether on the right or on the left, that deny the Herderian/Whorfian/Kallenian vision (and, I might add, the Hebrew prophetic vision of 'seventy peoples and seventy languages' even 'in the end of all days' when the earth will be full of the glory of God), a vision of ethnolinguistic pluralism as a value in its own right. So yes, I will continue to struggle for bilingual education stressing its enrichment potential for all children, rather than merely its transitional use en route to English-only in the school, a compensatory use that I predicted a dozen years ago would be self-destructive for bilingual education [Fishman, 1973]). Only enrichment bilingual education will gratify the social and cultural mobility goals of the middle class for its children and turn that class into allies, rather than sullen enemies, of bilingual education. I will oppose the terribly, destructively misguided 'English Only/English Official' efforts, although I think they may yet experience some further local victories in the short run, before the courts and the new *Zeitgeist* that is coming catch up with them. But I will also continue to oppose American uniformity under any guise, political, ethnic, religious or philosophical. If a turn toward reform is coming, and every time I read the headlines it seems to me to be simultaneously overdue, impossible and inevitable, then I hope to have introduced enough Herderian/Whorfian/Kallenian thought into the awareness of a younger generation of students and colleagues (see for example Fishman *et al.*, 1982) to convince the reformers that it is not enough to be *anti*-'English Only' or *anti*-'English Official'. Ethnolinguistic diversity is something I hope they will be *for*, as a public good (as it is in Australia, where the personality principle is just as dominant and the territoriality principle is just as inoperative as they are in the USA), as something that is in the national interest and in the interest of all our children and, therefore, as something that reform needs to champion when it again finds its place in the sun, just as conservatism should, both being 'indissoluble partners in the great adventure of [American] democracy'.

Neither major partner in the American idea and the American experience has done right in so far as fostering linguistic pluralism is concerned. Each has to be taught that in the American tradition *unum* and *pluribus* go hand in hand. The *unum* grows out of *pluribus* but does not replace it! The *unum* ideal and the *unum* reality pertain to our love for and loyalty to America and its fundamental political institutions and commitments. The *pluribus* ideal pertains to our substantive values, to our religious commitments, to our problem-solving approaches, to the living ethnic heritages, the costreams of American life and American vision that remain alive for million upon millions of our citizens. In a system of checks and balances, it is the *pluribus* ideal that counterbalances the *unum* ideal. Each saves the other from its excesses, and it is the *pluribus* ideal that requires bolstering in America today. The 'protectors of *pluribus*' must rally their forces of conviction and of persuasion, because pluralism

is the very genius of America: pluralism of political jurisdictions, pluralism of educational jurisdictions, pluralism of religious faiths (most of
which, by the way, are ethnically focused as well), and pluralism of
intellectual and philosophical outlooks. It is this broad-minded and
good-hearted pluralism that have made America great and no mean-
spirited, ghost-battling, witch-hunting, frightened bullyboys can long
deflect it from the patrimony of *pluribus* that has made it great in the
past and that will keep it so in the future.

## Note

1. This article is a revision of a keynote-address originally prepared for the
   California Association of Bilingual Education (CABE) Conference, January
   28–31, 1987, Anaheim, CA. Since its preparation, EPIC (English Plus Information Clearinghouse) has been organized by the National Forum and The
   Joint National Committee for Languages (227 Massachusetts Ave., N.W. Suite
   #120, Washington, D.C. 20002) to coordinate popular and scholarly efforts on
   behalf of culturally pluralistic language policy in the USA.

## References

Australia: Commonwealth Department of Education (1982) *Towards a National
    Language Policy*. Canberra: Australian Government Printing Service.
Barthes, Roland (1972) *Mythologies*. New York: Hill and Wang.
Churchill, Stacy, and Smith, Anthony (1986) The emerging consensus. *Language
    and Society/Langue et société* 18, 5–11.
Clyne, Michael G. (ed.) (1985) *Australia, Meeting Place of Languages*. Canberra: ANU
    Pacific Linguistics.
Fishman, Joshua A. *et al.* (1968) *Language Problems of Developing Nations*. New York:
    Wiley.
——. (1973) Bilingual education: what and why? *The Florida FL Reporter* (Spring/
    Fall), 13–14, 22, 43.
—— *et al.* (1977) *The Spread of English*. Rowley, MA: Newbury House.
——. (1982) Whorfianism of the third kind: ethnolinguistic diversity as an inter-
    national societal asset. *Language in Society* 11, 1–14.
—— *et al.* (1985) *The Rise and Fall of the Ethnic Revival*. Berlin: Mouton de Gruyter.
—— and Solano, Frank (1988a) Cross-polity perspective on the importance of lin-
    guistic heterogeneity as a 'contributory factor' in civil strife. *Proceedings of the
    Hyderabad Conference on Language and National Development*. Hyderabad:
    Osmania University.
—— and Solano, Frank (1988b) Cross-polity perspective on the importance of lin-
    guistic heterogeneity as a 'contributory factor' in per-capita gross national
    product. *Proceedings of the Heslington Conference on Sociolinguistic and Social
    Change*. Heslington: University of York.
Garcia, Ofelia, and Otheguy, Ricardo (1986) The education of language-minority
    children: impressions of London from a New York perspective. *Primary Teaching
    Studies*, 2, 81–94.
Heath, Shirley, B. (1985) Language policies: patterns of retention and maintenance.
    In Walker Conner (ed.) *Mexican-Americans in Comparative Perspective*, (pp. 257–
    282). Washington: Urban Institute Press.
Kachru, Braj B. (1982) *The Other Tongue: English Across Cultures*. Urbana: University
    of Illinois Press.

Linguistic Minorities Project (1983) *Linguistic Minorities in England*. London: University of London Institute of Education.

Marshall, David F. (1986) The question of an official language: language rights and the English language amendment. *International Journal of the Sociology of Language* 60, 7–76.

McRae, Kenneth, and L'Allier, Jean-Paul (1986) Youth speaks out. *Language and Society/Langue et société* 18, 12–19.

Pauwels, Anne (ed.) (1988) The future of ethnic languages in Australia. *International Journal of the Sociology of Language* 72 (entire issue).

Schlesinger, Arthur M., Jr. (1986) *The Cycles of American History*. Boston: Houghton Mifflin.

Smitherman-Donaldson, Geneva (1987) Toward a national public policy on language. *College English* 49, 29–36.

Turi, Giuseppi (1977) *Les dispositions juridico-constitutionnelles de 147 états en matière de politique linguistique*. Quebec City: International Center for Research on Bilingualism.

Veltman, Calvin (1983) *Language Shift in the United States*. Berlin: Mouton.

Webster, Noah (1790) *A Collection of Essays and Fugitiv* [sic!] *Writings*. New Haven.

Woolard, Kathryn A. (in press) Sentences in the language prison: the rhetoric of an American language debate. Paper presented at the American Anthropology Association annual meeting, December, 1986, Philadelphia.

*Chapter 11*

# On the Limits of Ethnolinguistic Democracy[1]

## The Principle of Ethnolinguistic Democracy

The various fargoing political and economic realignments that have recently swept over Europe, both Western and Eastern, make it necessary for all who have previously advocated ethnolinguistic democracy to try to rethink the practicality and the advisability of this ideal. The growing prospects and problems of democratization in Eastern and Southern Europe and the increasing integration of the European (Economic) Community often lend a particular urgency to either broadening or restricting the principle of ethnolinguistic democracy and simultaneously raise cogent questions as to the justifiability of its invocation in one context or another. Clearly, the extent to which this principle has been examined and implemented in Western and West-Central Europe has very definite implications for its examination and implementation elsewhere. Accordingly, I will base my comments, below, on Western and West-Central European examples; I do so, however, only as a matter of metaphorical parsimony. The issues, as well as the dimensions, that I will discuss and posit also have, I firmly believe, rather general and even worldwide relevance.

## What Exactly is the Principle of Ethnolinguistic Democracy?

On 11 December, 1990, the European Community's Parliament adopted the 'principle of complete multilingualism' with respect to its own operations. This resolution goes beyond any previous policy or resolution of the European Community (hereafter: EC) in that it posits this principle to be 'consistent with the respect which is owed to the dignity of all languages which reflect and express the cultures of the different peoples who make up the EC' (Argemi, 1991). Admittedly, this resolution was adopted due to Catalan pressure (as evidenced by 100,000 signatures delivered to the President of the EC's European

Parliament in 1987, in support of granting Catalan some sort of official standing in the EC organization's operations), but its adoption three years later was justified on grounds going far beyond the Catalan position, namely as being appropriate in order that the 'people of Europe do not regard European institutions as being out of touch with and foreign to them' ... but, rather, that they 'look upon them as important elements playing a part in the daily life of the citizens' (Argemi, 1991).

The implications of this position go far beyond the EC organization alone, and even far beyond language use in official institutions. Presumably, the cultures of the peoples that make up Europe should be even more basically enabled and assured of their right to *conduct their intra-cultural affairs in their own languages*, since such enablement must precede and provide the foundation for any rights or enablements to use their languages in inter-cultural affairs, such as those of the EC. The latter without the former would merely be a dishonest display, a Potemkin village built over a festering wound, just as the former without the latter is an affront to that 'respect which is owed to the dignity of all ... cultures'. In addition, it should be noted, the resolution is couched within a principle (the principle of 'complete multilingualism') that posits the view that all parties to a particular sphere of joint interaction should be able to engage in that interaction in their own language and that appropriate provisions for bi-directional communication must flow from that principle rather than dictate or limit its feasibility. Both the intra-cultural and the inter-cultural assumptions mentioned above, taken together, constitute the principle of complete ethnolinguistic democracy.

Note, however, that at the same time as the European Parliament's new resolution was adopted (a resolution that was fully in agreement, by the way, with its previous resolutions in recent years), it did not grant Catalan official status within EC operations. In essence, in operational organizational terms, the resolution merely served to encourage Catalans to continue exploring some sort of recognized status. Short of the full official status now recognized for nine languages, there is also possibly the status of 'working language' insofar as relations between the Autonomous Catalan Community and the EC are concerned. The principle of ethnolinguistic democracy does not require that all languages be declared equally important and equally privileged in all functions, i.e. at some point in the total interaction matrix that is imaginable between them, some consideration of proportionality between them may still be appealed to and implemented. Therefore, while acknowledging the principle of ethnolinguistic democracy, the European Parliament also recognized that within its own operations (and, implicitly, within any complex multilingual framework) some notion of limits must also exist, very much as notions of limits have existed in all theories of political democracy and individual rights from the very earliest times.

Just where and when the the limits of democratic rights should be drawn, be they linguistic or more general, can well be viewed as a dilemma within the democratic ethos itself. Limits can be set in self-serving ways and those who wield greater power are particularly likely to have a disproportionate say in the establishment of such limits. Establishments are more likely to limit others than to limit themselves, and, therefore, to appeal to or to implement any notion of limits primarily for the preservation and furtherance of their own power, rather than to permit others to have access to power by engaging in power-sharing.

In this last connection, the dilemma faced by the European Parliament is actually a global one. Languages are not merely innocent means of communication. They stand for or symbolize peoples, i.e. ethnocultures, and it is not obviously apparent to what extent administrative or econotechnical structures (cities, regions, states, international organizations) can, in practice, actually recognize, empower and/or assist them all. Languages may very well all be equally valid and precious markers of cultural belonging, behavior and identity, while nevertheless being far from equally valuable or viable as vehicles of either intergroup or econotechnical communication. Whether, where, when and how to draw the line between the two, i.e. between ethnolinguistic democracy, on the one hand, and ethnolinguistic equality, on the other hand, is often a matter frought with tension, guilt and outright conflict as well.

## The Principle of Ethnolinguistic Democracy at the Suprastate Level

Suprastate organizations, we must bear in mind, are originally and basically the creatures of states. As such, these organizations are rarely, if ever, strong enough to impose their own will on the strongest of their own creators. Thus, when the EC came into being, it quite understandably designated the official state languages of all of its creators as its official languages. As the EC has expanded, over the years, it has correspondingly expanded the number of its official languages. Thus far this has been feasible, but it has already become difficult (not to say expensive). After all, 72 different translation skills are called for in order to handle nine different but theoretically equal languages in all possible directions (although, admittedly, a few of these directions are seldom if ever called for in practice, whereas others are so common as to virtually represent the norms; see Haselhuber, 1991). Indeed, the Language Service has become one of the EC's largest administrative budgetary items. However, a more parsimonious approach, e.g. the adoption of a subset of one or more 'administrative' super-languages for the public operation of the European Parliament, has thus far proved to be absolutely impossible. Obviously, French, German, Italian and Spanish – but particularly French – cannot bring themselves to recognize English for what it has generally become, namely, *primus inter pares*. To do so would be viewed and experienced as an act of relative demotion for the others, even though their customary functions and perquisites, both at home and throughout the world, would in all probability remain unchanged. An administrative 'Big Brother' (or even 'Big Quintuplets') for the EC would smack of 'internal colonialism' and that would be the kiss of death for the EC *per se*, particularly since French still retains disproportionate prominence in conjunction with the EC operations in Brussels (as distinct from the European Parliament's operations in Strasbourg).

The UN, however, from the very outset, unabashedly differentiated between a small subset of 'working languages' (English and French) and a somewhat larger cluster of 'official languages' (English, French, Russian, Chinese and Spanish). All other languages received no official standing or recognition whatsoever. More recently, the UN added Arabic to its short list of 'working languages' and whereas the Secretariat continues to use English and French alone, various other UN bodies use various other 'working languages' as well. Thus the 'working languages' are a subset of the 'official languages' and both clusters taken together are no more than half a dozen and quite Eurocentric in nature. Its worldwide purview obviously led the UN away from any attempt at formulating a principle of 'complete multilingualism' from the very outset, just as its super-power origins led it from the very outset to make distinctions between the super-powers (with their permanent seats and veto-power in the Security Council) and the lesser powers.

By contrast, the EC, with a much smaller membership, also has integrative responsibilities even in the social and cultural realms, responsibilities that the UN does not even contemplate. These integrative responsibilities heighten authenticity sensitivities and these sensitivities render any linguistic distinctions (such as 'administrative' or 'working' vs. 'official') apparently impossible for the immediate future. Thus far, the EC must follow the 'equal in principle' approach *vis-à-vis* all of its *state* languages, even though it is quite clear that these languages are by no means equal insofar as their European and worldwide inter-state functions and utility are concerned (Haarmann, 1991). The states insist on considering the EC organization as one in which they are completely equal in principle and, accordingly, one in which the state languages too are completely equal and equally indispensable for all symbolic EC purposes. While it is generally true that all adopted EC decisions become binding as national laws in each member-state and that, therefore, they must be authoritatively translated into all the official languages of the member states, the internal operation of the EC organization *per se* is paying a very heavy price for this particular intra-state function, a price which its own bureaucrats attempt to escape from 'unofficially' for internal and closed EC operations, but for which there is no public 'official' relief.

What will this principle of 'complete multilingualism' mean when the EC is further expanded, as now seems absolutely predictable, given that Austria, Sweden and Finland are certainly assured of membership, with membership for Norway almost equally certain? Membership for Hungary and Czechoslovakia (or separately for Bohemia-Moravia and Slovakia) is also already under discussion. If the six new official languages of these additional states (six new languages and not seven, because the state language of Austria is already represented in the EC) are also to be treated as equal in principle with the current nine, that would result in 210 directions of translation between 15 languages. If all other European states are ultimately admitted, even barring separate membership for the subdivisions of the former Yugoslavia and USSR, the application of the unlimited principle of 'complete multilingualism' would result in fully 420 directions of translation for the official communications between 21 members in the EC. If the Soviet subdivisions too are admitted, 600 directions of translation would obtain between 25 official state languages! Clearly, some theory of limits must be invoked, perhaps via a distinction between administrative ('working') and official languages, even when equally sovereign states are involved in inter-state or supra-state activities (Leitner, 1991). But it is very difficult for sovereign states to agree to limit themselves, and even more difficult to do so once their organization has been established precisely on the principle of ethnolinguistic equality.

## The Principle of Ethnolinguistic Democracy at the Sub-State Level

The Council of Europe, on the other hand, has a much more varied and inclusive membership than the current EC. Furthermore, unlike the EC the Council of Europe has no legal standing within its own member states. As a result, it should come as no surprise that it not only uses only English and French as its official and working languages, but that within the limits of its 23 member states there are fully 85 non-state languages (counting only those whose speakers are of pre-World War II autochtonous vintage; Verdoodt, 1991). Given a number this large, it should also come as no surprise that these sub-state languages and their ethnocultural communities are differentially recognized (or ignored) and differentially treated (or maltreated) by their corresponding state authorities. Many Catalans  –  their own language being more prestigeful within the Autonomous Catalan Community than is the language of the Spanish state – may be less than fully satisfied by their less than fully autonomous status within Spain (not to mention their less than fully equal status within the EC organization). But their lot would be considered quite a fortunate one by the Catalans in France and, indeed, by the Occitans, Bretons and Basques in France, not to mention the Frisians in the Netherlands, the Ladins and Friulians in Italy, and a large number of quasi-recognized and entirely unrecognized regional ethnolinguistic concentrations throughout the member countries of the Council of Europe.

By and large, many members of the autochtonous sub-state ethnolinguistic communities in Western Europe (not to mention other, less democratically-oriented parts of the world), do not believe that the principle of ethnolinguistic democracy is being applied to them even *vis-à-vis* their *intra*-communal lives, let alone the principle of complete multilingualism or complete equality of languages. These languages are very often not recognized even for educational, media, judicial, legislative or other public services, even in their very own areas of concentration, insofar as the state authorities and state funding are concerned. Indeed, many of these ethnolinguistic communities are already in such weakened circumstances that very carefully pinpointed and informed efforts are required in order to salvage even the intimate family–home–neighborhood foundations of their intergenerational mother-tongue continuity (Fishman, 1991). Barring such informed efforts at reversing language shift – efforts which are difficult to plan precisely because they must focus on the elusive processes of informal/private intra-familial and intra-communal life during the early childhood years prior to and *pari-passu* with elementary education – even the genuinely 'good intentioned' acts of supporting some instructional, publication and/or media efforts in threatened languages predictably bear little intergenerational fruit. Obviously the states are even more reluctant to apply the principle of ethnolinguistic democracy *below* (or within) the level of the state than they are to set aside the principle of ethnolinguistic equality above the level of the state.

States manifest concern about the possibility of disruptive ethnic unrest, on the one hand, and pyramiding costs, on the other hand, should the principle of ethnolinguistic democracy be recognized to any significant degree below the level of the state, in addition, states often shed crocodile tears as to the lamentable corpus characteristics of those of their sub-state varieties that claim language (i.e. not merely dialect) status, characteristics which presumably always make these sub-state languages patently unsuitable for school, media or public administration use. The Netherlands is very certain that Nederlands is as good a language as English for the operation of the EC, but it is not sure that

Frisian is as good a language as Nederlands for the operation of local public services in Friesland. In other words, states are not slow to apply to languages lower in the pecking order than the state-languages *per se*, the very same notions of limits that the state languages are so unwilling to apply to themselves *vis-à-vis* the EC organization's operations.

There is a double standard here, the concept of limits being vociferously put off in one context (the 'manageable' inter-state case) and prematurely applied in the other (the 'obviously unmanageable' intra-state case). And, as always, the implementation of a double standard leads to self-confirming hypotheses, i.e. it results in perpetrating cumulatively increasing harm to the statuses and the corpuses of the sub-state languages involved, without offering them the benefits of the same kind of corpus planning in which the state languages themselves engage in order 'to be intertranslatable with English'. Friulian does become less and less suitable to be the language of public institutions the longer it is denied this function and the corpus planning it would require. The above sorry picture – certainly sorry insofar as providing 'the respect which is owed to the dignity of all languages which reflect and express the cultures of the different peoples who make up the EC' (to once more use the EC's wording) – does not even include the indigenous minorities outside of Western/Central Europe, not to mention the immigrant languages of this continent. The latter, the immigrant languages, are truly low-men on the ethnolinguistic democracy totem-pole. They benefit neither from *primum mobile* nor from ideologies that tend to contribute to the conservation or democratization of cultural resources at the intrastate level.

## Sociolinguistic Repertoires in Search of Ethnolinguistic Democracy

It is clear that many autochtonous European ethnocultural minorities (even Western European ones) do not as yet approximate what the Catalans of Spain may well have to settle for in the EC organization, namely, some overt sign of respect for and acknowledgement of the mother tongues that represent and express their ethnocultural identities (even though these signs may fall short of officialization). What way out of their dilemmas should and could an enlightened language policy attempt? Quite obviously, the principle of ethnolinguistic democracy will come up against different objective limits at the levels of individuals, of peoples (or cultures), of regions and of states. At the lowest or smallest ethnolinguistic levels, the problems of critical mass must come into play very early (as they often do even with the delivery of postal, medical and other vital social services that are provided by recognized regional or central authorities). Mail and medical services too are not always delivered to the door in the smallest and furthest outlying points. But setting such considerations aside, as involving an obvious and too often utilized excuse for official inaction, there is yet another consideration to keep in mind, namely, the status of the particular local/regional languages when viewed in a larger, more inclusive perspective.

In Northern Italy, German, French or even Slovenian can more easily be acknowledged for authoritative regional social services – even if they are not always so acknowledged – than can Valdostian, Friulian or Ladin which are often co-present in roughly the same areas. Speakers of the former require no more than a one language supplement in order to function both at a broader regional as well as at the national level. Those starting with German, e.g. need add only Italian as a second language, an addition which usually occurs at or before the elementary school level. However, those starting out with a variety of Friulian, need not only to add Italian and French or German, but these Friulian speakers cannot even take Friulian for granted in most localized social services. Obviously, local/regional languages themselves vary greatly in total size, status and support possibilities, both from within and from without the particular states in which they find themselves.

The smaller the total speech community, combining both those members within and those without the boundaries of any given state, the more serious are the problems of fostering even its intergenerational mother tongue continuity, let alone its use for out-of-home functions. The more pressing, therefore, are the reasons why various other, larger languages must be resorted to among the mother tongue speakers of the smallest languages, in order to enable these speakers to participate effectively at regional, state and supra-state levels. The larger the total speech community, the more likely its language is to be a state language somewhere. Therefore, even if another state language as well as supra-state language will need to be learned (e.g. among German speakers in Northern Italy), the mother tongue itself still possesses the corpus and status resources necessary for variegated modern functioning. Only the speakers of unquestioned international 'super languages' can *pretend* to be totally effective in modern life while remaining monolingual. Thus, clearly, those who start off *weakest* are required to protest the *most vigorously* at three levels, in order to (a) secure ethnolinguistic democracy in intra-communal affairs, (b) engage in the minimally adequate corpus planning required by local government and new media, and (c) attain access to national and international roles in their intergroup lives. The price they have to pay is a considerable one, not because it is difficult for individuals to learn several languages, but because it is difficult for societies to maintain several languages simultaneously, particularly when these languages differ greatly in functionality and when the width of the linguistic repertoire characterizing a speech community is demonstrably inversely related to its econotechnical autonomy and its sociocultural self-regulation.

## The Dilemmas of the Smallest Mother Tongues, Namely Those that are 'Non-Governmental' Everywhere that they are Spoken

Sub-state mother tongues, particularly mother tongues that are non-governmental everywhere that they are spoken, are obviously often viewed as 'multi-problem languages', whether in Western Europe or elsewhere (Mackey, 1991), even though their problems are far from self-inflicted but derive from their less than sympathetic neighbors. Unfortunately for the future of ethnolinguistic democracy, these very languages constitute the vast majority of the world's languages and they pertain to approximately a quarter of the world's population. These languages most commonly lack even any effective legal conventions to either protect or assist them. Most of them have no written functions or very meager ones, and, therefore, no standard orthographies or grammars to bridge their dialect differences. They lack budgets for audio-visual media and, even if such exist, their media programs cannot compete, either in number or in quality, with those of their surrounding 'Big Brothers'. At present they have very little econotechnical value. Above all, they may even lack sufficient demographic concentration in the very districts in which they are autochtonous, i.e. 'sufficient' in order to make intergenerational mother-tongue continuity the effortless and normal experience that it is for speakers of the state languages.

Others are always looking over the shoulders of sub-state languages, particularly when we consider those that are sub-state languages everywhere, in order to decide if they are 'worth the time and effort' required in order to keep them going. Worst of all, this literally 'existential' question is often answered for them by outsiders. Ethnolinguistic democracy, or (again in the words of the Parliament of the EC) the principle of 'respect owed to the dignity of all languages which reflect and express the cultures of ... different peoples', requires that insiders make this decision under unpressured circumstances and with equitable access to the general budget for local cultural efforts and social services. The smallest sub-state languages will always entail additional burdens and call for additional dedication on the part of their speakers, but decisions concerning the futures of these languages should therefore be made by those most likely also to value the integrative blessings of such languages as well, blessings in the form of relatively undislocated ethnocultural identities, belongingnesses, and intergenerational ethnolinguistic continuities.

When all is said and done, the question of the limits of ethnolinguistic denmocracy usually raises its head first for those who are speakers of the smallest sub-state languages, the ones that are sub-state everywhere that they are spoken. Furthermore, the subdivisability of both human ethnocultural identity and ethnolinguistic expression is fairly infinite, corresponding to the gradients of intensity of human interaction under the influence of various economic, geographic and historical circumstances. Even relatively small written languages often subsume several different spoken varieties and the speech communities utilizing these varieties can, under certain circumstances, each strike out on their own, developing their own written standards, stressing their own distinctive authenticity and, possibly, even their own political aspirations. In principle, this process never runs its course, not even in the light of the uniformizing effects of modern mass-markets and mass-media. Further subdivisions are always possible, though perhaps less probable, even where shared political and econotechnical institutions and experiences exist. The over-arching resources and powers of the state seemingly reach their integrative limits much earlier than do the multiple identity capacities of humankind.

We are, all of us, simultaneously, identified as individuals, as family members, as neighborhood residents, as members of communities that may involve a considerable variety of religious, occupational and political sub-networks, as regional participants, as state citizens and, more recently, as supra-state participants as well. We often feel little conflict between such multiple roles and identities, but should such conflict arise, any of the smaller identities can become not only contrastively available but even salient as well, and their linguistic counterparts can, sometimes rather quickly, become part and parcel of new and mobilizable language and ethnicity linkages that had previously been quiescent or even non-functional.

## Conclusion: Resolving Tensions Between Broader and Narrower Identities

Smaller ethnocultural and ethnolinguistic units are obviously under pressure to re-ethnify and relinguify in the direction of the more powerful reward-systems that surround them. It is the fear of just such potentially dislocative re-ethnification and relinguification that keeps the member states of the EC from overtly adopting just one, two or three overarching languages of administration. However, this same type of fear characterizes the sub-state languages *vis-à-vis* the state languages. Indeed, in some regions there are sub-regional ethnolinguistic aggregates that experience this same fear *vis-à-vis* the regional languages that surround them, albeit the latter themselves are also minority languages within their respective states. Thus, just as some Nederlands speakers fear being relinguified and re-ethnified by English, so some Frisians fear relinguification and re-ethnification by Nederlands, and, startlingly enough, some Stellingwerfsk speakers fear being relinguified and re-ethnified by the Frisians that surround and outnumber them.

Nevertheless, the co-occurrence of both broader and narrower identities and loyalties are not only often possible but inevitable, and the further down one goes in the scale of ethnolinguistic and ethnocultural identity, the more (rather than the less) such co-occurrences of part-identities are encountered. 'Down there', in the deepest reaches of small ethnocultural identity, the notion of limits quite frequently seems more flexible, more expandable and more multiply-rewarding than such identity seems from above. More Frisians also consider themselves Netherlanders than main-line Netherlanders suspect. Of course, the view from above *has to be* a different one than the view from below. Indeed, the obvious advantages of multiple identities, when conceived of most generally, are often very apparent to mainstream individuals, although they may not as frequently conceptualize these identities along ethnolinguistic lines. That is precisely why the limits of ethnolinguistic democracy should never be defined from the top alone. Rather, these must be significantly defined from the bottom as well. Certainly, the smaller members of the EC would appreciate being consulted before any subset of administrative super-languages is selected by the super-powers among them. Similarly, all EC members must learn to consult the sub-state speech communities within themselves if fairness in ethnolinguistic affairs is ever to be more than a null set.

It is unfortunately true that very few people (including most of their own speakers) care about the impending demise of small languages. Modern language consciousness is a byproduct of the nationalist response to the widespread social change attributable to urbanization and industrialization. Accordingly, this consciousness is not evenly distributed throughout the world and is very seldom applied to 'other people's little languages', not even by the most enlightened co-participants in intercultural processes. Very few people pause to consider what it is that is lost when a language is lost, particularly if it is someone else's language. But what is lost when a language is lost, especially in the short run, is the sociocultural integration of the generations, the cohesiveness, naturalness and quiet creativity, the secure sense of identity, even without politicized consciousness of identity, the sense of collective worth of a community and of a people, the particular value of being 'Xians in Xish', rather than 'Xians in Yish' or Yians in Yish, even when the conveniences of daily living are 'greener in the other field'. The loss of the above characteristics exacts a price via elevated levels of alienation, via injury to both corporeal and mental health in two or more generations, via a vastly increased incidence of social dislocation manifested as civil and criminal offenses, and via elevated public costs in order to overcome or contain such dislocations (many of which have come to constitute the warp and woof of much of modern life). Finally, what is lost is the cultural creativity (in song, story, theater, myth, dance and artifacts and in the representational arts) that ultimately enriches not only the immediate vicinity in the original language but also the total human experience in a myriad of translations. The loss of all of the foregoing is survivable, but, in many ways, the result of such loss amounts to a seriously lowered quality of life, including the very meaning of life itself. It is the particular gift of the most threatened languages and cultures to make us all more aware of this issue, but it is the peculiar responsibility of the largest and most secure languages to respond constructively and magnanimously to this universal problem in human cultural-ecology.

The EC organization needed the prodding and the protests of the Catalans in order to expand its previous concept of 'complete multilingualism'. Those who care for small languages and identities (e.g. Stauf, 1991) and who treasure the intimate ethnocultural patrimonies that these languages index, symbolize and implement, those who willingly accept the extra stimulation and enrichment – and burdens and tensions – that multiple memberships entail, they deserve all of the assistance that a generous theory of limits can provide so that, to quote the European Parliament for the last time 'the people of Europe [and of the world at large – JAF] will not regard ... [their] institutions as being out of touch with and foreign to them' ... but rather 'look upon them as important elements playing a part in the daily life of its citizens'. On the other hand, if limits and accommodations *are* sometimes necessary in applying this declaration at the sub-state level, then it should be remembered, such limits may well be equally or even more necessary at the supra-state level. The arbitrariness of power must be opposed, in the ethnolinguistic arena, just as it must be opposed in the political and economic realms of which the EC is apparently more aware.

## Note

1. This is a revised version of a paper originally presented at a celebration honoring the 700th anniversary of the Swiss Confederation, Disentis, August 1991, at the Symposium on Linguistic Human Rights, Tallinn (Estonia), October, 1991, and at the Tenth Annual Conference on Language and Communication, New York, December, 1991, i.e. before the separation of Czechoslovakia, Yugoslavia and the Soviet Union into constituent independent states. I am indebted to many members of the audience at all of the above meetings and, most particularly, to Tove Skutnabb-Kangas, Robert Phillipson and Humphrey Tonkin for their helpful comments which have enabled me to substantially improve my original presentations.

## References

Argemi, A. (1991) European recognition for Catalan. *Contact: Bulletin of the European Union for Lesser Used Languages* 8, 1 and 6.

Fishman, J. (1991) *Reversing Language Shift*. Clevedon: Multilingual Matters.

Haarmann, H. (1991) Monolingualism vs. selective multilingualism: On the future alternatives for Europe as it integrates in the 1990s. *Sociolinguistica* 5, 7–23.

Haselhuber, J. (1991) Erste Ergebnisse einer empirischen Untersuchunkgg zur Sprachsituation in der EG-Komission (February 1990). *Sociolinguistica* 5, 37–50.

Leitner, G. (1991) Europe 1992: A language perspective. *Language Problems and Language Planning* 5, 282–296.

Mackey, W.F. (1991) Language diversity, language policy and the sovereign state. *History of European Ideas* 13 (1–2), 51–61.

Stauf, R. (1991) *Justus Mosers Konzept einer deutschen Nationalität*. Tübingen: Niemeyer.

Verdoodt, A. (1991) Writing and schooling in the regional languages of the member states of the Council of Europe. In O. García (ed.) *Bilingual Education: Festschrift in Honor of Joshua A. Fishman on the Occasion of his 65th Birthday* (pp. 61–71). Amsterdam: John Benjamins.

# Chapter 12
## *Language Spread and Language Policy for Endangered Languages*

Having contributed, over the course of many years, to the study of language spread, on the one hand, and to the study of language maintenance/language shift, on the other hand, it has generally been clear to me – and, I suspect, to others as well – that these two topical concentrations generally deal with quite different macrolevel language situations. Language spread calls to mind the dynamic of English as an additional language, particularly in its role as the worldwide language of technology (both popular and advanced) and of huge chunks of youth culture in most modern and modernizing contexts; the dynamics of Russian as an additional language in the Soviet Union (particularly among minor Asian peoples who have no other means of access to the world of modern ideas and technology, but among all other Soviet peoples as well, for ideological and lingua franca purposes); the dynamic of Swahili as an additional language among many Anglophones (particularly young Anglophones) in Canada; of Spanish as an additional language among enclaves of Latin American Indians; of Mandarin/Potinhua as an additional language among non-Han peoples in Mainland China, etc. Many additional examples of language spread can be given, particularly if we go back in history (e.g. to the spread of Latin – initially as an additional language – in the Western Roman Empire, and the partially contemporary and partially even earlier as well as later spread of Greek as an additional language for High Culture in Rome itself and throughout the Eastern Roman Empire). The common factor among all of these examples of language spread is that they focus upon contextually more powerful languages whose spread is (or was) facilitated precisely by the doors they can (could) open, the broader vistas they can (could) provide, the more statusful roles they are (were) associated with (at least potentially or referentially if not immediately), the promise they hold (held) to change the lives of their new speakers (initially: under-standers and, ultimately, perhaps also readers/writers) in desired directions.

The mood in language spread studies is generally an 'upbeat' one, precisely because it takes its point of departure from the perspective of the spreading languages themselves and their sponsors. If we care to glance below this surface, however, the efforts related to language spread are also full of open or hidden tales of personal dislocation, of social dislocation, and of cultural dislocation when viewed from the per-spective of at least some of those to whom these languages spread. However, we tend to be so convinced that 'you can't fry omelettes without breaking eggs' that no other, less destructive metaphor occurs to us. We quickly, too quickly, place our hope in the ultimate beneficial effects of the sociocultural revolutions that necessarily accompany language spread. We all love winners and the study of language spread is replete with accounts of their prowess in bringing new products, technologies, ideologies, curricula, appreciations, opportunities (includ-ing creative opportunities) to the populations exposed to them (more quickly to elites and more slowly to masses). We tend to (or want to) forget that 'spread' is one of those anesthetic terms that numb us and lull us from feeling or even recognizing the multitude of pains and sins that they cover. If we add to our interest in 'spread' an interest in 'language policy', as I have been bidden to do in this paper, then we run the risk of overlooking another matter, namely, that spread not only involves conscious 'language policy', but unplanned spread as well, via Zeitgeist trends that can contribute as much or even more to spread than language policy *per se*. There is often a momentum to spread, a momentum to which social mobility aspirations contribute, as do the hungers for material and for leisure time gratifications, as does the appar-ent stylishness of the pursuit of modernity itself. All in all, it is the complex processes of culture contact, cultural diffusion, culture change and culture conflict, and their dislocation of everyday life in all of its manifold activities, rather than language policy alone, that are involved in language spread. To reduce these manifold processes to the narrow parameters of language spread and language policy is, therefore, not only to impoverish our understanding of the broader context in which these parameters are implanted but also to impoverish our understanding even of these parameters themselves.

If the affective tone surrounding the study of language spread is a triumphalist one, then the mood surrounding the study of language shift often becomes quite sombre. We now focus on the sorrows of the losers, on their endangered languages and on their anguish, trauma and travail. We often sympathize with those whom history has defeated ('history' too, by the way, is a euphemism; otherwise we might have to admit that the cruel victors were flesh and blood, not only like us, but perhaps even our own forebears). However, as long as the vanquished are/were not flesh of our flesh and blood of our blood, we generally prefer to move on to less painful topics. Even the intellectualization of other people's pain (and intellectualization is the very heart of our enterprise, otherwise we may be taken for journalists or propagandists) is far from a happy or pleasant topic. There aren't many Nancy Dorians around who care to go back, time after time, to dying language communities, even for research purposes, although such communities contain the answers to many of the best, the most difficult and the most important questions: the questions of limits (of where and how to draw the line between dying and changing, between illness and health, between death and life). But, whether we attend to them or not, the endangered languages, i.e. languages with a large, sustained and uncontrollable negative balance with respect to the discrepancy between their intergenerational influx and their intergenerational outflux of speakers, are there and their number is legion, as any reader of *Cultural Survival Quarterly* or *Survival International News* can plainly see, issue after issue, year after year.

Efforts to ameliorate the woes of endangered languages, to help them arrive at a *modus vivendi* (as opposed to a *modus 'morendi'*) with their more powerful competitors nevertheless go on, insufficient and thwarted though they may be. Often these efforts are in the hands of sociolinguistically untrained or only partially trained caretakers. Few language planning specialists read (or can read) what they write 'in those funny little languages of theirs', and comparative studies or theories of assistance to endangered languages (i.e. language policy on behalf of endangered languages) are few and far between. However, it seems to me that if we are sensitive to the loss suffered by our collective 'quality of life' on this planet when endangered animal species are further decimated, if we strain to do something on their behalf so that their natural habitats will be protected and their life chances improved (like holding off the repair and replacement of the West Side Highway in New York for over a dozen years because certain species of fish would never recover if their current breeding grounds were destroyed), then the need to look steadfastly and act affirmatively in connection with endangered languages should be even more obvious. Theoretically, there need be no conflict between language spread and language maintenance. Language spread may pertain to the acquisition of socioculturally new ('modern') functions, usually H-type functions, rather than to the displacement of speakers from their 'traditional' L-type functions. However, true though this may be theoretically, and I myself have testified many times to this theoretical truth, the complementary distribution of functions that it depicts is very often only an early and fleeting stage in a process which, if left unattended, easily develops into a subsequent stage in which that which is not theoretically necessary nevertheless, predictably, comes to pass: the spreading language initially associated with newer, more statusful roles and pursuits, soon competes with and also begins to erode the remaining functions originally allocated to the language(s) previously employed by the speech community. It is at this point that the danger begins.

The possibility of stabilization is there, of course. We call that possibility 'diglossia', namely, the copresence within an ethnolinguistic community of a widely implemented, generally accepted, and long-lasting complementary functional allocation of languages. We can all give examples of such consensual societal arrangements (even examples like Swiss German/High German, where no traditional religious props or social class advantages (like the monopolistic 'traditional' or premodern restriction of literacy) are available to provide the impetus for the continuation of such arrangements). But, after all is said and done, the diglossic solution to the problem of endangered languages is a very difficult one to arrive at under any circumstances, whether philosophically or empirically, all the more so under typically modern circumstances. And that brings me back to 'language policy'.

How can language policy be implemented so that endangered languages can find a safe harbor for themselves, tossed and battered as they soon are by the advancing functional spread of competitor languages associated with far greater status rewards? I know that there are those who take the view that 'survival of the fittest' should prevail in the language arena, as it does in the jungle. I know there are those who declaim against language policy on behalf of endangered languages, considering it useless, seeing in it tendencies toward excess and toward fostering and exacerbating intergroup tensions, an interference with the rights of the majority to rule and an implicit vote of 'no confidence' in the inherent fairness of the majority if left to its own devices (i.e. without imposing laws requiring the protection of endangered languages). However, I happen not to agree with these folks. I do not really believe in the 'survival of the fittest', precisely because it is the law of the jungle and I have always tried to follow a higher law than that. Although I don't fully put my trust in princes in order to even the scales between the strong and the weak, I also do not expect much 'inherent fairness' toward lambs on the part of wolves. I know that my advocacy of endangered languages will be interpreted as reflecting a vested interest on my part (I admit it; I feel aggrieved that my own mother tongue is an endangered language and I have vowed to do what I can on its behalf); nevertheless, I feel that I can make as much claim for acting in the public good as can my opponents, and I suspect that they too must have a vested interest or two up their sleeves (interests which they insist on not disclosing and even on hiding) in championing a majority that really needs no support. So I return with unbowed head to my original question: given that language spread is not an unmixed blessing, leading in many cases to language shift and to endangering the very existence of smaller languages engulfed by the processes of sociocultural change in which language spread itself is a coparticipant, how can language policy be utilized on behalf of fostering a stabilized coexistence between the weak and the strong, between the lambs and the wolves?

Since considerable attention has already been directed at our meeting toward the English Official/English Only movement in the United States, a movement that seeks to utilize language policy on behalf of a powerful language (English in the United States) and against weaker languages in our country, I will attempt, at the particular request of our sponsors but hardly against my own will, to draw my examples from several other contexts that I have come to know rather well over the past few years, namely, the cases of Basque, Frisian, Irish and Yiddish, all of which raise in my mind questions of limits, i.e. are there stages of decline and conditions of endangerment beyond which the spread of a stronger competitor can no longer be contained? Or, to put it another way: can a better fit be engineered between language policy efforts on behalf of weaker languages and the particular functional circumstances in which such languages find themselves? In what follows, I ask you to keep in mind non-Western examples too, because although the specifics of my discussion will not apply to them, the general principles that I advance are, nevertheless, quite applicable.

## The Spread of Endangered Languages

If one examines the language status efforts on behalf of many endangered languages, one cannot help but be struck by the fact that they generally attempt to fight fire with fire. Faced by the progressive encroachment of a competitor within the gates of their own ethnolinguistic community, faced by the well-nigh complete control of the domains of power and modernity by this competitor, the loyalists to and the advocates of endangered languages commonly (all too commonly) lay plans to capture (or, in some cases, to recapture) 'the terrain of power and modernity'. Basque advocates work on terminologies for the natural sciences in higher education, because, presumably, that will advance the day when a unilingually Basque 'Basque Country' will arise again on both sides of the Pyrenees. Irish protagonists lay plans for governmental offices and agencies operating primarily in Irish, as befits 'the national and first official language' of their country. Frisian loyalists seek to conquer the secondary schools and the town councils, and Yiddish protagonists, from at least the time of the Tshernovits Language Conference of 1908 to this very day, are concerned with dictionaries and grammars, modern poetry and *belles-lettres*, theatre and intellectual journals, and with corpus planning at least for purposes of popular science and inter-translatability with *The New York Times*. Although it is clear to those who adopt such policies for themselves, and to those who advocate them for others, that the time and effort invested in spreading their endangered language into the uppermost functions of modernity will (a) initially attract few who are both willing to and capable of using that language for these functions and (b) do little if anything to stem the ongoing attrition with respect to the primary determinants of intergenerational language transmission (in Western or Westernized society: home, neighborhood, elementary school, work sphere, religious domain), nevertheless, such efforts continue unabated and represent major language policy decisions. Suggestions that a more modest target be aimed at, i.e. that the primary intergenerational arena be focused upon and shored up, are met with the scornful charge of 'folklorization', i.e. with accusations that such a narrower focus would be tantamount to surrendering the power- and status-related interactions of modern life (and, therefore, of language life) and of opting for trivialization via a focus on the rural past (old wives' tales and the folksongs and dances of a bygone age). The modern world, its genres and pursuits, has a tremendous fascination for language policy authorities, and understandably so, since they themselves are almost always modernized élites who have been fashioned in the crucible of modern tensions and aspirations.

## The Double 'Approach-Avoidance' Dilemma

Actually, by the time a language is an endangered species, almost any proffered status planning solutions to its problems involve a high level of risk relative to the likely benefits to be gained thereby. Solutions that stress entry or reentry into modernization pursuits and interactions imply a policy of direct competition and confrontation with a stronger (and often increasingly stronger) competitor. Understandably, relatively few ordinary individuals are ready, either linguistically or philosophically, to embark on such a confrontation, particularly when the forces that foster it are primarily linguacentric in nature. Studying (or teaching) astrophysics in Irish certainly proves that 'there is nothing deficient about our language; if we do not use it for astrophysics it is *we* who are at fault and not the language'. However, the huge amount of time, effort and funds necessary in order to reach that goal (both in connection with perfecting the necessary terminologies and texts, and in connection with getting teachers themselves to learn and to use them) and the small number of individuals who will ever use Irish (or Xish) for that purpose, seriously raises the question of whether that is a wise policy or not, particularly when at the very time that astrophysics is being stressed, the attrition on the 'home front' is still going on among many, many more individuals than will ever hear of astrophysics, let alone be enlightened by it. However, no sooner is the wisdom of pursuing such confrontational and multi-modern-functional priorities questioned and alternative emphases suggested focusing upon the family, the neighborhood and the elementary school, i.e. upon the very domains and role relations that are at the core of socioculturally patterned language acquisition and, accordingly, upon the domains and interactions that are central to intergenerational ethnolinguistic continuity, no sooner are such emphases suggested than the bugaboo of 'folklorization' raises its head. If Frisian and Yiddish are to be related only or primarily to the vernacular intimacy of hearth and home, if they are to be denied meaningful roles in the world of modern concerns, aspirations and statuses, then are they anything more than anachronistic spinning wheels and pious formulas in an age governed by computers, rockets, and the devil take the hindmost? Who wants spinning-wheel languages? Who needs them? Who stays with them after passing through adolescence and leaving home to find one's fortune in the big city? Isn't anything that might be won initially by this approach of shoring up the home front, ultimately lost in spades as the traditional and sheltered premodern world of parents and grandparents is left behind (even rejected) in a mad scramble to join the present and, better yet, the future?

Clearly, endangered languages and their custodians are damned if they do and damned if they don't, no matter what it is that they do or don't do in the language policy arena. Whether they fight language spread fire with fire or whether they fight it with water, the risks are apparently equally great and the outcomes equally dubious. They are buffeted by the double dangers of folklorization, on the one hand, and Irelandization on the other hand, and the more they seek to avoid the one, the more they risk gravitating toward the other. What can and what should a sociolinguistically informed language policy effort on behalf of endangered languages do? Is there any way out of their impasse?

## Reasonable and Reasoned Compromise in Language Policy for Endangered Languages

If it is erroneous to pretend that 'nothing can be done for them by the time they are endangered', it also does not help to pretend that 'it is never too late' to rescue endangered languages, for, indeed, it often *is* too late relative to the amount of social control that the policy planners who labor on their behalf either can or should exercise. However, it is definitely not automatically too late (as some misinformed observers would have it) merely because the 'endangered' stage has been reached. Even in our modern age, when speech communities are so highly interrelated and interdependent, a judicious combination of direct community-building efforts (these are indispensable; no language should be dependent on direct language policy efforts alone), on the one hand, and direct language policy efforts, on the other hand, can (re)stabilize speech community networks and the borders between networks. However, as in the case of all 'emergency first aid', the hemorrhaging of the main arteries must be stopped first, well before major attention is devoted to poetry journals, to astrophysics, and to the world of international power politics or even middle level technology. However, the central domains of inter-generational mother tongue continuity must also not be defined too narrowly either; they include not only hearth and home but neighborhood (i.e. residential concentration), elementary schooling, work sphere, and, often, the religious sphere as well. Taken together, these are the societal foundations that one inherits, that define community, and that one hands on to the next generation on a societal rather than merely on an individual basis. Given the Euro-American focus that we have adopted for our discussion, these are the primary societal institutions, and when a language is safe within them it has at least a generation's worth of breathing time and space. These are the initial institutions that transmit values and, therefore, these are the ones that transmit the values, loyalties, ideologies, philosophies and traditions out of which a sense of community arises and is maintained, from which the call to loyalty to the necessarily interpreted ethnolinguistic past (as interpreted by the language loyalists) and the call to custodianship *vis-à-vis* the desired ethnolinguistic future are derived, are inculcated, are reinforced and are legitimated.

Material and materialistic beings though we be, we still have not totally lost either the capacity or the need to live for ideals, for loved ones, for collective goals. It is via the primary sociocultural institutions that language is first related to the verities that make life worth living and it is to these institutions that policy makers must turn if they are to reconnect language with those verities. Every language needs an idea – a goal and a vision above the mundane and the rational – to keep it alive. The basic and minimally essential 'idea' is the imperative of remaining a separate ethnolinguistic entity, and a struggling language community must safeguard this idea before all others. In healthy languages the 'idea' need not even be consciously recognized by the bulk of the speakers; in struggling languages, consciousness of personal responsibility for the language (the symbolic integrator of all that is good and precious), needs to be developed early and stressed repeatedly. The family, the neighborhood, the elementary school and the church need to be urged, instructed, rewarded and guided to play their irreplaceable roles in this connection. There is no substitute for them, nor for the ideas that they can espouse from the very earliest and tenderest years and, thereafter, throughout the life span (ideas such as the inherent right to continue, the duty to continue, the privilege of continuing the language-in-culture association of any community's historic preferred collective self-realization), no substitute, certainly, if vernacular functions are to be stabilized. These social functions are absolutely necessary and they must be reconquered first, because without them there are no vernacular functions at all that are intergenerationally transmitted, not even if quite a large number of people study astrophysics in Basque. But the family, neighborhood and elementary school are not enough. They are necessary but they are not sufficient, least of all for 'moderns'.

'Man does not live by bread alone', the *Sayings of the Fathers* teach us, but also 'If there is no bread there is no learning'. Just as corpus planning without status planning is an empty game of silly linguists, so mesmerization by hearth and home is a romantic infatuation of ethnic innocents. Even while home and neighborhood are being revernacularized (via language associations of parents active in neighborhood nurseries and kindergartens, via language associations related to shopping and to fishing, to knitting and to reading, via language-related local sports teams for toddlers and singing contests for adolescents, via prizes for language-championing essays at every grade level and prepaid vacations for language-insistent and language-successful parents, via recognition in church and recognition in school in the many ways that dedication, piety and excellence are normally recognized by every self-respecting society, but in this context: in connection with language), at this very same time the work sphere – particularly the lower and entry-level work sphere – must also definitely be staked out early for language-related recognition, rewards, promotions, raises and preferences of all kinds. The serious world of work and careers starts here and the bulk of the citizenry spends the bulk of its time over the bulk of its years in this world. This is the first area of language spread into which formerly endangered languages must be enabled (nay, must be shelteringly engineered) to expand. For many, it will be the last significant language spread they will experience, particularly so if we count the world of mass entertainment (whether sports or performing arts) as normally falling within the secondary rather than within the primary institutions of language maintenance, i.e. within the institutional structures that are generally not societally or familially transmitted from one generation to the next, institutions with a weaker moralistic flavor and institutions that individuals generally enter only after adolescence.

The world of work has no limit. It goes from entry level 'all the way up' and it is more likely than not that the further up it goes, the more it will be dominated by the competing language of greater power. The weak are always more likely to be bilingual than the strong, and those from the endangered language community who have the ability and seek the rewards related to the upper work sphere will definitely need to show versatility in the intra- or intersocietally competing language of wider communication. There may, indeed, be room for a poetry journal or two in Yiddish or for an organic chemistry text in Frisian, but I seriously doubt whether these need to be priority concerns, until and unless we are no longer dealing with endangered languages but with communities of sufficient autonomy, above and beyond cultural autonomy, to provide the dynamics for language spread into many of the higher and more powerful reaches of society. In most cases, however, such autonomy is not only not a realistic early goal, but on the contrary, it is actually a counterproductive early goal for languages in the endangered state. To pursue the social and political policies that such a goal implies, when the language itself is still seriously struggling for its very existence and when the higher reaches of power and authority are still far outside its grasp, rather than actually or even nearly within it, is to confuse the essential with the visionary, the immediate with the pot of gold at the end of the rainbow. It is also tantamount to providing ammunition to the opposition that is always waiting exactly for such errors in judgment in order better to be able to shoot down the entire restoration effort. It is tantamount to not recognizing that a functionally dislocated language needs generations of quiet and stability in the primary domains of intergenerational language continuity, rather than more turmoil, more dislocation, and more disturbance of the intimate patterns of daily life which nurture both a distinctive ethnocultural pattern and its traditionally associated language.

The most important lesson to remember and, apparently, the most difficult one to learn initially, is the following one: the intimate domains are also the most sheltered; they nurture intergenerational continuity, even if these domains are not the major movers and shakers of the modern world. On the other hand, the most powerful modern domains are also the most exposed to the vicissitudes of power confrontation; they do not lay the foundations of community, precisely because their impact upon us comes developmentally later in life and their aim is higher and their grasp is of greater scope than that of the immediately experienced speech community. Endangered languages must assume control of the former – the intimate spheres of family and community – even though they may never attain control of the latter – the status spheres of supralocal power and authority. Assuming control of the home and community domains means (re)building those domains via the endangered language, becoming inseparably interpenetrated by them, inextricably associated with them. In short, it means community building, community policy, community well-being, community institutions, community life, community activity, rather than language policy alone, language policy *ad nauseam*, language fears and dreams and nothing more. Language always exists in a cultural matrix, and it is this matrix that needs to be fostered via policy rather than the language *per se*. Not even linguists live by and for language alone; ordinary mortals are ever so much less capable of doing so. Language policy must maintain a fine balance between directness and indirectness, between figure and ground, between vinegar and honey. 'Lingua sana in communitas sana' is the only realistic goal for endangered languages; they must not become fetishes; rather, they must be intimately tied to a thousand intimate or small-scale network processes, processes too gratifying and rewarding to surrender, even if they do not quite amount to the pursuit of the higher reaches of power and modernity.

## Conclusions

'A man's reach must exceed his grasp, or what's a heaven for?', Robert Browning opined, but that is a counsel that is tailor-made for those who can afford to fall flat on their faces if they reach too high. At the outset, and it is particularly the enfeebled outset that I am stressing because it is the stage of greatest risk, language policy for endangered languages must be more circumspect than that, more cautious, more calculating along risk-benefit lines. At the outset, before they acquire a dynamic of their own, all language policies must be sensitively harmonized with the functional profiles and the most crucial functional prospects of the languages on whose behalf they are formulated. Among endangered languages the hemorrhages in the realm of home and immediate community must be stopped first and quickly. The danger of folklorization, if, indeed, it exists (as in the rare case of 'nativization' movements), can be coped with later and more leisurely than can the danger of losing the remaining thinning ranks of mother-tongue speakers. 'What profiteth it man to gain the world and lose his soul?' What profiteth it Irish or Basque to gain astrophysics and to lose the Gaeltacht or the casarias? The 'dangers of folklorization' become real only after the primary ethnocultural domains have been fully secured. Until such time, the dangers of Irelandization are infinitely greater than those of folkorization.

An exaggerated abhorrence of 'folklorization' (exaggerated, certainly, if this designation is pejoratively and indiscriminately applied to the necessity of giving priority to the pursuits of hearth and home, and of daily life more generally, for languages that are still threatened in these very functions) undercuts the very sense of uniqueness, the sense of ethnolinguistic authenticity and distinctiveness, that are at the experiential foundations of ethnolinguistic continuity. Our kith and kin, our neighbors and friends, our colleagues and clergy, our regular customers and employees, our child socialization patterns and our local collective memories, festivities, customs and traditions – these are the ultimately irrational *raisons d'être* and building blocks of separate ethnolinguistic existence. A computer and an atom smasher by any other name are really exactly the same thing, but an ethnically encumbered interaction (such as the celebration of a festival, a birth, a birthday party or a marriage ceremony) in a language other than the historically associated one, signals a different family culture, a different everyday reality, a different interpretation of and involvement in the tangible past, and a different view of the future. In short, as I first indicated 20 years ago in my *Language Loyalty in the United States* (1966), and as I subsequently theoretically elaborated in my *Language and Nationalism* (1972): a different language in the ethnoculturally encumbered interactions is indicative of a differently realized and implemented ethnocultural identity, a differently enacted and expressed ethnoculturally contrastive context, even if the same ethnic label is still utilized due to the elements of continuity that remain even after language shift occurs.

Living cultures and languages are always changing, of course, but language shift is indicative of a culture's inability to control or significantly influence the rate and direction of its change. Efforts to foster endangered languages represent the will of endangered networks that are conscious of the dangers in which they find themselves and that are eager to influence yet other networks that are not yet conscious of those dangers, to hold on to and to increase the historically validated content of their lives, or some more traditional version and interpretation thereof, rather than just to their identity-metaphors devoid of such historically validated content, to significantly control, influence or guide their intercultural relations rather than to be merely the playthings, the by-products, the targets and captives of such relations under the control of others. Few of us, even the most powerful, are fully masters in our own homes; but none of us willingly settle for being strangers in our own homes, servants, dispossessed ghosts. It is not an ethnic label that we seek, but an ethnic content that strikes us as befitting the label, that seems to us to harmonize with it, that fits it in accord with our own historic image of 'goodness of fit' rather than in accord with someone else's.

Language policy on behalf of endangered languages must assure the intimate vernacular functions first, and, if possible, go on from there, slowly building outward from the primary to the secondary institutions of intergenerational mother tongue continuity. The entry-level work sphere is a must; the more advanced work sphere is a maybe. Diglossia is a must (with safely stabilized spheres exclusively for the endangered language); monolingual economic autonomy and political independence are maybes. Widespread reconquest of the vernacular intimacy functions is a must; language spread into the higher reaches of power and modernity is a maybe. The rationalization of language policy for endangered languages is a must; the maximization of results from such policies is, at best, a maybe, because under conditions of rapid social change and dislocation, there are always multiple other forces and other considerations to contend with, above and beyond language policy on behalf of such languages.

And of what value is this entire exercise for all of those, and, probably, for most of us, who may actually be more interested in English and in French, in Latin and in Greek, in Spanish and in Potinhua, in Swahili and in Hindi? Is talk of minor, endangered languages which have a meager chance of surviving and even less chance of spreading) a fitting way to start off a conference on the unlimited horizons for language spread and language policy? Indeed it is, for just as illness teaches us about health, and just as psychopathology teaches us about what is normal in everyday mental life, so the problems of endangered languages teach us about the extreme delicacy of language policy and the extreme complexity of language spread. And while it behooves us to help these languages because they need our help most, because by doing so we become more human, we should also note that our involvement with them will also benefit us by making us more sensitive, more humble and more cautious language policy researchers and language policy implementers as well, researchers and implementers more likely to realize that for every gain there is a loss; for every self-satisfied smile, a despondent tear; for every glorious triumph, a tragic defeat.

## References

Fishman, J.A. (ed.) (1996) *Language Loyalty in the United States: The Maintenance and Perpetuation of non-English Mother-tongues by American Ethic and Religions Groups*. The Hague: Mouton.
——. (1972) *Language and Nationalism: Two Integrative Essays*. Rowley, MA: Newbury House Publishers.

## Chapter 13

# 'Business as Usual' for Threatened Languages? (On Planning Economic Efforts for the Greater Benefit of Reversing Language Shift, or 'Keeping Your Eyes on the Ball')

My *Reversing Language Shift* (1991) may well have launched a new area of sociolinguistic specialization (RLS for short), but it admittedly paid scant attention to the economic dimension inevitably associated with such activity (as with all other human activity). The economic dimension undergirding RLS was simply subsumed either in stage 6 or, more commonly, in stages 3, 2 and 1, i.e. it was treated either as a component of family–home–neighborhood and community, on the one hand, or, on the other hand as a component of the regional and national worksphere, media effort and governmental activity. The time has now come to focus on the economic bases of RLS more explicitly and to attempt to harmonize RLS efforts and economic pursuits in such a way that the former will benefit maximally from the support of the latter.

## Modernization: Beneficent or Dislocative?

The title of this discussion is intended to ask whether the wellbeing of threatened local languages would be helped or hindered by an ever-closer association with the most advanced econotechnical methods and processes of production and distribution that undergird the globalization revolution of much of daily life in the modern world. This question has been asked in one ethnocultural context or another for many centuries. It is encapsulated in Cicero's famous rhetorical dictum: 'The whole world would like to become Roman! Who would not want to profit from Roman roads, Roman commerce, Roman peace?' This pronouncement clearly reveals his underlying assumption – restated since then in many different ways and in many different corners of the world – that rewarding and stable commercial links lead to transethnification in the direction from which such rewards emanate. If this was true then, then it is now ever so many times even more so: modern econotechnical practices and processes are increasingly heading toward the globalization and the uniformation of both business and ethnocultural identity, the latter doing so in the direction of the major engines of modern production, distribution and consumption. Westernized (not just Anglo-American but very substantially so) styles, tastes and aspirations lead not only to economies of scale but to uniformation of values in directions that have not inaccurately been labeled 'Cocacolonization, Macdonaldization and CNNization' by their opponents. The issue raised by Cicero (namely, that ethnic identity is changeable and that it inevitably drifts in the direction of the obviously greater economic reward, since every people know on which side its bread is buttered) had not been recognized – and would undoubtedly have been rejected by the great Hebrew and Greek thinkers that preceded him. They had both assumed that ethnicity was set in sanctity and that authenticity to primordial identity was its own reward: an honorable and authentic life among one's own people.

Cicero's new assumption about ethnicity, as continually constructed and reconstructed via economic reward, has been rendered simultaneously not only more urgent but more complicated by 19th and 20th century efforts to overthrow imperialist political and cultural hegemonies. But the nationalist revolutionaries also wanted to partake of the good things of modern life (some of them admittedly of a philosophical and ideological nature) which the empires had nevertheless introduced into their former colonies. This ambivalent striving for self-definition (ambivalent because it was so often of a 'both–and' nature, rather than of an 'either–or' nature), often encompassing both cultural autonomy and political self-governance in the face of the Western juggernaut, has been pondered by Chinese, Japanese, Arabic, Hindu, Javanese and other spokespersons for indigenous 'Great Traditions' in Africa, Asia, Latin America, the Pacific area and Eastern Europe. All of them recognized essentially that some line had to be drawn if local identities, beliefs, customs and practices (including their traditionally associated languages) were not to be totally engulfed and eclipsed. But it was not usually quite clear *just where* this line was to be drawn.

## Western Tools vs. Non-Western Soul

While Western devices were initially deprecated as merely 'soulless tools' (note the Yiddish folklike song[2] about an alarm clock which is 'a set machine, without desire and without a will of its own. When the time comes it must alarm, it has no feelings of its own'). In this respect they were morally inferior to most of indigenous culture with its totally ethnoreligious interpenetration. Nevertheless, precisely because of their moral emptiness, Western tools had a totally devastating dislocative capacity, a capacity eminently great enough to destroy the local 'cultural soul'. In the face of the onslaught from endlessly additional tools of foreign provenance, a domino effect was hypothesized linking the traditionally associated language and local historical consciousness, ethnocultural identity, indigenous way of life, moral philosophy, values, spirit and *raison d'être*, etc. On many occasions it has been claimed that the acceptance of foreign tools leads inexorably to the acceptance of foreign language, culture and identity, although where the process of cultural change was slow enough, it also became clear that this was not always the case by any means and that a variety of combinations (both in degree and in kind) were, indeed, possible.

## Marx and Weber on Technology and Identity

Somewhat earlier, in the mid-19th century, the issue of the direction of causality between technology and identity had been argued in the West itself. Karl Marx proclaimed that any collective identity (such as cultural identity or ethnic identity) that is not based upon control of the tools of production was a false identity. Such false identities were malevolently planted among the working class by the bourgeois and aristocratic classes in order to fractionate the proletariat and rob it of its strength. Local identities divide the working class which would otherwise unite on a worldwide basis and cultivate its only true identity: its proletarian identity. Max Weber, on the other hand, espoused a more complex and circular causal relationship between sociocultural identity and the means of production, in his justly famous Protestant Ethic, he viewed both of these as aspects of culture and, therefore, inherently interrelated. Just as the means of production helped form collective consciousness of culture and cultural identity (ethnicity), so local cultures deeply influenced the means of production that their members devised and found acceptable. Religion and ethnic identity were also pails of culture, Weber pointed out, and, therefore they too play a decided role in influencing the ways and means of production that are locally acceptable and possible.

Even without reading Weber, the Hindi poet and philosopher Rabindranat Tagore intuitively recognized that the Western penchant for speed reflected the impact of Western culture more generally. The view that 'time is money' leads to perfecting express elevators that can get to the 50th floor a few minutes faster than the local elevators do, but these elevators do not help their riders consider the significance of those few extra minutes for the purpose of arriving at a definition or a more meaningful life. Similarly, Gandi's old-fashioned spinning wheel represented both his control over material passions in his own life as well as his self-liberation from being colonized and exploited as a market for British manufacturing. Surely this is an example of culture determining the means of production as well as the identity that this culture pursues.

## Moving Toward the Center

Although many late-liberation movements still ponder the causal direction between the means of production and ethnic identity, there has more generally been a slow movement toward the center (i.e. toward less extreme and monodirectional causality assumptions) with respect to the link between language advocacy and protection and economic involvement in the globalization process, on the other. Most of the RLSers I have met (and by now I have met thousands of them in all parts of the globe) are neither language determinists nor economic determinists. They want their traditionally associated languages and identities to thrive but they also want their modernizing economies to thrive, without focusing entirely on either one alone. They have avoided what could be a cruel dilemma by moving toward the center, a position that is well known in American politics, particularly in election years. Indeed, does anyone have the courage to be a Gandi today? Does anyone really believe that merely having native terminologies for all foreign-derived tools and ideas will, *per se*, fully preserve indigenous identities, beliefs and practices? Aside from such rare examples as the Old Order Amish, Mennonites and Hutterites, on the one hand, and the Ultra-Orthodox Khasidim, on the other, all of whom have established non-participationist 'sealed societies' in order to separate themselves as completely as possible from the modern 'Godless' world, most speakers of smaller languages throughout the world have already been profoundly influenced by Western modernity and must, therefore, ask themselves how far can we afford to go in this direction before we lose ourselves? They must not only examine if they can continue to be 'Xians via Xish' if they continue unceasingly along the slippery slope to Westernization, but to ask themselves if they will even continue to be Xians at all if the core of their culture is not essentially Xian (even if by some chance their language still remains Xish).

In part, this is a question of where to draw the line *vis-à-vis* seeking the gratifications of globalization, but in part it is also a question of 'damned if you do and damned if you don't'.

If networks of individuals that utilize small language-and-culture systems are drawn too far into the Western orbit, they inevitably lose part or all of their authenticity and come to suffer, in their own eyes and in the eyes of others, the guilt of treason. But, if these same networks belonging to small language-and-culture systems reject the ways of the West too vigorously, they are accused of preferring a spinning wheel life, a rocking chair life, one that is insufficiently rewarding, particularly for the young in their midst. 'Life is unfair' for threatened languages. They are destined to fight a difficult and prolonged two-front war: pursuing just enough but not too much modernization on the one hand, and cultivating and safeguarding 'authenticity', on the other hand. Authenticity, whether viewed as real or recognized as being constructed, is at the very heart of the appeal that separate ethnolinguistic identities have to their believers and the goal of authenticities is to differ as much as possible from other cultures all over the globe. On the other hand, westernization and econotechnical globalization exist only as one kind. All over the globe – the Anglo-American kind – which is what frightens even the French, the Japanese and the Scandinavians, not to mention the Basques, the Catalans and the Frisians. These two irreconcilables (Pan-Westernization and local authenticity) are attainable only by compartmentalizing each of them, so that the one does not violate the other. This is a notoriously hard thing to do. As my father told me several times: 'It is better to be born into a large, wealthy and strong people, than into a small, weak and poor one'. Unfortunately, hardly any of us have any choice in this connection.

## Compartmentalization

Clearly, all small cultures who climb onto the 'modernization/globalization express' have a bear by the tail. That is a notoriously risky position to be in. But to let the bear go entirely is also intropunitive in very material ways. By and large, there has been only one even partially successful solution to this quandary. It is a tripartite solution made up of (a) bilingualism, (b) with a careful and studied compartmentalization of the languages involved, and (c) with a complementary distribution of the societal functions allocated to each of them. Unfortunately, during the past generation the pressures of modernization and globalization have become so dynamic as to constantly appear to be decreasingly compartmentalizable. This is particularly true among the non-state-forming lesser used languages. State-forming languages reinforce their own cultural boundaries by means of their political boundary controls, and, as a result, not many state languages are among that half of all of the worlds languages that are threatened by extinction during the coming century. Clearly then, it is up to the non-state-forming languages (languages that are not the official or national languages of polities anywhere in the world) to undertake an unabashed sociocultural and ethnolinguistic compartmentalization between the economically vital and rewarding languages and lifestyles of globalization and their own authenticity striving toward traditional languages and cultures. There are several problems in this connection. Any such effort at compartmentalization is likely to be construed and characterized as 'apartheid', even when practiced by the weak in self-defense against the strong. But the major question is whether any effective compartmentalization is possible even when it is judged to be desirable?

Since it is only natural for co-territorial living things to interact, it should be expected that hermetic compartmentalization between co-territorial cultures is not possible. But, just as there are degrees and levels of compartmentalization, so there are degrees and levels of Western-nization. Rates of change and cultural areas of change need to be con-trolled with respect to many non-linguistic behaviors as well as linguistic ones: customs, moral and legal codes, self-governing insti-tutions, religious practices, traditional artifactual skills, decorative designs, musical patterns, aesthetic conventions. All these, when taken together, and the identity that goes with them, undergird and express a separate way of life and only a separate way of life really makes a separate language not merely possible but it makes one necessary as well. All this is what is lost, in a fine-grained way, when a culture loses its traditionally associated language, because no culture can be fully alive and continuous in translation. But this does not mean that modern global pursuits need to be altogether taboo in the smaller worlds that also prefer their particular Xian-via-Xish identities. Even the Old Order Amish use electricity for pasteurizing the milk that they send to market, although they don't use it at home because they believe that such use would expose their private and intimate domain to worldly intrusions and worldly depen-dency. Furthermore, they refrigerate their food at home, but their refriger-ators are powered only with replaceable batteries which are fully under their own control. Horse drawn plows are considered acceptable farming-related technology, but gasoline powered tractors are not. So where do the Old Order Amish 'draw the line' between permitted and excessive modernization? They seem to conceive of a cultural line that prohibits any power that links them to the outside world and makes them overly dependent and interactive with it. The exact location of this line has changed during nearly three and a half centuries of their pre-sence within easy access of New York, Philadelphia and Washington (indeed, at one time buttons too were taboo), but it is their line to define and they continually do so at the level of controllable, man-in-the street technology. Every culture must draw this line of accommo-dation to pan-Westernization and globalization for itself, if it seeks to survive in an authentic fashion (with 'authenticity' also being culturally and contextually self-defined).

While all smaller, non-state languages need not fall back on Gandian or Old Order Amish maximalist rejections of modern life and of interactions with global society, neither can they aspire to harbor Microsoft headquarters in their own midsts. While daily visits to the wide-wide-world are not necessarily all bad, societal reality must be such as to provide ample satisfaction 'down on the farm' even 'after they've seen Paree!' This kind of reward structure can be designed and attained only via a more complex, rather than via a more simple, type of ethnocultural identity. Western-driven technology and globalization are so powerful that their rewards, values, practices and artifacts are sometimes seen as engulfing also by larger state-building languages and cultures. Some of them – *viz* France and French Canada – have had to reinforce their own cultural boundaries, via trade agreements, tariffs, educational curricula, signage requirements and immigration policies, in order to defend their own particular authenticity strivings. How much more careful must seriously threatened, smaller and non-state languages and identities be of extending full *carte blanche* to those who would come bearing gifts of western econotechnology?

## A Different Drummer

Marching to the tune of a different drummer, to the tune of one's own drummer, requires the elaboration and incorporation of a more complex ethnolinguistic identity when and if a small and authentic language and culture are also to be successfully defended. Bilingualism and biculturism are more rather than less complex identities than those of the more-often monolingual mainstream. But, if the truth be told, that mainstream also has a more complex intracultural identity that it usually acknowledges. Gender roles, family roles, political participation roles, professional roles, avocational roles, citizenship roles, good-neighbor roles, smart consumer roles, sports-fan roles, these are all part of almost everybody's modern Western identity. However, bicultural identity also has all of the above roles and multiplies many of them by a factor of two. Such an identity may sometimes require more identity consciousness, but it often yields many more rewards in the realms of music, art, literature, customs and Weltanschauung or cultural outlook on life than do the less complex identities. Nevertheless, the higher and more complex yields of biculturalism exact a price. The price is the maintenance of a complementary compartmentalization of languages and cultures so as to guard against the undercutting of the authenticity and intimacy-related roles which threatened languages must reserve for themselves. Such careful compartmentalization, is necessary if a viable corner of authenticity is to be retained in a world dominated by western econotechnical globalization in most of the extracommunal walks of life.

## Some Econotechnical Principles for RLS-Focused Economic Development

RLS advocates on behalf of threatened languages must pursue their efforts via face-to-face demographic concentrations ('real' communities) rather than through virtual communities. The latter are of no use in mother-tongue acquisition and, therefore, in intergenerational language transmission of the most crucial kind. Face-to-face communities for both children and adults, on the other hand, are not only *sui generis* insofar as intergenerational mother tongue transmission is concerned, but they also provide authenticity socialization and reinforcement far beyond any individual's power or resources. Particularly for the young (infants through to adolescents) face-to-face communities have an enormous power to encourage, reinforce, reward, validate and integrate the authenticity bonds which form cultural identity and which provide a foundation for the Language associated with such authentic identity.

In order to maintain RLS face-to-face communities at their maximal power and influence, local and nearby regional occupations must be stressed. Such occupations require low rates of parental and other adult-worker absence from spouses, children and voluntary community-involvement groups. 'Community' is both a place of life and a way of life. It constitutes a Gemeinschaft, wherein residents have common goals, values, cultural traditions (including language use) and cultural identities (such as being 'Xians-via-Xish'). Working at home via computer is a modern facilitation of community and provides major support/resources for community institutions such as schools, teams, clubs and self-governmental infrastructure. On the other hand, its linkage-capacity with the outside world poses dangers which may be far easier for adults than for children to avoid. Self-discipline for adults and careful supervision of children are inevitable prices that must be paid for RLS-focused cultural and economic community development. Intra-communal self-employment, self-financing and self-regulation of cultural, productive, distributional and other types of business and administrative activities are to be preferred for RLS-purposes' overinteractive dependency associations with Yians-via-Yish or even Xians-via-Yish.

Government too often needs to be held at arms length, to avoid the bureaucratization, interference, regulation and dependency that government tends to breed. Particular vigilance is required in connection with the slippery slope between 'governmental funding' and 'governmental intrusion', including linguistic intrusion via meetings, hearings, inspections, documents, reports, etc. Autonomy from Yish in all cultural matters is an RLS goal devoutly to be pursued, although association and cooperation with other RLS Gemeinschaften is very much in order.

Xish must be the language of local work and local record, as well as the language at home, in the streets and playgrounds, sportsfields, in the community store(s) and in the community school(s) and meeting place(s). An example must be shown by community leaders and elders (full or part-time teachers, administrators, group leaders, teachers-helpers, board-members, elective or appointive officials, committee chairs, etc.) in this very connection and Xish oralcy, literacy and exemplary RLS leadership behavior must be conditions of attaining and retaining office.

Self-taxation ('tithing') via funds, goods or services for the community ('giving back to the community') must become a norm in RLS communities. Such practices will both lessen governmental dependency and foster the sense and the sinews of dedication to the Xian-via-Xish goal. This practice should start in early childhood and be continued throughout one's adult working life.

Many of the above points may sound strange to those focusing on economic issues *per se* (see, e.g. Grin & Vaillancourt, 1999; van Langevelde, 1997). There may seem to be nothing very economic about most of them. Their goal, however, is to foster language, culture and ethnolinguistic identity boundary maintenance or contrastivity as the interactive norm. This should become the defining stance for association with the world of overriding and unlimited modernization. The underlying premise of the above points is that Xian-via-Xish is the governing consideration in intra-communal business, industry and the local economy as a whole. For RLS to succeed, it must come first and cost-benefit analysis only second. 'Business as usual' may not be an approach that RLC homes, neighborhoods and communities can ever fully utilize. Yians-via-Yish don't really have to worry about RLS (although France and French Quebec sometimes demonstrate that they do), but those who are concerned to foster RLS for Xians-via-Xish have to conduct all of their economic pursuits within a total awareness of how those pursuits will contribute to and will fit into the community's RLS-enterprise first and foremost.

## Notes

1. Currently also Visiting Professor of Linguistics and Education, Stanford University, Visiting Professor of Linguistics, Graduate Center, CUNY, Visiting Professor of Bilingualism and Biculturism, New York University and Visiting Professor of Education, Long Island University (Brooklyn Campus).
2. May-ko mashme-lon. 1915. Words by Avrohom Reyzin (1875–1953) and music by N.L Saslavsky. (See Eleanor Gordon Mlotek and Joseph Mlotek, 1988. *Perl fun yidishn lid-Pearls of Yiddish Song*. New York, Arbeter Ring, pp. 116–117.)

## References

Fishman, Joshua A. (1991) *Reversing Language Shift*. Clevedon, Multilingual Matters.
——. (ed.) (2001). *Can Threatened Languages be Saved? 'Reversing Language Shift' Revisited*. Clevedon, Multilingual Matters.
Grin, Francois and Francois Vaillancourt. (1999) *The Cost-Effectiveness Evaluation of Minority Language Policies: Case Studies on Wales, Ireland and the Basque Country*. Flensburg, European Centre for Minority Issues (Monograph #2).
van Langevelde, A. (1997) *Bilingual and Economic Development in West European Minority Language Regions: A Dooyeweerdian Approach*. Groningen, University of Groningen (Graduate School/Research Institute Systems, Organization and Management).

*Part 4*
# *Yiddish Language and Culture*

# Chapter 14
# The Holiness of Yiddish: Who Says Yiddish is Holy and Why?

My Yiddish interests predate my sociolinguistic interests by many years, although my more general sociolinguistic research predates my Yiddish sociolinguistic research (again by many years). Nevertheless, regardless of what the dates of publication might be, the one has always influenced and, indeed, nourished the other. The sociology of language deals with the relationship of any two or more of the following: language usage, language users, language uses (functions), attitudes toward language and overt behaviors toward language (e.g. overt behaviors of a fostering or of a prohibitory nature). This chapter pertains to a specific sub-category of language attitudes, 'positive ethnolinguistic consciousness,' i.e. positive beliefs expressed toward a particular language (Fishman, 1997).

There are several other topics that pertain to ethnolinguistic consciousness beyond those that I will deal with here. There is also, of course, negative ethnolinguistic consciousness. But, more complexly, there is the question of the incidence of their presence or co-presence and, finally, the determination of their contextualization: culturally, historically, economically, in discourse, topically, etc. All in all, this is truly a complex area and one which sociolinguists have only begun to untangle. In this article I will focus, therefore, on only one substantive topic within positive ethnolinguistic consciousness: the attribution of sanctity. Other topical attributions are ethnicity related (i.e. cultural and historical uniqueness), functional attributions (e.g. educational, legal, religious or technological functions) and a wide variety of corpus attributions (cultural 'good-fit', lexical wealth, grammatical simplicity, phonological euphony).

## Sanctity of Languages

Nearly three quarters of the languages extant today are viewed by some portion of their historically associated speech-and-writing communities as sanctity-linked. This is particularly true of languages in the

233

European orbit, with their well-established classical and romantic heritages. The number of sanctity-linked languages is actually growing, whether by diffusion from the Euro-Mediterranean heartland or via independent genesis elsewhere. Seemingly, it is an idea which appeals to more and more ethnolinguistic aggregates, perhaps as a counterforce to the pressures of modernization and globalization. As Table 14.1 indicates, on the basis of a non-purposive sample of 76 languages from throughout the world,[1] the percentage of sanctity-linkage is highest and oldest in Europe and is correspondingly lower and younger in other regions. Of course, the exact notion of sanctity differs over time and culture. Accordingly, in any attempt to compare cultures or subcultures with respect to sanctity claims for their languages, one must proceed on the assumption that sanctity is socio-culturally constructed. I will offer no a priori culture-bound or culture-free definition of holiness, as have many distinguished scholars before me [e.g. Rudolf Otto (1917) and Emile Durkheim (1912)] and will simply let holiness be defined contextually, i.e. as its claimants use it. That approach would seem to be mandatory for exploring my main question: What claims or views do markedly different claimants have in mind when they claim that 'Yiddish is holy'.[2]

But perhaps we should back up a step before proceeding further. Is it really possible that 'holiness' has been attributed to Yiddish, given its history of rejection, abandonment and neglect (lasting into the modern period and even to this very day (see, e.g. Weinreich, 1974; Fishman, 1991) and its co-existence within the same sociocultural space as the undeniably prior and greater sanctity of Hebrew and the 'miraculous' revival of modern Israeli Hebrew? It may help put the answer to this question

**Table 14.1** Sanctity linkages and average year of their literary occurrence, by region (Fishman, 1997: 301–303)

| *Region* | *Number of citations* | *Proportion (%) with sanctity theme* | *Average year of citation* |
|---|---|---|---|
| Western Europe | 18 | 17 | 1901 |
| Other Europe | 22 | 25 | 1919 |
| Combined Europe | 40 | 42 | 1912 |
| Americas | 16 | 12 | 1961 |
| Africa | 12 | 8 | 1961 |
| Asia/Pacific | 33 | 38 | 1954 |

into a broader cross-cultural context if we keep in mind that such still derided vernaculars as Black English and Haitian Creole have also been viewed as holy (and still are so viewed in some quarters; see Fishman, 1997) as were such now powerful but once lowly vernaculars as English, German, Italian and endless others. Holiness not only varies along a historical continuum (hitherto non-holy languages having holiness bestowed upon them and, in the opposite direction, once-holy languages being secularized and desanctified), but holiness can also be a matter of degree and of startlingly different imagery in different social circles that are contemporary. The foregoing dimensions of contrast and dimensions of developmental change are particularly important *vis-à-vis* Yiddish.

As a first effort at the comparative study of sanctity claims directed toward Yiddish, I will use both a time contrast (before and after the Holocaust) and a social contrast (secular and Orthodox/Ultra-Orthodox).[3]

**Table 14.2** Sanctity claims collected pertaining to Yiddish, before and after the Holocaust and in secular vs. Orthodox/Ultra-Orthodox circles

|  | *Secular ('Yiddishists')* | *Orthodox/Ultra* |
|---|---|---|
| Before the Holocaust | (a) 20 | (c) 20 |
| After the Holocaust | (b) 12 | (d) 28 |

Phi = 0.21

Table 14.2 reveals the distribution across these two dimensions of the first 80 claims as to the sanctity of Yiddish that I have encountered.[4] There is a weak tendency for the number of Orthodox/Ultra-Orthodox attributions of sanctity to Yiddish to increase after the Holocaust and for secular attributions to decrease. There are also more Orthodox/Ultra-Orthodox attributions of this kind, among those that I have encountered, all in all, than secular ones. I will only present a representative handful of all 80 claims in this article, so that the reader can have an idea of what these claims amount to (substantively and stylistically) and so that we can have a common data pool to analyze and discuss.

## Secular (Yiddishist[5]) Claims for the Sanctity of Yiddish, Before and After the Holocaust

I will start not with the earliest secularist citation that I have located from the pre-Holocaust period (quadrant (a) in Table 14.2), but with the most famous one. It is from the gifted pen of Avrohom Lyesin (1872–1939), who fled to the United States from Czarist Russia where he had been an activist in Jewish revolutionary circles. In the USA, he became a prominent labor leader in the Jewish trade-unions and also the long-term editor of the prestigious socialist literary journal *Di tsukunft* (which still appears today and is now in its 110th year of publication). The poem, 'Der nes' [The miracle], was first published in 1922 and immediately became and remained popular in all four Yiddish-secular school movements in the USA;[6] its popularity far transcended party lines as is also evidenced by its being reprinted in textbooks of all four movements.

The poet relates that the angel of Yiddish[7] awoke him one night, speaking with the voice of his mother, as he remembered it when she read the Pentateuch in Yiddish[8] on Sabbath days. The angel reviews the help that Yiddish has been to the Jewish people over the ages: providing lullabies about the Torah for children still in their cradles, the vehicle of all popular translations and commentaries, oral or in print, which enabled those not literate in Hebrew (mostly women and the poor) to follow the lection in the synagogue (the commentary of 'the holy Alshikh'[9] is mentioned explicitly), the means by which itinerant preachers brought consolation and comfort to towns and townlets throughout central and eastern Europe, the vehicle of spontaneous prayers and requests, the tongue of holy martyrs and of those who struggled heroically against discrimination. 'If the purest sanctity is reflected through suffering and pain, then I am your holiest of all', the angel proclaims. For all of these services past and present, the angel appeals only for one promise: that the author (and the reader) 'remain a link in the procession of generations that lived for holy scrolls and even died unflinchingly for them' (Lyesin, 1922).

Clearly, Lyesin largely locates the sanctity of Yiddish in very traditional contexts: hallowed texts, practices and places, holy martyrs and the entire history of Jewish resistance to poverty and persecution. The latter may be considered to be a reflection of Lyesin's socialist convictions (although the millennial struggle against poverty and persecution is by no means socialist or even secularist concerns alone), but the former, the clear majority of instances of staunchly tradition-embedded sanctity claims, are particularly noteworthy in the light of further evidence for this period. Indeed, all of my other pre-Holocaust quadrant (a) citations asserting holiness of Yiddish (some by very outstanding literary figures such as K. Hayzler, B. Lapin or M. Ravitsh) are very similar to those of Lyesin in their overwhelmingly traditional contextualization of that sanctity, at a time when the tradition was still largely intact in its own heartland and when organized Jewish secularism was at its height there and roundly rejected traditional beliefs and practices.

Shifting our attention now to post-Holocaust secularist claims (quadrant (b) in Table 14.2), let us look briefly at one of many such poems by Leyb Faynberg (1897–1969). Faynberg is particularly instructive because he was not only an outstanding poet both before and after the Holocaust, but he had also been a Communist and a Yiddish-secularist cultural activist in the USSR before World War II and did not leave the Party until 1939. His *Mizmer shir lemame yidish* ([Sing a song to Mother Yiddish], 1967), is a paean to Yiddish throughout the centuries, utilizing and paraphrasing passages from the Book of Psalms for this purpose. While Faynberg associates Yiddish with many personages (authors, playwrights and famous story-tellers) who pioneered the literary modernization of Yiddish, as well as with the Jewish experience of overcoming persecution and adversity throughout the centuries, most of his associations with sanctity are drawn, once again, from the Orthodox world. Yiddish was the vernacular of the intellectual giant the *Gaon* [genius] of Vilna (1720–1797),[10] is associated in every Jew's mind with such towns as Mezhebezh[11] and Bratslev,[12] from which major varieties of Jewish piety and mysticism went forth into the world, with such major religious works as the *Kedushes-leyvi*[13] and the *Tanye*,[14] and, ultimately, with the sanctity of the Sabbath and the supreme goodness of God.[15] It is quite striking that a secularist, particularly one of Faynberg's political background, would utilize such traditional images and associations in supporting the sanctity of Yiddish. Notably, however, he does not invoke the Holocaust. He pointedly does not associate Yiddish with the death of its speakers, but with their pre-Holocaust creative life. The link between Yiddish and the Holocaust is clearly made, however, in the next (and final) secular example.

A.A. Roback (1890–1965) arrived in the USA as an adolescent, obtained a doctorate in psychology at Harvard, and became a world-class academic psychologist and psycholinguist. At the same time as he published an authoritative reference on the History of Psychology and many other scholarly volumes in this field (all in English), he also published works on both literary analysis and literary history in Yiddish throughout his adult life. I would like to bring a passage from his essay *Yidish-koydesh* [Holy Yiddish] (1958), because I believe that Roback is the first person to have formulated this expression as a parallel to the traditional reference to Hebrew as *loshn-koydesh* [holy tongue].[16] Roback claimed that:

A language becomes holy when there is written in it a letter such as the one the Rabbi of Blazheve[17] received:

With the help of heaven, 13/1/1943

Dear beloved R' Israel Shapero, *shelita*,[18] may you be well: The brush-factory in which we are, about 800 Jews, has now been surrounded and we are to be killed. They are trying to decide whether to shoot us or burn us. I beg of you, dear Rabbi, when you will be privileged to come to the Land of Israel, please insert a small stone somewhere on that holy ground, with my name and the name of my wife, so that our names may not be forgotten. Or write a Torah scroll for us. With this messenger I send you fifty dollars. I am in a hurry because we are being told to undress. I will send your fond regards to your holy ancestors, and ask them to intercede for you and to grant you length of days. Your servant, Arye ben Leye.

This style of writing connects generations and eras through a bond of holiness ..., heroism ..., concern for others and for one's own responsibilities. And now, can anyone still deny that Yiddish is a holy tongue?

For the secularist Roback, Yiddish has been rendered holy because of the Holocaust, not only because it was the vernacular of the lion's share of all of its Jewish victims, and not even because of their terrible anguish and suffering, but because of the moral values and holy teachings that they never abandoned, clinging to them in Yiddish, even in the shadow of certain and horrible death. Secularists believed that they remained devoted to such values even after they abandoned traditional beliefs and practices.

Space limitations make it impossible for me to bring further secularist claims concerning the sanctity of Yiddish (quadrants (a) and (b) in Table 14.2). It will be easier to summarize the essential features of those claims after we have also sampled a few of the most characteristic Orthodox/Ultra-Orthodox claims in this connection. Let us, therefore, turn our attention to examples in quadrants (c) and (d).

### Orthodox/Ultra-Orthodox Claims of the Sanctity of Yiddish, Before and After the Holocaust

Once again, my first citation is not the oldest that I have encountered, but, perhaps, the most influential that I have located in quadrant (c). It is by Sore Shenirer (1883–1935), the founder of the *Beys-Yankev* Schools for Girls (*Kruke* [Cracow] 1917). She was a feminist of sorts within her Orthodox milieu, pioneering a thorough Jewish education for girls against considerable rabbinic opposition. She soon became a charismatic figure for many traditional Jewish women, but most particularly for her students (whom she referred to as her 'sisters'). Two years before her untimely demise, she spoke (and wrote) to them as follows on the topic of *Yidishkayt un yidish* (Jewishness and Yiddish):

The Yiddish language is obviously dear to us because our mothers, grandparents and great-grandparents spoke in this language. We are obliged to speak Yiddish simply out of filial piety. However, in addition, Yiddish is also holy for us because so many righteous and virtuous folk, so many Torah-giants, have spoken it for hundreds of years and speak Yiddish today, that it necessarily becomes holy thereby. A language is also the outer apparel, the garment of the soul ... Among us Jews, the outer must be firmly tied to the inner. Just as one's modest Jewish dress and one's modest behavior are the best indicators of a truly Jewish soul, so language is also related thereto ... Just as one counts *sfire*[19] every day, one should similarly take stock every day as to whether one has improved in some way with respect to the matter of Yiddish. And, God willing, we will all certainly meet in Jerusalem [1933].[20]

Shenirer has both repeated and surpassed some of the previously mentioned claims by secularists concerning Yiddish. Like Lyesin, she links Yiddish with close kin and, like Faynberg and Roback she associates it with great figures and works of eternal religious significance. Like Lyesin and Faynberg, she explicitly relates it to the sanctity of the services. However, she goes beyond anything we have encountered before by calling for action on behalf of Yiddish ('take stock every day as to whether one has improved in some way with respect to the matter of Yiddish'). In all of these respects she was not unlike other significant contemporary Orthodox leaders in Poland, e.g. Nosn Birnbaum (1861–1937) and Eliezer Shindler (1892–1950), who called for sanctity-reinforcing activity both through and on behalf of Yiddish. Such action is always a component of the Orthodox notion of sanctity.

For the post-Holocaust Orthodox examples [quadrant (d) in Table 14.2], I have selected statements by the two most outstanding Orthodox personages of the latter part of the 20th century. Rabbi Yoysef Dov-Ber Soloveytshik (often referred to in English as Rabbi Joseph Soloveitchik, 1903–1993), known to his disciples throughout the world simply as '*der rov*/the Rav', and Menakhem-Mendl Shneyerzon (a common English spelling is Schneerson, 1902–1994), more widely known as the *Lyubavitsher rebi*. Although both *rav* and *rebi* mean rabbi, they connote the worlds of non-khasidic and khasidic Orthodoxy, respectively.

Rabbi Soloveytshik was the leading rabbinic teacher and rabbinic arbiter in Modern Orthodox circles[21] after the Holocaust. As a preeminent Talmudic master, he begins by applying the Talmudic distinction between two kinds of sanctity to the case of Yiddish (1961):

I am not a Yiddishist who believes that the language per se constitutes an absolute value. But I am a Talmud-Jew and I know that holiness and absoluteness are not always identical. The *halokhe*[22] has formulated two concepts of sanctity: sanctity per se and vessels that contain sanctity. It ruled that if there is a fire on the Sabbath, one must rescue[23] not only the Torah scroll itself but also the mantle in which it is wrapped; not only the phylacteries but also the pouch in which they lie. Accordingly, even though not included within sanctity per se, Yiddish as a language certainly belongs in the category of sanctified vessels which are also holy and must be protected with all our might. Is there a better vessel in which the holiest Torah scrolls were and are still wrapped than Yiddish? In this language the Re'ma,[24] The Meharsha'l,[25] the *Vilner goen*,[26] Reb Khayem Volo'zhiner,[27] and others who were Torah giants of their generations, learned Torah. In Yiddish the Bal-shem-tov,[28] the Magid of Mezritsh,[29] and the Old Rebi[30] explained the secrets of creation. In simple *mame-loshn*,[31] the Jewish masses expressed their faith, their simple love and loyalty. To this very day, great Torah sages deliver their Talmud discourses in Yiddish. Such a vessel is certainly holy, even if its sanctity is not absolute, but rather a sanctity by association, in the category of sanctified vessels. To preserve such a vessel is certainly a great privilege.

In Soloveytshik's defense of the sanctity of Yiddish there is much that we have already encountered: great figures of the world of Torah learning (indeed, many of them have already been mentioned by others), by implication: the great works with which these luminaries are associated, and, last but not least, basically, the entire, everyday world of kinfolk and ordinary men and women of Jewish eastern Europe who were fully committed to their faith and practices. What is new about Soloveytshik's presentation is his application to Yiddish of the Talmud's two-way division of sanctity into sanctity in and of itself and sanctity by association with sacred objects. This division is not at all unlike the first two parts of Rudolf Otto's somewhat earlier three-way dichotomy (1917) into (a) God/God's Word, (b) holy vessels associated with the former and (c) holy/saintly individuals. Although Otto's third kind of sanctity is not separately identified in Soloveytshik's dichotomy (indeed, many, and perhaps even most, scholars of Judaism would consider it to be distinctly un-Jewish to consider any human as holy), nevertheless, Soloveytshik proceeds to rest most of his case for sanctity on an extensive list of Torah scholars, a practice which we have also encountered in Sore Shenirer and even, to a lesser degree, in Lyesin and in Roback. And although there is no doubt in Soloveytshik's mind that Yiddish is only of a second order of sanctity, it is precisely because of that sanctity that Yiddish is not only worthy of use but of defense and protection, even in the case of a fire on the Sabbath, i.e. in difficult and dangerous times such as ours.

It is only fitting that we not leave quadrant (d) without considering the words of Soloveytshik's counterpart in the khasidic world, R' Menakhemmendl Shneyerson [Schneerson] (1902–1994). Just as Soloveytshik is *der rov*, so Shneyerson is *der rebi*, and, arguably, the most influential Jewish leader of the 20th century. Knowing Hebrew, Russian, German, French and English fully and well, he nevertheless delivered his famous *sikhes* (discourses) in Yiddish, and they were often (re-)broadcast to his followers around the world in Yiddish along with simultaneous translation. This is what he had to say about Yiddish (1991):

Among the seventy languages,[32] there are certain ones that possess a special merit, as the Talmud mentions with respect to *halokhe* in Greek and in Aramaic.[33] And there is reason to believe, along those very lines, that this also applies to the language which is called Yiddish. The very fact that during so many generations – also in our own generation – the majority of Ashkenazi Jews, including the Ashkenazi Torah giants, spoke in this language (to such a degree that it came to be called, at the very least during the past generation, Yiddish [Jewish]), while we do not find this for Aramaic in the time of the Talmud, nor for Arabic in the time of the Rambam,[34] neither before nor after him, nor for French in the time of Rashi,[35] implies that it possesses an advantage relative to other languages ... Another asset of Yiddish is that it has a special relationship to Torah-matters that are both revealed and hidden. As is well known, the Old *Rebi*[36] states in *Igeres hakoydesh*[37] that the Bal-shem-tov,[38] may his memory be for a blessing, would talk of Torah in Yiddish and not in the Holy Tongue. And it is well known that this was also the practice of his pupil *Harav Hamagid,*[39] of the old honorable holy one, our master, our teacher and our rabbi[40] himself, and of the *rebis* after him, up to and including my teacher and father-in-law, our master, our teacher and our rabbi,[41] they all spoke of khasidism in the language of Ashkenaz, in Yiddish. Precisely because our teachers and our leaders spoke of khasidism in Yiddish, they increased its merits even further than they were before. The special relationship between Yiddish and the holy teachings of khasidism is stressed even further in the *Seyfer tanye*[42] – the written Torah of khasidism ..., and the beginning of the revelation of all matters pertaining to the holy teachings of khasidism ... Also, even those things that our teachers and leaders originally wrote in the Holy Tongue were initially [said] in Yiddish.

Although the *Rebi* never actually claims sanctity for Yiddish in so many words he does strongly stress its 'special merit' due to its close and pro-longed association with Torah, khasidism and the great and holy *rebis* and sages who formulated and propagated khasidism. The *Rebi's* repeated contextualization of Yiddish in the company of holy writings, holy leaders and holy revelations places this discourse squarely within the very same framework of sanctity claims and associations that we have reviewed before.

## Preliminary Reflections

Although there are many, many more citations that could be cited here, particularly Orthodox ones since the Holocaust, they would add few new perspectives on the nature of the sanctity claims for Yiddish. In terms of the two major dichotomous dimensions on the basis of which our sample was selected, the similarities stand out much more clearly than the differences. Before the Holocaust, both Lyesin and Shenirer claimed sanctity for Yiddish by virtue of its centuries of close association with (i) cultural heroes, mainly Torah sages and holy martyrs, (ii) major hallowed writings and authors, and (iii) the closest of kin and the simple, pious Jewish everyman. The similarities in the metaphors and images of such otherwise ideologically widely different spokespersons are really very striking and surprising. Often the very same holy books and saintly folk are mentioned in the religious and in the secularist camps. Perhaps it should be pointed out that the pre-Holocaust secular-ists all had received religious (even Yeshiva) educations and it may be from that world of religious ideas and metaphors that they draw when sanctity is claimed for Yiddish. It may also be that the reason sanctity claims for Yiddish quickly dry up among secularists and then disappear entirely very soon after the Holocaust is that the post-Holocaust generation of secularists (writers and readers alike) completely lacked the religious concepts, associations and metaphors that were available to their predecessors born and traditionally educated before the Holocaust. We must remember that Roback and Faynberg are of the pre-Holocaust vintage of secularists, even though we have quoted from what they wrote after the Holocaust had ended.

But there are important differences too. Only Lyesin claims sanctity for Yiddish before the Holocaust by virtue of its association with a millen-nium of Jewish suffering and persecution, a link that Roback strongly reinforces after the Holocaust. Both of these figures are secularist, and, indeed, the Holocaust itself seems to be a secularist preoccupation in connection with the sanctity of Yiddish. Roback stresses this most starkly, of course, but the progression from Holy Yiddish (*yidish-koydesh*) in Faynberg to language of the holy martyrs (*loshn-kedoyshim*) in Roback is indicative of a kind of linguistic *yizkoyr* service[43] that secularists resonate with. The Holocaust destroyed the secular Yiddishist heartland and none other of similar centrality and robustness has ever arisen. On the other hand, only Shenirer called for pro-Yiddish action before the Holocaust, a call which Soloveytshik also supports after the Holocaust. Clearly, they are both from the Orthodox fold, i.e. from a cultural context in which all values somehow connected to sanctity must have corresponding commanded actions. This is not to imply that the religious were and are unfamiliar with Jewish suffering and that the secular were and are strangers to pro-Yiddish social action. Nothing could be further from the truth! But when it comes to sanctity claims for Yiddish the secularists and the Orthodox differ noticeably in the extent to which sanctity judgments are expected to require externalized behavioral implementations.

## Modernization vs. Exceptionality

The metaphor of sanctity by association with holy and pious books as well as righteous and scholarly sages is a very old one in Jewish tradition. As early as 1815 (three-quarters of a century before the secular/religious split began) Shmuel Yankev Bik (1772–1831), one of the very first defenders of Yiddish among Eastern European *maskilim*,[44] did so, in part, by relating Yiddish to renowned and holy rabbis over the centuries, as well as to popular books that had brought Judaism's hallowed Hebrew classics to ordinary readers in Yiddish translation. He believed that only books in Yiddish could ultimately help the masses to modernize via a secular literature of their own. A century later, secular Jewish modernizers also strongly made this point, although usually without explicitly making the association with sanctity that Bik had proposed.

However, the custom of claiming sanctity for Yiddish by associating it with previously sanctified books and personages was also very much in evidence among those who opposed Jewish modernization. One of the latter was Rabbi Yehoyshua-Leyb Diskin (1817–1898). Writing from Jerusalem, in 1871, he criticized those Jews who dared to speak Hebrew and proclaimed that 'every day that we are still in exile, Yiddish will continue to be spoken, and because Yiddish has always been our protector against assimilation, then it is the holy tongue itself' (cited by Glinert, 1991: 79; also see Glinert *et al.*, 1999). This claim had previously also been made by the famous *Khsam Soyfer* (Rabbi Moses Schreiber, 1762–1839), who, in the 1820s, struggling against the success of German-speaking Reformed rabbis in Presburg (Bratislava), reminded his followers that one of the major merits thanks to which the Jews had been rescued from their bondage in ancient Egypt by God himself, was that 'they had not changed their language'. He forbad his German speaking but Yiddish mother tongue followers (chiefly in Hungary and Slovakia) to attend synagogues in which rabbis delivered German sermons and he commanded them to zealously safeguard Yiddish if they were to safeguard their very existence among the nations.[45] This same call for action on the part of fathers to provide their sons with Yiddish books and not to permit them to read English (or secular Hebrew) books ('preserving the boundaries between the sanctified and the secular, is to merit the coming of our true Messiah, speedily and in our days, amen') is explicitly found in a 'Holy Appeal' signed by 14 khasidic rabbis and published in several of New York's Ultra-Orthodox Yiddish newspapers in 1996.

Sore Rubin (the *sulitser rebitsin*[46]) also calls for action in connection with her appeal to mothers to speak only Yiddish to their daughters and require them to reply in Yiddish as well.

> I appeal to all Jewish mothers and daughters to organize a committee to be named 'Ascend higher: Speak *mame-loshn'*. Then every Jew will suddenly feel that from this small spark coming from the hearts of mothers there has flared up a mighty fire of holiness and that the spirit of God rests in their homes. By drawing closer to the generations past we will also draw closer to the Creator and we will hasten redemption. Remember: because of the merits of righteous women Israel was saved (in Egypt).

Thus, Yiddish is not only clearly located within the sanctified fold but its intergenerational safekeeping will merit the supreme reward: living to witness the coming of the Messiah and the redemption of all the faithful. The link between Yiddish and the messianic age, when those who safeguarded Yiddish will merit to meet on the streets of Jerusalem, as well as the link between Yiddish and non-assimilation, are links that we have already noticed in the cited words by Sore Shenirer,[47] above. Note also that this final rubric, with its somewhat different implication, namely, the message of withstanding the modernization and secularization necessarily inherent in a language of wider communication, nevertheless continues the Orthodox orientation to behaviorally express and actively reinforce their conviction as to the sanctity of Yiddish. Such calls continue to this very day but have never been paralleled in secular treatments of the sanctity of Yiddish.

## Summary and Conclusions

The views that we have examined here concerning the sanctity of Yiddish also throw some light on the spreading tendency to attribute sanctity to profane vernaculars. The association of the language with individuals whose sanctity cannot be doubted (in the case of Yiddish,

Torah sages, the very closest of kin and the unquestioning piety and religious devotion of simple folk) and with texts of unimpeachable authorship (the major rabbinic writings in Yiddish or translated into Yiddish to foster their accessibility) are predominant in both religious and secular claims.

A distinctly secular claim to sanctity for Yiddish is based upon its association with Jewish suffering, their long struggle for freedom and dignity and, finally, the Holocaust. The Holocaust was particularly devastating for Yiddishist secularism, but seems not to have resulted in Yiddish sanctity claims among the Orthodox, most of those who weathered the Holocaust reestablished major Yiddish-speaking communities afterwards. However, the Orthodox also present two types of sanctity claims which are peculiarly theirs. The first of these is the contribution of Yiddish to Jewish distinctiveness and, thereby, to Jewish survival. The second is the obligation that is incumbent upon all Orthodox folk to actively support and implement the sanctities that they hold dear. The secular and the Orthodox experienced the Holocaust together, but they came out of it, as they had gone into it, with quite distinctive views of how Jewish sanctity in general and the sanctity of Yiddish in particular are constituted. Sanctity of language claims do not begin to exhaust the varieties of positive ethnolinguistic consciousness that are associated with particular languages (Fishman, 1997). Such claims can apparently also coexist with a variety of negative views as well. Simultaneous support for conflicting views is a common human and cultural characteristic. Finally, positive views of an other-than-sanctity nature do not stand in any implicational relationship with the sanctity views, whether within or between languages. The orthogonality of sanctity views toward language is an important hypothesis suggested by our data.

Younger secular Yiddishists, coming to the fore after the Holocaust were generally bereft of traditional Jewish exposure, whether at school or at home, and the sanctity of Yiddish ceased to be a metaphor with which they were comfortable after 1972 (the date of our last secular citation). They still actively foster and champion Yiddish but they express their efforts on behalf of the language along well-known modern lines, focusing on ethnonationalist, ideological, ethnohistorical and cultural creativity associations (Fishman, 1972). These are dimensions that receive far less, and certainly less exclusive, Orthodox attention and, furthermore, they are not necessarily linked to sanctity at any overt behavioral level.

Of course, the claimed sanctity of Yiddish does not take an iota away from the traditional sanctity of Hebrew in Orthodox communities. Nevertheless, the continued Orthodox claims for the sanctity of Yiddish and their efforts in support of the language (its active use, protection and reinforcement in family, neighborhood, school and synagogue) cannot but help Yiddish stay off the endangered languages list for the foreseeable future. What for secularists is or was a metaphor of supreme endearment, albeit often traditionally expressed, is and was for the Orthodox a veritable link to a veritable category of sanctity and, accordingly, carries with it a behavioral obligation too.

It would be unwise to generalize too widely on the basis of the Yiddish case. On the other hand, each and every case is valuable in that it suggests previously unsuspected hypotheses worthy of follow-up investigation. The recent worldwide growth in the number of vernaculars to which claims of sanctity are applied may be attributable both to spreading notions of metaphorical sanctity and behavioral sanctity. The former is by far more common than the latter. Sanctity metaphors regarding life (or death), the forces of nature and, most particularly, imbeddedness in a sanctified historical or cultural past and its resulting fidelity imperatives are particularly widespread. The co-presence of a prior sanctified classical tongue seems to pose no barrier to the development of vernacular sanctity as well. The transition from such metaphors to normative behavioral sanctity is a more uncommon development, but one which the increased use (or co-use) of vernaculars in religious contexts, texts and practices may well foster.

## Acknowledgments

An earlier version of this article constituted the 'Third Annual Lecture in Yiddish Studies', in the series sponsored by the Program in Jewish Studies, Stanford University, November 19, 1996. I owe special thanks to Itshe Goldberg, Yosl Mlotek and Bernard Spolsky for encouragement and assistance.

## Notes

1. Methodological and sampling issues are discussed in Fishman (1997), which was based on 141 citations collected by the author and his correspondents.
2. Like English, Yiddish calls upon two different lexical sources in designating that which is holy. In English these sources are Germanic (holy) and Romance (sacred, sanctity). In Yiddish, they are Germanic (*heylik*) and Semitic (*koydesh, kedushe*). In neither language do these doublets imply differences in degree. Yiddish is mostly written in standard Hebrew characters (a few of them being somewhat modified) and its transliteration into Roman characters in this article follows the standard established by the United States Library of Congress (USLC) and the YIVO (Yidisher Visenshaftlikher Institut) Institute for Jewish Research. Stress in Yiddish is normally penultimate and therefore only exceptions to this rule will be indicated via an apostrophe after the stressed vowel (e.g. *sha'besdik*). A different transcription system is normally utilized for Hebrew but Hebrew-origin words that have

been merged into Yiddish are also transliterated in accord with the USLC/YIVO system.

3. There is no litmus test to differentiate Orthodox from Ultra-Orthodox across time and space. The boundary between them is a relatively recent, shifting and perspectival one. If we go back a century the difference between the two is less clear than it is today (see, e.g. Heilman, 1989, 1992). Yiddish has been much more commonly (although not universally) retained, as a vernacular, as a medium of Talmud study (*lernen*) and as a medium of instruction, among those generally viewed as Ultra-Orthodox (*khareydi, khasidic*).

4. All ascriptions of sanctity are texts in print, unless otherwise noted. Whether or not such ascriptions correspond to spoken convictions is assumed but undemonstrated. Their authors are indubitably more literate than the average members of their speech communities, but the higher status of these authors also lends more norm-setting impact to their views.

5. This designation is commonly applied to non-religious or, at times, anti-religious Jews for whom Yiddish is the sole or supreme definer of their Jewishness. That is how this term will be utilized in this article, although it is also encountered today to designate, more generally, anyone interested, competent or specializing in Yiddish. The secular/Ultra-Orthodox distinction is reflected both in beliefs and practices.

6. The four major Yiddish secular school-movements in the USA included one each affiliated with socialism, Labor-Zionism, communism and educational non-*partisanism*. See the website (http://www.fsysa.org) that has been developed for the Secular Yiddish Schools in America archival collection at Stanford University Libraries, Department of Special Collections, containing the records, publications and memorabilia pertaining to these school movements.

7. There is a Jewish folk-belief which maintains that God converses with the 70 ministering angels via the 70 tongues that correspond to the notions of 70 languages and 70 peoples in the world. Each angel is the guardian of its particular language (Steinschneider, 1903). Lyesin was the first to suggest that there is also an angel for Yiddish.

8. A Yiddish translation of the Pentateuch written for women, referred to as 'the *khumesh-taytsh*' [Pentateuch translation], was a very common book in pre-Holocaust eastern European Jewish homes. The most popular of these was the *Tsene-urene* [go forth and see], early 17th century and still in print (after over 120 printings/editions in Yiddish alone), which also includes commentaries, tales and the readings from the Prophets related to the weekly lection. Men not well-versed in Hebrew also made use of it, or of similar texts (see below).

9. Named after its 16th century author (compiler), R' Moyshe Alshikh, it was held in such high repute that it was widely referred to as 'the holy Alshikh'. The *shul*-reader would translate it into Yiddish for adults who could not follow it in Hebrew, when the upcoming weekly Torah lection was reviewed in advance.

10. The *Vilner goen*, also known as *Hagoen r'eyliyohu* or *Hagra*, acquired such fame, authority and distinguished students that *Vilne* (now Vilnius, the capital of Lithuania) became the preeminent center of Torah studies and was widely referred to as 'the Jerusalem of Lithuania.'

11. Mezhebezh, located in the Ukraine, was for many years the place of residence of the Bal-shem-tov (c. 1700–1760), the founder of khasidism, a branch of Orthodoxy which has come to be of great importance in the modern Jewish world. It has been strongly associated with Yiddish, orally and in print, from its very origins. Although the many branches or types of khasidism

differ from one another in details, they are generally all characterized as a reaction against the academic formalism of concurrent rabbinic Judaism. By stressing the loving-mercy of God, encouraging joyous religious expression via song and dance, and de-emphasizing the centrality of traditional (Talmudic) study, it spread rapidly among the poor and less educated. More recently, khasidim too have come to accept the importance of studying the Talmud.

12. Bratslev is the town in Poland from which a particularly mystic variety of khasidism, inspired by R' Nakhmen Bratslever (1772–1811), was disseminated. The Jewish cemeteries in both Mezhebezh and Bratslev are visited annually by followers of the two varieties of khasidism mentioned above, to observe the anniversaries of their rebi's demise. The Bratslever khasidim never proclaimed a new rabbi and are, therefore, also known as 'the dead khasidim'.

13. The *Kedushes-leyvi* was an influential book by R' Leyvi Yitskhok Berditshever (1740–1809). It was either authored in or quickly translated into Yiddish and was widely read.

14. The (*Seyfer*) *Tanye* is a widely studied text by R' Shneyer Zalmen of Lyadi (1745–1813). It is a systematic exposition of khasidic belief and is considered the principal source (the written law) of the Lyubavitsh movement (see below). It was also either authored in or quickly translated into Yiddish and widely read.

15. The title and the penultimate line of Faynberg's poem paraphrase a line from the Sabbath morning service ('*mizmer shir leyoy'm hashabes*') the source of which is Psalms, 92.1. The final line, also from the Sabbath morning service, is taken from Psalms, 136.1.

16. Another commonly encountered designation of Yiddish, one that is also contrastive to *loshn-koydesh*, is *loshn-hakedoyshim* [language of the martyrs]. This too, of course, is a sanctity association.

17. Blazheve: a Polish town west of Lodzh and south of Reyshe, both of which are more easily located on maps of Poland.

18. *Shelita* is an acronym for *sheyikhye leyomim tovim, omeyn* [may he live to good days, amen] that is a common honorific for great rabbis.

19. *Sfire* is the ritualized counting, at the morning and evening services, of the 49 days between the second night of *Peysekh* (Passover, the religious holiday which celebrates the liberation of the Jews from Egyptian bondage) and the first night of *Shvues* (Feast of Weeks, the holiday commemorating the Jews' acceptance of the Torah at Mt. Sinai, i.e. the goal and climax of that liberation).

20. Many Orthodox Jews believe that after the coming of the Messiah, the righteous of all peoples, living and dead, will come to praise God at the Holy Temple in Jerusalem. By associating this apocalyptic vision with the speaking of Yiddish, Shenirer thereby hugely reinforces her view that Yiddish is holy.

21. The exact boundary of Modern Orthodoxy is difficult to define and changes over time. Arising in Germany and in the USA in the early decades of the last century, some of its defining characteristics have been the acceptance of modern, secular subjects (including college education) as necessary for a good education of both males and females and the pursuit of greater female study of traditional sources and their greater participation in religious services.

22. *Halokhe* (also spelled *halaha* and *Halacha* in English) refers to the entire body of Jewish law and tradition, Biblical, Talmudic and post-Talmudic, as interpreted by rabbinic authorities.

23. 'Rescue' here implies to carry out from the synagogue into the street on the Sabbath, although Orthodox Jews are prohibited from transferring objects

on the Sabbath from a private domain (their homes or places of worship) into a public domain.

24. The Re'ma (Rav Moyshe Iserlis) was a 16th century Torah luminary and author of several books of rabbinic commentary.

25. Meharsha'l (*Moreynu harav* [our teacher, rabbi] Shloyme Lurye), 1510–1573, halakhic arbiter and author of Talmudic commentaries.

26. See footnote 10 above.

27. *Reb* Khayim Volozhiner (1749–1821), founder of the famous Volozhiner Yeshiva (1802), an institution of advanced Torah learning in which many subsequently famous secular and religious leaders were students (e.g. the Hebrew-Yiddish writer Khayim Nakhmen Byalik [1873–1934] and the first Chief Ashkenazi Rabbi of the Land of Israel, Avrohom Kook [–d.1935]).

28. See footnote 11 above.

29. A *magid* is an itinerant preacher. The *Magid* Dov-ber of Mezritsh (–d.1772) was one of the most important early disciples, and later the successor, of the Bal-shem-tov.

30. The Old *Rebi* was Shneyer-Zalmen of Lyadi (1745–1813), a student of the *Magid* of Mezritsh, who subsequently went on to become the founder of Lyubavitsher khasidism.

31. *Mame* has two syllables (ma-me). *Mame-loshn* [mother-tongue] is an affectionate term for Yiddish in contrast to the more formal (and Germanic) *mutershprakh*.

32. The traditional Jewish belief is that after the great flood the children of Noah spread throughout the world and, after the tower of Babel, there ultimately arose seventy peoples and seventy languages. The tower of Babel story implies that the Lord intends these to be everlastingly separate, until the end of all days.

33. Both the Talmud and the *Rebi* have in mind only Judeo-Aramaic. Various other varieties of Aramaic developed and, by the 10th century had spread from the Mediterranean eastward all the way to Tibet.

34. The Rambam (1135–1204), Rabbi Moyshe ben Maymon or Maimonides, was the preeminent medieval codifier of Jewish law. Although most of his major works were authored in Hebrew (e.g. *Mishne Toyre*, his encyclopedic systematic arrangement of all Talmudic law) others were written in Arabic (e.g. his famous *Guide for the Perplexed*) and had to be translated into Hebrew in order to be accessible.

35. Rashi (1040–1105), Rabbi Shloyme Yitskhaki, famous commentator on the Bible and the Talmud, noted for his simple clarity. Was born and died in Troyes (France) and his use of French words throughout his commentaries, as glosses of obscure Hebrew words, often constitute the very earliest sources for French that scholars have thus far found from a period in which French was as yet seldom written.

36. See footnote 30 above.

37. *Igeres hakoydesh* is a posthumously published collection of letters (1814) by R' Shneyer-Zalmen of Lyadi.

38. See the section of footnote 11 above, that pertains to the Bal-shem-tov.

39. This is the popular name of the Mezritcher Magid, see footnote 29 above.

40. The 'Old *Rebi*'. See footnote 30 above.

41. R' Yoysef-yitskhok Schneerson (1880–1950) was the Lyubavitsher rebi prior to the author of this citation.

42. See footnote 14 above.

43. *Yizkoyr* is the traditional Jewish memorial service for the revered dead, particularly for one's deceased parents or other close family members,

which is recited in Hebrew at the (Orthodox) morning service on the concluding day of every major festival.

44. A *maskel* (plural: *maskilim*): a member of a loosely organized group of early 19th century Jewish modernizers in Eastern Europe. They generally supported modern, secular studies for Jews and most realized that this could only be realized via Yiddish since Jewish proficiency in Hebrew or the co-territorial official language was too meager for either of them to be widely useful as vehicles of modernization.

45. The *Khsam soyfer* is cited along these lines both by Vaynraykh/Weinreich (1973) and by Glinert (1991).

46. A *rebitsin* is the wife of either a *rov* or a *rebi*.

47. See the citation from Sore Shenirer in our discussion of quadrant (c), above.

## References

Bik, Yankev Shmuel ([1807] 1833) In defense of Mendl Lefin. *Kerem Khemed* 1, 96–99.

Durkheim, Emile ([1912 French] 1915) *Elementary Forms of the Religious Life*. London: Allen & Unwin.

Faynberg, Leyb ([1954] 1975) Mizmer shir lemame-yidish. Reprinted in Sh. Rollansky (ed.) *Fun revolutsye tsu tshuve: Musterverk fun der yidisher literature*, Vol. 64 (pp. 141–142). Buenos Aires: Ateneo Literario.

Fishman, Joshua A. (1972) *Language and Nationalism*. Boston: Newbury House.

——. (1991) *Yiddish: Turning to Life*. Amsterdam: Benjamins.

——. (1997) *In Praise of the Beloved Language*. Berlin: Mouton.

Glinert, Lewis H. and Shilhav, Yoseph (1991) Holy land, holy language: A study of an Ultraorthodox Jewish ideology. *Language in Society* 20, 59–86.

Glinert, Lewis H. (1999) We never changed our language: Attitudes toward Yiddish acquisition among Hasidic educators in Britain. *International Journal of the Sociology of Language* 138, 31–52.

Heilman, Samuel C. (1989) *Cosmopolitans and Parochials: Modern Orthodox Jews in America*. Chicago: University of Chicago Press.

——. (1992) *Defenders of the Faith: Inside Ultra-Orthodox Jewry*. New York: Schocken.

Lyesin, Avrohom ([1922] 1967) Der nes. Reprinted in Sh. Rollanski (ed.) *Yidish in lid: Musterverk fun der yidisher literatur*, Vol. 33 (pp. 57–59). Buenos Aires: Ateneo Literario.

Otto, Rudolf (1917) *Das Heilige*. Munchen: C.H. Beck. [*The Idea of the Holy*. New York: Oxford University Press].

Roback, A.A. (1958) Yidish-koydesh. In *Di Imperye Yidish* (pp. 107–110). Mexico City: Mendleson Fund.

Rubin, Sore (*Di sulitser rebitsin*) (1992) Ascend higher: Speak mame-loshn. *Dos yidishe vort* 52.

Sawyer, J.F.A. and Simpson, J.M.Y. (2001) *Language and Religion*. London: Pergamon.

Schneerson, Menakhem-Mendl ([1981] 1991) Hoysofe, Bs'd. Misikhes shel parshe yisro, htshm'a. In *Lekutey sikhes al parshiyos hashavue* (pp. 10–15). New York: Likutey Sikhes.

Shenirer, Sore (1931) Yidishkeyt un yidish. *Beys-yankev*, 8, 71–72.

Soloveitchik, Joseph (1961) Vegn yidish. *Der tog*, February 24, 4.

Steinschnider, Moritz (1903) Die kanoinischen Zahlen 70–73. *Zeitschrift der deutschen Morgenländischen Gesellschaft*, 57, 479–505.

Vaynraykh, Maks (Max Weinreich) (1974) *Di geshikhte fun der yidisher shprakh*, 4 volumes. New York: YIVO.

## Chapter 15

# 'Holy Languages' in the Context of Societal Bilingualism

### Times and Tides in the Study of Bilingualism

There is no better place to begin this discussion than to marvel at the Zeitgeist change during the past quarter century *vis-à-vis* considerations of societal bilingualism. In the mid-sixties to the mid-seventies the climate of opinion was still overwhelmingly a negative one. My earliest efforts to provide a more balanced perspective on immigrant-based bilingualism in the USA (Fishman, 1966) were met with substantial incredulity. The two favorite 'flies' in the bilingual ointment were (a) purportedly lowered intelligence and (b) penalized foreign accentedness. When I demonstrated that there was no necessary link between intelligence and bilingualism (Fishman, 1965) and that everyone always spoke their local languages (whether L1 or L2) with some kind of accent, the demonization of some accents being a form of rank social prejudice, this was considered to be an admission of 'guilty as charged', rather than a clarification of the issue. I think I may have been among the very first (and perhaps actually the very first modern day researcher) to point out that the bulk of the human population was and had always been bi- (or multi-) lingual and that elitist bilingualism was and had always been considered a badge of refinement and lifelong advantage, rather than a stigmata of poverty and marginality. We have come a long distance since those days, with the pluses of bilingualism finally being given the attention that they fully deserve. The journals devoted to this area, the conferences, the academic programs and this very book itself are all evidence that there has been a sea-change in our understanding of the individual, societal and cultural ramifications and correlates of bilingualism. Bilingualism really is a many-faceted human phenomenon, some of its aspects (as is also the case of all human phenomena) being inevitably selectively perceived as more positive than others.

251

## Bilingualism as a Sociocultural Norm

We owe to the sociolinguistic enterprise the realization that bilingualism is not only an individual or even a social class phenomenon, but that it may very well be the sociocultural norm. I am using 'norm' here not only in the sense of *commonality* or *frequency*, but also in the more interpretive sense of *normality* or *desirability*. A great founding father of modern sociology, Emile Durkheim, recognized that every social norm had within itself not only an indication of what was considered socioculturally 'expected' of members in good-standing, but also a behavioral aspect according to which members were judged to be good, proper, decent, i.e. morally proper or improper according to sanctified traditions and standards. Durkheim realized that exactly what it is that is considered holy may well differ from one culture to another, but believed that in every case it is related to normified behavior which expresses notions of the ultimate 'good' or 'desirable' in life. It should come as no surprise then, that languages, constituting the main symbol systems of all human cultures everywhere, have often come to be considered holy too. As a result, in many bilingual settings, one language or even both have had this supreme attribute ascribed to it (or them) by the members native to that setting and incorporated normatively and moralistically into their communicative conventions. Durkheim would say that not only is bilingualism implicitly holy wherever it corresponds to the sociocultural norm, but that in many of these settings it involves one or more languages that are *explicitly* holy too. The latter settings are the ones that we will particularly explore in this chapter.

## Types of Holiness

Notions of holiness differ from culture to culture. English, because of its hybrid linguistic nature, is one of a very small sub-set of languages that has two etymological roots pertaining to this notion. The words *holy* and *sacred*, from the Germanic and the Romance components of English respectively, give us two different glimpses of what this term can connote. Holy implies wholeness, completeness, perfectedness, hallowedness, i.e. a specialness far above and beyond any human approximation to such goals. Sacred, on the other hand, is more explicitly otherworldly in its conceptualization, referring to sanctity, saintliness, godliness. The triliterate root for the Hebrew term that is glossed as 'holy', K-D-Sh, reoccurs in meanings that imply separated off, set aside as (or dedicated to being) special, extraordinary. Accordingly, when languages are referred to as 'holy' we must, strictly speaking, investigate the semantic (rather than only the etymological) field of the original term that is translated into English as 'holy', in order to find out what exactly the indigenous imagery implies. Although we cannot pause here to do that in each case, we can at least agree that 'holy is as holy does', i.e. that in each case it may mean something somewhat different (i.e. connote or denote different attributes and be applicable to different referents, situations or circumstances). Nevertheless, there is sufficient commonality of meaning underlying the term that we can not only utilize it cross-culturally, but even suggest reoccurring clusters of meanings or associations that the designation has in cultures around the globe. There is no human culture without language and no human culture without the notion of the holy. As a result, these two notions co-occur and are joined in many cultures. Naturally, they also co-occur in the writings of Durkheim, although viewed from his more theoretical perspective that does not even require that the notion of sanctity be perspectivally present to members of any given culture.

## Types of Holy Languages[1]

### When One of the Two Languages is Considered Inherently Holy

All religions derived from Judaism, the so-called 'Abrahamic religions', recognize as holy the language(s) of revelation and of their respective holy scriptures. In each of these cases the language (or the 'variety' of the language) that is revelation and scripture related is by now (and has been for over a millennium a 'religious classical', i.e. a variety not employed for quotidian vernacular purposes and, in most instances, no longer employed for quotidian written purposes either. Other such languages are Classical (i.e. pre-Christian) Greek, Sanskrit, Geez, Pali, both Classical Tamils and Classical Mandarin, all of which can also be related to purportedly revealed and hallowed *texts* or to initially *oral traditions* that may only have been committed to writing centuries after their oral initiation. These languages are holy because of having been the vehicles of materia sancta, whether orally or in writing. Their very structure and corpus is assumed to have been transformed or shaped by their unique 'holy vessel' function. Like all holy phenomena these languages are considerable unalterable, just as are their texts. This fixed-once-and-for-all nature of religious classicals ultimately contributed to making them unsuitable for daily secular life, even assuming that they had been so used before their revelatory role began. The obvious by-product of this situation is the necessary bilingualization of a sociocultural aggregate, one of whose languages is strongly sanctity linked, while the other is not. No genetic relationship between the two is necessary, although is often present, as Ferguson (1959) has demonstrated.

## When Another Language Becomes Holy by Dint of Association with the One that is Already Holy

Precisely because holy languages either never were used for everyday speaking, reading and writing, or have not been used in such functions for centuries, other community languages have had to be put to use to teach, translate and explain the languages of direct revelation, as well as any other hallowed texts originally and most significantly identified with them. It is in this fashion that a progression of languages of everyday use can come to partake of holiness, because they are the means whereby subsequent generations have had materia sancta translated, taught and explained to them. Even Latin and Ecclesiastic Greek may be primarily in this category of 'holiness one step removed', depending on just how much of the Vulgate and the early Greek Bibles are believed to contain the actual words of Jesus and of his disciples, rather than merely subsequent translations of those words. The Old Church Slavonics definitely belong in this second category, as does 'Luther German' for the Hutterites, Old Order Amish and Mennonites (and for many Lutherans too) and as does Yiddish for Talmud study among almost all Khasidic Jewish groups. This is one of the processes by which the universe of holy languages grows. The Protestant Reformation inspired and required vernacular translations of the Bible and of the books containing the church services. In so doing, the sanctified status of English, German and the Scandinavian languages was substantially contributed to (but long maintained only in the case of German). Such growth is probably inevitable for all successfully continuous religious cultures. However, the 'sanctified by association' languages (or the varieties most directly associated with materia sancta translation, e.g. The King James version of the Bible) also come to resist further change and, therefore, can be replaced for everyday use by varieties or languages that are not yet significantly religiously impacted. Once again, in such circumstances the sociocultural patterns involved are, of necessity, bilingual. In such bilingual circumstances, one spoken language will be sanctity linked whereas the other will not (or, at most, will be far less so).

## Holiness Via Ethnic Kinship Identity, Life/Death Metaphors or Other Very Special Experiences and Associations

Finally, more and more vernaculars are coming to be regarded as holy due to their association with heightened ethnic contrastivity, historical ethnic grievances and traditional ethnic identity. Such developments are often communally patterned, rather than merely individual experiences, and, as such, frequently prompt positive ethnolinguistic consciousness for the 'ethnic mother tongue', even long after an intrusive language has been adopted for everyday life. The struggle for the life of the ethnic collectivity (or any other collectivity that comes to be connected by a kinship myth or sentiment) begins to make use of the metaphors of human life and death. Since the latter are linked to sanctity (for example 'life everlasting', 'undying love', 'immortal soul', etc.), the former too is discussed in such sanctity suffused terms. Similarly, expressions of endearment and intimacy, usually reserved for the closest kin, putative kin or kin-to-be, are transferred to the ethnicity-linked language, even when (or particularly when) its secular use has become attenuated and many of its erstwhile workaday functions are being discharged by another language still linked to the hurly-burly of daily life. The tendency toward psycho-ostensives is particularly notice-able among recessive ethnicity-linked languages (Matisoff, 1978) and, so also, is the tendency toward calls for acts of moral obligation and for the discharge of duties due to one's own dearest and nearest of kin. Meta-phors pertaining to the beauties of nature, to the return of spring, to the inevitable waxing of the moon, the reappearance of seasonal flowers and animals, are all part and parcel of the tendency to romanticize and to sanctify the 'ethnically own' language in comparison with the worka-day one more recently borrowed from the outside. As a result, we are once again faced by bilingual populations in which one language is viewed (consciously or unconsciously) as much more within the pale or penumbra of sanctity than the other. It is in precisely this sense that for 'true believers' Irish is holy whereas English is not, Basques is holy and Spanish is not, Breton is holy and French is not, Frisian is holy and Dutch is not, Ainu is holy and Japanese is not.

## When Both Languages are Holy

When the language of materia sancta *per se* and the language in which sanctity is learned, understood and appreciated are both considered holy, there may be cultural recognition of greater holiness and lesser holiness. Hebrew and Yiddish are often viewed in precisely this fashion among many Orthodox Jews. Both Rabbi Joseph Soloveitchik and the Grand Rabbi of Lubavitch have pointed out that while Yiddish is not as holy as Hebrew is, nevertheless it too has a very definite and vital sanctity of its own. Urdu is so enriched by Persian and Arabic that Urdu too basks in the sanctity that emanates from the former. This recognition may even be more spontaneous in Orthodox Christianity (e.g. Old Church Slavonic and Russian, Old Church Bulgarian and Bulgarian, Ecclesiastic Armenian and Armenian, Ecclesiastic Greek [Katherevousa] and Greek, etc.) and in Hinduism (Sanskrit and Hindi, Sanskrit and Bengali, Sanskrit and Gujerati, etc.), where both languages are etymologically related. This is also the case in much of Islam (Koranic Arabic and Modern Arabic) and Judaism in Israel (Classical Hebrew and Modern Hebrew) and was also the case in the Western Church before the Latinate-vernaculars became fully secularized (e.g. French and Latin, Spanish and Latin, Portuguese and Latin and, of course, Italian and Latin). The use of the same 'Chinese' writing system throughout much of China has transferred some of the holiness of Classical Mandarin to Han and even to some non-Han languages as well.

## When Neither Language is Holy

Bilingualism today is spreading most rapidly and most significantly due to the spread of Western languages of modernization and globalization. English, e.g. is now far from being considered holy (even though it may have been so considered briefly, at the time of the founding of the Church of England and the publication of its Book of Common Prayer). As a result, when English forces its way into daily technological, consumerist and youth culture on all continents, its appeal in Cuba, Indonesia, Taiwan, Madagascar and the Philippines has as little to do with sanctity as does the staying power of the locally spoken vernaculars. The entire notion of the sanctity of a language is still more frequently Western than non-Western, when the world as a whole is considered. Nevertheless, most of the growth in language sanctity claims has occurred in the non-West within the past half century or so. Indeed, the very idea of the sanctity of the local language often seems to be adopted in almost pristinely Herderian terms. In resisting the Western-derived erosions of local life and identity, the local language comes to be viewed as 'the genuine spirit of the people', a 'mystic essence' enabling them 'to remain true to their own way of life', a 'sacred trust and responsibility', a 'key to preserving their own authenticity', etc. However, there are still huge sections of the globe where no such appeals are known, even though bilingualism may be quite widespread. Africa, Latin America and the Pacific provide most examples of such totally secular bilingualisms, whether in connection with the spread of Western or local contact languages.

## The Consequences of Language Sanctity Beliefs

Language sanctity convictions do not operate in a vacuum. Whether or not they are accompanied by parallel notions of sanctity of the people and/or sanctity of the land, language sanctity convictions have mobilizing, rallying, activating, rousing, energizing potentials. These potentials are employed in conjunction with collective efforts on behalf of democratization through local vernacular status elevation, language maintenance consciousness raising, reversing language shift and language corpus modernization. The practical utility of language sanctity convictions in the political arena has probably also contributed to the steady growth in such convictions, sanctity being every bit as much socially constructed as other societal beliefs and convictions. However, although language sanctity notions may help activate popular ethnic consciousness, these very same convictions also tend to complicate or restrict language modernization efforts, constraining them to be more 'authentic', purist, ausbau and indigenous in orientation rather than following along the lines of 'internationalization' (adopting paradigms from English and other Western languages) which corpus planning for modernization normally pursues. Modernization movements and ethnic authenticity movements often co-occur among bilingual populations. These populations may well become conflicted as to which of their two languages should have the upper hand and just how holiness and power are to be separated.

The result of ethnicity driven 'introspective' or 'self-distancing' corpus planning is to make the two languages of bilingual speech communities less similar, counteracting the common tendency for languages in contact to interact with each other, not only lexically but also phonologically, grammatically and semantically. Furthermore, within the sanctity-impacted language, the varieties that are written are likely to be most stringently regulated (by schools, churches and governments) and, therefore, most puristic of all and most distant from 'the other language' of bilingual sociocultural aggregates. Of course, where both languages are considered holy in some way, their self-distancing efforts will be mutual and reciprocal, at the same time that a complementary allocation of functions exists between them to avoid societal conflict. When such a complementary allocation of functions falls apart (e.g. when both languages seek governmental, educational or modern written functions), then a longer or shorter period of conflict must ensue until a monolingual victor or a new complementary bilingual distribution is established.

## The Staying Power of Sanctity

More than fifteen hundred years after the collapse of the Roman Empire, Latin continues to be learned and used – by bilinguals who already speak, read and write some other language(s). Even more miraculous is the staying power of Hebrew within a dispersed and persecuted minority culture, all of whose members spoke – and many of whose members also read and wrote – other languages (some for within-group and others for between-group purposes). Because sanctity is upheld by and linked to major and powerful societal institutions, it is not a 'here today and gone tomorrow' phenomenon. It quite understandably has extraordinary staying power and this same power is transferred to the languages most intimately suffused by it. Languages of direct sanctity live on in their holy texts and, as such, are not subject to the winds of change and of influence (or interference) from other languages in the way that spoken languages are. While it is not the case that they do not change at all (as a result of the fact that they come to be written by individuals who are thinking in another language), it nevertheless remains true that the holy texts themselves constitute a mighty 'corrective' pulling all subsequent texts back into their structural orbit.

But the staying power of sanctified languages within bilingual repertoires is also noticeable in yet another way: they do not come and go the way quotidian vernaculars do. They wax and wane and have a seemingly phoenix-like capacity to arise again out of their own ashes. This latter capacity too is a reflection of the sanctity attributed to them. Every sociocultural system has its own frustrations, disappointments and defeats. Religion is a system of comfort, resetting of priorities, decentering of one's own importance in the grander scheme of life and recentering on a greater design and a Supreme Designer. As a result of such recentering experiences, there have been cycles of 'return to religion' or of 'renewed fundamentalism' throughout human history. During such 'renewal' or 'rebirth' periods the original sacred texts are 'rediscovered' and the languages of these texts, seemingly peripheralized, lost and/or forgotten, are again focused upon, studied and pondered by growing numbers of adherents. Although almost never revernacularized (because the bilinguals who read and study these texts already have perfectly functional vernaculars), their most striking expressions, figures of speech and turns of phrase are frequently adopted by their accompanying vernaculars, thereby adding another touch of sanctity to the latter as well.

## Conclusions

All in all, the realm of sanctity is doubly influential in connection with sociolinguistic processes: (1) it both maintains and renews the vitality of the language most impacted by religion and (2) it appreciably influences the accompanying language as well, if for no other reason that the speakers of the latter are exposed during so many hours, days and years to the texts, translations or elucidations of the former. This process of 'sanctification of the vernacular by dint of long term association with the language of materia sancta' is commonly much stronger than the process of 'secularization of the sacred'. Obviously, some of the latter also may occur over time, given that the languages of the same community can rarely be fully compartmentalized, and particularly so if the language of religion also comes to attain widespread secular reading and recording functions. On the whole, however, secular vernaculars have come and gone throughout human history, whereas religious classicals and the vernaculars that they have influenced most thoroughly (e.g. the 'Luther Bible' of the trilingual Old Order Amish) seem to dig-in and hang-on almost 'eternally'. The full or partial sanctification of one or more languages within multilingual societies is a factor which contributes to the stability of societal bilingualism *per se*, to the longevity of language movements world-wide and to authenticity strivings within corpus planning more generally. There is a particularly high likelihood that the H variety within diglossic societies will be religion related and that more learned realizations of the L variety will also be implemented by borrowing lexical and grammatical items from the H.

The secularized monolingual sociocultural world occupies a distinct minority status in the world at large, in which religion impacted societal bilingualism is the quantitative norm.

## Note

1. Numerous examples of languages involved in *each* of the three types of societal bilingualism discussed below, in which holiness is ascribed to one or both languages, may be found in Fishman (1996). The section on Sanctity in that book is organized in a manner that closely follows the organization of the present paper. There the reader will find scores of references to sanctity-claiming quotations pertaining to languages from all parts of the globe.

## References

Ferguson, Charles A. (1959) Diglosia. *Word* 15, 325–340.
Fishman, Joshua A. (1965) Bilingualism intelligence and language learning. *Modern Language Journal* 49, 227–237.
——. (1966) *Language Loyalty in the United States*. The Hague: Mouton.
——. *(1996) In Praise of the Beloved Language: The Comparative Study of Positive Ethnolinguistic Consciousness*. Berlin/New York: Mouton de Gruyter.
Matisoff, James A. (1978) *Blessings, Curses, Hopes and Fears: Psycho-Ostensive Expressions*. Philadelphia: ISHI Press.